FISCAL POLICY
AND POLITICS

Fiscal Policy

and

Politics

by

PAUL J. STRAYER

Princeton University

HARPER & BROTHERS   PUBLISHERS   NEW YORK

FISCAL POLICY AND POLITICS

Copyright © 1958 by Paul J. Strayer

Printed in the United States of America

L-H

Library of Congress catalog card number: 58-13961

38566

To My Father

CONTENTS

PREFACE   ix

I. INTRODUCTION   1

II. THE GREAT DEPRESSION   11
   The Impact of the Depression

III. THE IMPACT OF WORLD WAR II   22
   Direct Controls

IV. WAR FINANCE AND TRANSITION: 1939–1946   40
   Tax Policy
   Government Contracts
   Transition Period: 1945–1946
   Conclusions

V. BETWEEN WARS, AND THE IMPACT OF THE KOREAN
   WAR: 1947–1951   56
   The Impact of the Korean War: June 1950–June,
      1951

VI. 1951–1958   81
   The Republican Administration

VII. THE UNITED STATES ECONOMY: 1958   93
   Basic Commitments

VIII. THE POLITICAL AND ECONOMIC FRAMEWORK   104
   Maximization of Economic Product
   Maximization of Social Welfare
   Maximization of Political Welfare

Federal Structure of Government
Administrative Aspects
Conclusions

IX. STABILIZATION THEORY AS A POLICY GUIDE   133
Fiscal Policy
Debt Management
Monetary Theory
The Conflict Between Price Stabilization and Full
    Employment
Conclusions

X. PUBLIC EXPENDITURE POLICY   167
Government Expenditures and Economic Welfare
Economic Stabilization
Political and Administrative Aspects
Conclusions

XI. TAX POLICY I   202
Tax Theory
Tax Limits
The Ideal Tax System
Current Issues and Possibilities of Reform
Equity

XII. TAX POLICY II   228
Distribution by Income Class
Stabilization Policy
Effects of Taxation on Incentives and Growth
Conclusions

XIII. STATE AND LOCAL TAX PROBLEMS   259
Conclusions

XIV. SUMMARY   279
A Positive Program of Reform

INDEX   297

PREFACE

The increased power of government in our economic life needs to be more certainly recognized. Yet there are few individuals who have been willing to discuss some of the limitations of the power of government. Those who use national income models to make recommendations for the stabilization of the economy often neglect the fact that it is politicians who decide what will be done. Throughout this book emphasis will be on the limitations of the power of government. In other words, this is a study in the field of political economy. One of the greatest dangers we face today is the growing power of pressure groups to act for the benefit of the group concerned. As a result the unorganized are neglected and their interests are not represented.

This book was completed before the depression of late 1957–1958. It is of interest to note that the government has failed to act with vigor to stimulate the economy. The administration has not asked for an all-out attack on the depression. Congress has also failed to act to reduce tax burdens or to take other steps within its power. I believe that the failure of either Congress or the executive branch to act is a reflection of the fear that they will overcompensate. In both cases I believe that they will act only after conditions have grown much worse.

Still another problem is the inability of Congress or the executive branch of government to develop the degree of flexibility required to meet current conditions. Too often action has been taken for the wrong reasons at the wrong time. A reversal of policy, if it is in the best interest of the country, must be made respectable. Too little is known about the effects of any govern- mental action in relation to the amount of stimulus or restraint that is required. Government must learn to respond to actual conditions not merely to forecasts.

Finally, we must pay more attention to the methods used to redistribute income and to maintain a stable economy. The choices we make today will have a profound effect upon the economic, political, and social structure for years to come. There is danger that the measures used will have adverse effects upon the maintenance of democratic institutions and the preservation of a market economy. If individuals wish to change the economic and political system, they should do it with their eyes open, not as a result of a failure to anticipate the results of actions taken today in the name of stability. The problem is one of leadership. It also requires the reuniting of politics with economics. Such leadership has not often been found among the leaders in politics, industry, labor, or agriculture.

To those who read this manuscript my debts are great. They are: Marver H. Bernstein, Lester V. Chandler, and Joseph R. Strayer. Their criticisms and suggestions have helped make this a better book. I also wish to acknowledge the assistance given me by the Princeton University Research Fund. The grants from the fund made this book possible. For any errors or shortcomings that remain I have only myself to blame.

PAUL J. STRAYER

August, 1958

FISCAL POLICY
AND POLITICS

CHAPTER I

Introduction

In no other country has the role played by government in the economy changed more rapidly than in the United States. The change began with the Great Depression of the 1930's and has continued to the present time. The first part of this book is an attempt to find out why this change has occurred. The implications of this change upon the long-range growth and stability of the United States and some of the dangers that may arise from government efforts to influence the economy are then considered.

The approach used in this book is that of the political economist. No attempt is made to develop new economic data. The primary focus is upon the practicality of the various suggestions that have been made for stabilizing the economy and upon some of the dangers of trying to operate under existing political institutions a government which intervenes actively in the economy. Particular attention is devoted to the dangers in abuse of governmental powers and to some of the threats to the stability of the economy and of political institutions.

The growth in the role of government can be documented in a variety of ways. Government has a profound influence upon the character of the output of the economy. It is also responsible for the stability of the economy. Finally, it continues to exercise a substantial influence upon the distribution of income, as taxation, subsidies, and transfer expenditures affect the share of income going to different groups in society.

In the event of a serious depression there is no longer any doubt that government will assume responsibility for the restoration of prosperity. In the event of war, government must assume responsibility for the direction of the entire economic system. Neither business leaders nor individuals can make important decisions without regard to the policies pursued by government.

One of the remarkable facts about the change that has occurred is the brief period in which the transition was made. Between 1929 and 1939 a large part of the growth had been accomplished. Since then there have been substantial additions to the influence of government, but most of the additions have been related to defense needs or to the residual burdens resulting from World War II.

As recently as 1929 the prevailing attitude was that the government that interfered least in the affairs of business was the best government. In 1929 government did not assume responsibility for the stabilization of the economy. Social security and unemployment insurance were bitterly fought by the business community. The problem of relief was left to private charity or neglected. The policy of "let the buyer beware" prevailed in most of the financial and securities markets. Federal budgets were running in the range of $3 billion annually and national defense expenditures were about $700 million. State and local expenditures were more than twice as large as those of the federal government. It was at the state and local level that primary responsibility for most governmental functions was assumed. Great satisfaction had been derived by the Harding, Coolidge, and Hoover administrations in the reduction of federal tax burdens from the heights that had been reached in the period of World War I.

It is also interesting to note that before 1929 neither labor nor agriculture had achieved the power to influence legislation. The

Agricultural Marketing Act of 1929 sought to place agriculture on a basis of equality with other industries. But purchases in a declining market led to the failure of the plan in 1931. The American Federation of Labor had carefully kept out of organized politics and tried to play one party against the other as a means of accomplishing their objectives.

The desperate condition of the economy in March, 1933, led to rapid government action. Reforms that had long been considered were made in the field of finance and the organized securities markets. Direct responsibility for the unemployed was assumed by the federal government because of the breakdown in the capacity of the states to carry the burden of relief and the disintegration of private charitable organizations. Labor was given new status, first under the terms of the National Industrial Recovery Administration and later under the Wagner Act. The farmer became the direct beneficiary of numerous subsidies. Public works were advocated as a means of stimulating the economy while the federal government tried to salvage something for the little man through direct relief. Taxes were raised to heights never before reached in peace time.

The reasons for these changes are not hard to find. First was the reaction against the policies pursued by government prior to 1933. Second was the compelling demand for action. Little concern was expressed about the internal consistency of the steps taken as long as government assumed responsibility for the needs of people and the stimulation of recovery. The national debt grew and the orthodox worried about it, but each year there was hope that the budget might be balanced the next year. Business leaders became much concerned about the trends found in the New Deal but had little power to temper them or in any way affect the basic policies of the government.

The sharp depression of 1937 was discouraging and led to some changes in the policies pursued by government. But there was still a lack of any coherent philosophy within the New Deal or consistency in the policies it pursued. The fall of France and the growing involvement of the United States in the war finally brought recovery and a striking improvement in the standard of living of the average worker. In spite of the restrictions imposed upon the production of durable goods and the limitations upon new housing, few individuals failed to profit from a marked improvement in their incomes during the war period. This rise from the depths of the depression continued in the postwar period and is one of the special forces that may have given some workers and their leaders false ideas about the rate of growth that can be sustained in normal times. It is certainly one of the important factors that must be considered in any realistic appraisal of the prospects of the economy in the future.

For the duration of the war period the government not only ran the economy but, in the field of finance, made major innovations which permitted us to survive the period of tension that followed the war. The most important of these was the radical shift in the income tax so that the majority of the workers were brought within the tax base. This was done by putting the tax on a source collection basis and greatly lowering the exemption level. Without such a tax there would be little chance of raising the revenues now required without becoming directly involved in tax levies used by the majority of the states and local governments. In view of the difficulties states and local governments now find in raising the revenues required to meet current services, such competition between the states and the federal government would seriously embarrass the states and local governments. Other adjustments were made in the revenue systems, but none were of the same importance as the revisions of the individual income tax.

Perhaps the other major accomplishment of the war period was the ease with which the substantial deficits were met. The ability to create money was the direct result of the policy followed by the Federal Reserve System of maintaining a fixed rate of return upon all the securities issued by the federal government. The Federal Reserve also made sure that the banks were never without adequate reserves. Banks could therefore purchase the necessary amount of government debt. There was never any restriction imposed by the gold reserve position of the central bank.

The importance of bond supports for the duration of the war lay not only in the assistance it gave the Treasury but the problems it left for the postwar period. For the entire war period the central bank of the United States placed itself at the service of the Treasury and neglected its other obligations. Having become accustomed to such behavior, central bankers and many economists became concerned about the dangers of once more restoring to the central bank the power to use its conventional weapons of buying and selling securities in the open market and of changing both the reserve requirements and the discount rate. As a consequence, it was not until the spring of 1951 that the Federal Reserve started to act once more like a central bank. Since then, the policies of the Federal Reserve have been flexible and responsive to changes in economic conditions. Some allege that the changes have not been as rapid as they believe desirable; some would argue that the changes have been perverse. But for the most part those who believe in the effectiveness of monetary controls will generally support the broad outlines of the policies followed.

Following the termination of the war, hope for a return to more normal conditions was upset by the devastation in European countries and the inability to work out our differences with the U.S.S.R. As a consequence, first the aid to the war-torn European countries and then the various foreign aid programs have kept the United States heavily involved in the international field. Military preparation required the expenditure of much larger sums than had ever been spent in peaceful times, due to the growth in the complexity of armaments and the seriousness with which the country viewed the threat of the Russians. The final blow came with the outbreak of the Korean War.

The new interest in missiles following the Russian successes in this field has again pointed to the need for larger expenditures. What may be next is difficult to say, but so long as the "cold war" continues there is bound to be another period of tension and the necessity of large scale expenditures for purely defensive purposes. In addition there is evidently a need to spend large sums for basic research so that the balance can be maintained with the rapidly advancing technology of the Soviets. If, in addition, there is need to spend billions for shelters the magnitude of the job is well beyond anything that has yet been suggested to the public. Add to this the belief of many that a systematic dispersal of industrial plants and military bases must be followed to assure the protection that is required in the modern world, and the sums become astronomical.

After the end of World War II, the extent of the change in attitude of both Congress and the public during the last quarter century was indicated by the ease with which the Employment Act of 1946 was passed in both houses of Congress. This act requires the federal government to use all practicable means to assure both the maintenance of full employment and a growing economy. As a result the government cannot ignore a depression and must use all possible means of preventing another collapse of the magnitude of the Great Depression of the 1930's. It is now generally conceded that another depression of such dimensions would have repercussions which would threaten both the economic and the political framework of our society.

As a result of all the changes that have taken place since the early 1930's the federal government now spends more than twice as much as state and local governments combined. Important reasons for this are the requirements of defense, debt service charges, and veterans' commitments resulting from World War II. But in addition there is a growing realization that the welfare of all the people is one of the interests of the federal government. This increased government spending also reflects the growth in prosperity accompanied by a new concern for the realization of the basic concept of democratic government: the granting of an equal opportunity in life to all regardless of their family circumstances.

As a result of the changes cited above, the states and local governments are finding it increasingly difficult to raise the sums required to finance their rapidly expanding need for schools, higher education, highways, institutions and agencies, parks, and general governmental requirements. For example, there have been no new state income taxes since 1937; but indirect levies have multiplied as a means of raising more revenue in the least painless manner. Such developments raise the question of the capacity of the states and local governments to continue to expand their basic services without federal assistance. Still another problem is the growth of cycle-sensitive taxes which will leave the states and local governments in a poor position in the event of another depression. This suggests that there may well have to be some assistance from the federal government at certain stages of the cycle.

Another development of great interest is the growth in the dependance of certain industries upon government orders. Public construction is about as large as total private construction. Aircraft and missiles are almost completely dependent upon government orders for the bulk of their business. Unfortunately these industries tend to be concentrated in certain parts of the United States so that a decline in government spending may have a much greater impact in certain areas than in others. Of all business sales in the United States some 11 percent are sales to government. When the direct product of government workers is added to this total, the magnitude of government influence upon the total level of employment and total product is apparent. The value of government's own product valued at cost is almost equal to that of the purchases it makes from private firms. Direct employment at all levels of government is now 7,178,000 excluding members of the armed forces. If they are included the total is increased to 9,978,000. This number is more than twice the total employed by all governments in 1929. One must also remember that private employers producing for government are as much affected by government policies as are direct employees.

Still another way in which the government has affected the economy is in the area of transfer expenditures for such purposes as old age pensions, aid to the blind and dependent mothers, unemployment insurance, and aid to veterans. If interest payments and subsidies for such purposes as farm supports are included, this total amounts to approximately $23 billion annually. These payments affect income distribution directly through disbursements and indirectly through the taxes imposed to pay for them.

Add to the above-mentioned influences of government the dominance of the federal government in the money markets of the nation, and the full dimensions of the federal influences are revealed. It is no longer possible for the Board of Governors of the Federal Reserve System to ignore the effects of their policies upon the rate of interest and the general availability of credit throughout the United States. Federal Reserve officials must always be concerned about the influences of their policies upon the economic health of the nation.

All that has been said above suggests that no government can be indifferent to the repercussions of its policies upon income, employment, and prices. Taxes can have a decided influence upon the allocation of resources. Expenditures will have a similar effect. Debt management policies can make credit tight or easy. This widespread influence of government policies has created a great interest on the part of all members of the community in the policies pursued. What is not so well recognized is that it has also led to the formation of certain groups with an interest in modifying or manipulating federal laws to improve the position of their constituents. So long as taxes and expenditures remain high there will be strong pressures to influence the way in which taxes are imposed and expenditures allocated. Access to individuals with political influence can make the difference between success and failure for many industries and groups.

Further complications arise when the question of the means to be used in pursuing the commonly accepted objectives of government are discussed. Although most of us are in favor of full employment, there may be a vast difference in the methods used to achieve this end. Labor, industry, and agriculture all have a stake in the methods used to maintain stability. Some have an interest in inflation. Others would like to see a moderate amount of deflation. All this suggests that the cold logic of economics is often at a disadvantage when faced by the realities of politics. Too often the economist will find that his arithmetic comes out second best.

In the pages that follow, a detailed account of the growth of public expenditures will occupy the first six chapters and some of their implications will be considered as the analysis is being made. Then a chapter endeavoring to establish the basic political and economic framework for use in testing government practices will be attempted. When government behaves badly there is need for a consistent set of ideas against which to judge its behavior. The next four chapters will discuss successively the problems of achieving stabilization, public expenditure policy, tax policy, and finally the problems of state and local finance. A final chapter will attempt to summarize the main elements of the argument and state a few conclusions.

In all that is said there is an attempt to keep the longer-run implications of some of the newer policies uppermost. Only as this is done can the public really choose among the different ways of accomplishing the same end. Too often the public is interested in only the short run and gives little thought to the eventual consequences of different ways of achieving the same objective.

If, after due deliberation, the public wishes to make basic changes in the political and economic framework this is their privilege; but too often the full meaning of the act is not brought to their attention, and before they realize what they have done they may find that it is too late to modify the practices that have become traditional or so generally accepted that there is little chance of turning back.

The purpose of this book is to consider the implications of different means of achieving the same objective within a political and administrative framework that is slow to change and subject to abuse. All proposals are tested as they may affect the social, political, and economic institutions that now prevail. Much of the analysis must be tentative and of a subjective nature. But a failure to attempt such an analysis would keep many of the most important problems of current policy from being considered by the citizen who must make choices. I have tried to suggest that government cannot do everything and that governmental powers can be easily abused. More people need to realize that governments cannot give all things to all people without a price tag being attached. Very often the price paid is not worth the results obtained.

CHAPTER II

The Great Depression

The Impact of the Depression

The story of the Great Depression of the 1930's is usually told in terms of facts and figures—the number of unemployed, the product lost, the number of business and bank failures, the foreclosure of home and farm mortgages, the stock market collapse, the breakdown of international trade, and the growth of the public debt. The cost of these events in terms of human suffering and shattered families and hopes will never be measured, but it is the memory of these troubles that is of greatest influence today. The loss of product and the immediate reactions of the people affected are now a matter to be analyzed by historians, but the change in popular thinking and in popular demands upon government is still influencing the political and economic policies of our time.

In spite of the high levels of income and employment maintained since 1940, we are still preoccupied by our fear of depression. This has affected all interest groups and parties, so that when the Employment Act of 1946 was passed there was no significant opposition to the assumption by government of a commitment for the preservation of high level employment. It is of interest to note that the language of the Act required the government to maintain "maximum production, employment, and purchasing power." It is significant that the Employment Act made no mention of inflation. As a result, since the end of World War II any attempts to curb inflation have been resisted by many on the ground that such a program would endanger the maintenance of full employment. Only recently has there been a reaction and a general recognition that full employment may not be consistent with price stabilization.

Another by-product of the fear of another depression has been the tendency for many business, labor, and farm groups to feel perfectly justified in using all available means to better their position in the short run. They fear that the period of good times is temporary. This trend has perhaps been most important in the labor and farm sectors. On the other hand, many of the larger corporations have found that their public relations and longer-run economic interest dictate a policy of going along with, rather than leading in, the scramble for betterment of short-run position.

A further expression of this fear is the extent to which the government has become involved in specific measures designed to minimize the risk of failure and loss in the event of even a mild depression. Most of these measures have full justification in a welfare sense but they have become so widespread that there is danger that the "rule of no bankruptcy" will dominate. The most conspicuous example of this tendency is in specific applications of the farm price support program. The formulae are so rigged that the support policy encourages maintenance of a level of output that has no justification in the market. The potato support program of a few years ago is perhaps the most flagrant example, although there are others, and there will be more in the future unless the basic approach is changed. Another example may be found in certain governmental plans for housing finance, where the possibility of excessive private profit was maintained but the possibility of loss was effectively removed by the commitments of the federal government.[1] The old promoter financing his project with "other people's money" survives in new dress.

A somewhat less clear case is the growing tendency of government agencies to accept and to respond to the idea that a sick industry or region deserves special support in the form of subsidies or grants regardless of the basic reason for its difficulty or the efforts of the region or industry to cure itself. The revelations of the special privileges granted by the Reconstruction Finance Corporation discloses not only petty influence-peddling but general acceptance of the idea that government should support marginal business activities and guarantee them against the possibility of great losses. One of the most difficult policy issues of the day is that of the line to be drawn between government assistance which is necessary to prevent general deflation or to aid depressed areas, and assistance which prevents adjustment to shifts in supply and demand or technology.

This general trend results not only from the fears mentioned above but also from the fact that many of the policies instituted in the depression for sufficient reason have continued when the need was no longer so evident. The most obvious case is that of housing, where the use of government guarantees to make credit easier has been continued through the period of inflation. This policy can be justified in terms of the obligation of the country to the veteran, but the economic fact is that cheap money probably gave advantages to the real estate promoter but small benefits to the veteran who lost in higher prices for his house what he saved in lower interest rates. There is little question that the volume of housing constructed was not significantly increased by the greater ease of mortgage money for most of the period from 1946 to 1949.[2] The limits to new construction were manpower and materials more than money.

[1] Nathan Straus, *Two-Thirds of a Nation—A Housing Program*, New York, 1952, p. 128.
[2] Leo Grebler, "Stabilizing Residential Construction," *American Economic Review*, XXXIX (1949), 898-910.

Other examples of the continuance of measures suitable for depression in periods of inflation and full employment are numerous. As indicated above, many of the agricultural price programs now represent the influence of organized pressure groups rather than justifiable aids to a depressed sector of the economy. By far the most important, however, was the continuance of the easy-money policy initiated in the 1930's throughout the period until March, 1951. Among the reasons advanced for this policy are that easy money is necessary to maintain confidence in the government credit, to protect holders of government debt, and to maintain the rate of investment necessary for continued expansion and achievement of or maintenance of high levels of employment. The most extreme form of this doctrine was expressed by the Council of Economic Advisers through two of the original members, Keyserling and Clark. Modifications in this policy achieved since the outbreak of the Korean war are still opposed by those favoring cheap money and low interest rates, a state of mind which is one of the important heritages of the depression.

In general, the depression shattered the confidence of economists and government officials in the way in which things had been done in the past and encouraged a tendency to overcompensate for past errors or failures. The general reaction against dependence upon the use of restrictive monetary and credit policy and new interest in the use of fiscal policy or direct controls has been typical of much that has transpired as the result of the blow of the 1930's. Not the least of the influences leading to the general tendency to favor direct controls has been the loss of public confidence in the ability of business leaders. Suspicion of bankers became particularly acute as a result of the investigations of the 1930's and the record of bank closings and other financial failures. The failure of business to provide any leaders who could make plausible recommendations for the solution of the depression in terms that met the human needs of the period also strengthened the case for more direct governmental controls.[3] This was furthered by the leadership of President Roosevelt and the early New Dealers who seemed to embody the hopes of the public and their reactions against the "malefactors of great wealth" by taking direct steps to correct the major abuses of the past and to provide at least a subsistence for those in need. The lack of any orderly program or profound analysis of the economic problems troubling the country did not weaken the New Deal in the popular mind as long as its leaders responded directly to the individual needs and hopes of the mass of individuals who were unable to help themselves. Although the prestige of the financial and business world has improved since then and is once more ascendant, a reaction could set in much more rapidly if another period of adversity set in, even though it is a mild depression.

The experience of the 1930's led to a justifiable skepticism about the effectiveness of low interest rates, excess reserves, and favorable investment terms. The lack of response to the continuance of easy money conditions seemed comparable to the results achieved when one tries to push on a string. Business investment did not respond and unemployment continued until the outbreak of World War II.

It was under these conditions that the Keynesian position began to develop such appeal and the influence of Hansen became important in this country. Hansen's stagnation thesis, suggesting that investment demand would not recover and that public investment would have to fill the gap, seemed to fit the facts of the 1930's. It provided an elaborate justification for the direct intervention of the government in order to assure the sort of economic development that we believed our right and within our capacity. Salvation by government action had additional attractions because it had not been tried in recent times.

[3] The longer prosperity lasts the greater the influence of business leadership. It is also of interest to note that the Committee for Economic Development has done much to develop an articulate business view based on the best evidence available.

At the same time that new thinking about monetary and credit policy was evolving, the continued deficits of the 1930's led to the gradual acceptance of a new budget policy and a new attitude toward the growing public debt. Keynesian economic theory was an important part of this development, but in my opinion it was not the determining influence. The problems of debt management, deficit finance, and monetary and credit policy are all closely related. In the period under consideration, the continued deficits caused great debate within the government until the set-back in 1937, after the cash budget was balanced, and led to the growth in influence of those who favored the continuance of deficits as long as and as big as necessary to provide full employment. This same group favored the extension of public investment projects. They became a major influence favoring the transformation of the economy to assure the level of investment required to provide outlets for all the saving that individuals and business might wish to make under conditions of full employment.

Criticism of the growth of the public debt and fear of its consequences continued through this period. This, and the fact that a large part of the debt was held in the banks, making them the beneficiaries of the interest paid on it, led to great stress upon the advantage of maintenance of a favorable market and of preserving low interest rates. Thus the loss of faith in monetary and credit policy as a major instrument of recovery did not lead to the abandonment of a low interest rate program. Much was made of the fact that the annual cost of the growing debt was held low by the favorable rates of interest prevailing. There was also general agreement that the low rates were desirable although not sufficient to assure recovery in a period of depression. Thus the discounting of monetary policy resulted in a bias toward low rates and easy credit terms. Throughout the period there continued a growth of Treasury influence on both debt and monetary policy. Treasury balances, the stabilization fund, and gold policy all became important instruments of control affecting the basic monetary conditions in the country and the world.[4]

The shift in budgetary policy from the early days of the depression when deficits were regarded as evils to the last days when there was a growing tendency to accept deficits as a permanent feature of government finance was gradual and never completely accepted. What was accomplished was the shift to a stronger executive budget, with more adequate staff directly under the direction of the President. The creation of a Fiscal Division within the Budget Bureau also represented the influence of the newer thinking about the function of fiscal policy as a basic instrument of economic planning. Although the Budget Bureau did not achieve the place many thought it should have in the planning and coördination of the governmental program, it became an indispensable tool of management and served the President well. As a consequence, there will never be another period when the role of the budget director is confined to that of a general accountant or bookkeeper.

Nor is it likely that there will ever be a time when the general income effects of the budget can be ignored by either those interested in the total economy, or by those concerned about the specific impact of government upon their affairs.[5] The overwhelming fact of the period is the growth of the size of the federal budget in both absolute and relative terms. Although expenditures grew more rapidly than revenues, taxes increased in severity and extent, so that what had been a minor factor in the considerations of the business man and the wealthy individual became a major consideration. Also important was the change in attitude of the administration. Instead of a government favorably disposed to the wealthy and the business community, the New Deal was generally critical and consciously attempted to reduce the dis-

---

[4] G. G. Johnson, Jr., *The Treasury and Monetary Policy, 1933-1938*, Cambridge, 1939.

[5] Jesse Burkhead, *Government Budgeting*, New York, 1956.

parity of income distribution and to reduce the power and influence of the wealthy individual and large corporation. The violent reaction to this change of attitude is still evident in certain circles. The general belief of the wealthy that the tax policies of the New Deal were punitive and "antibusiness" has tended to divide the country further and has helped to justify an opportunistic policy by business.

The final major effect of the depression was to speed transfer to the federal government of responsibility for many of the functions that had been previously performed by states, local communities, private charitable institutions, or the family. These new responsibilities were in addition to the new functions taken on by the federal government which competed with or supplemented the role of private business. The most important transfer has proved to be that of the responsibility for individual economic security. First, the breakdown of local relief agencies required the federal government to take emergency action to prevent millions of people from starving. Then, the logical development of this program began to evolve in the form of the Social Security Act and its subsequent modifications.

The maintenance of state administration and considerable state independence in the financing of the unemployment insurance features of the act reduces the immediate commitments of the federal government. There is, nevertheless, a residual commitment that will again be assumed by the federal government in the event of another depression. The centrally financed and administered Old-Age and Survivors Insurance program and the extension of federal aid for public assistance programs to certain classes of needy represents a commitment that continues to be large in good times or bad.

Other federal programs that have taken over what used to be local responsibility are in the area of resource conservation and development. The Tennessee Valley Authority has not proved to be a model organizationally, but major federal power and water development, rural electrification, and soil conservation programs continued throughout the period of Democratic rule. The last major increase in federal commitments began slowly, compared with recent trends, but became a significant influence well before the end of the depression. This was the expansion of outlays for arms and defense-related purposes. It is of interest to note that under the original National Industrial Recovery Administration, funds were made available for the construction of naval vessels, later to become important elements of the fleet in World War II.

It would be wrong to conclude this discussion of the influences of the depression upon financial institutions without mention of the many institutional reforms in this period, particularly those strengthening our financial structure, such as banking legislation, securities regulation, the Home Owners' Loan Corporation, and the Reconstruction Finance Corporation, as well as the general improvement in the level of economic statistics. These reforms are of great importance, but cannot be considered within the limitations of this analysis.

It is also important to remember that many of the changes of this period were considered temporary by most of the public, including many within the New Deal. In 1933, Congress delegated extensive powers to the executive, responding, as did the public, to the leadership of Roosevelt and his staff. State and local governments were grateful beneficiaries of the benefits of federal programs and of direct grants and subsidies. But aside from the shift in the position of the Supreme Court from a negative to a permissive policy, few changes in the basic political structure of the country were made. As a result, when the emergency was over and Congress began to look with less favor on the delegation of power to the executive, the machinery of government began to show signs of stress. The President's opportunism and the decline in his control of his party organization aroused increasing tensions between the executive and legislative branches. At the same time, the states that had been saved from financial

disaster by the federal government began to see that their strength
had been weakened by the increase in federal powers and particularly by the great increase in federal financial demands. Sectional
interests, particularly in the South, began to react against the
imposition of federal legislation affecting their policies. Congressional procedures permitted minority groups to block legislation
and often to pass measures of sectional interest in face of the
opposition of the executive branch. The attempt of the President
to strengthen his party control by the purge of 1938 proved
abortive. The executive office did, however, gain strength by
the Reorganization Act of 1939, which built up the staff available
to serve the President.[6] The outbreak of World War II found
little change in basic governmental organization and required
resort to the time-honored custom of renewed delegation to the
executive in order to increase the power of government.

The failure to make more changes in the organization of the
federal machinery at a time when the functions and responsibilities of the central government were increasing reflects the historic
and deep-seated distrust of the American public of big government. We may place new burdens upon it and use it to gain personal advantage but, in matters of governmental organization, the
tradition of separation of powers and checks upon governmental
action continues unabated. Emergency requirements and awareness
of new needs were not enough to overcome the resistance to fundamental change in the basic organization, or procedure, of the
federal government.

At the present time it is impossible to say what would have
been the final influence of the changes of the depression period
had the recovery not been accompanied by war. Certainly the
impact would have been greater than that of a normal cyclical
movement. Much of the legislation of the period was needed
and merely brought the United States up-to-date in its response
to the requirements of a modern industrial society. A return to

[6] Clinton Rossiter, *The American Presidency,* New York, 1956.

II

The Impact of World War II

IIIIIIIIIIIIIIIIIIIIIIIIIIIIIIIIIIIIIIIIIIIIIIIIIIIIIIIIIIIIIIIIIIIIIIIIIIIIIIIIIIIIIIIIIIIIIIIIIIIIIIIIIII

The outbreak of war in Europe in the fall of 1939 had sur-
prisingly little effect on the immediate economic and political
conditions in the United States. The debate between the isolationists and the interventionists grew hot, but the pace of defense spending did not increase enough to change the general
economic picture. Prices were stable and unemployment was still
in the range of 9 million or 17.2 percent of the total civilian labor
force.[1] Business investment continued below normal, and the
recovery of housing and other construction did not grow enough
to change basic conditions. The lack of fighting in the winter and
the false predictions of those who asserted that Hitler could
not finance a full-scale war made many Americans, who did not
wish to think that they were to become involved in another world
conflict, believe that some settlement could be arranged. The
threat of Japan was generally discounted by the public, which
had a feeling of superiority with regard to the Japanese and a
belief that they would not dare fight. The investigations of the
1930's attempting to prove that wars were caused by munitions
makers and evil plotters seeking personal gain[2] had found a
receptive audience among persons disillusioned by the depression

[1] Joint Committee on the Economic Report, *Historical and Descriptive Supplement
to Economic Indicators*, Washington, 1953, p. 15.
[2] Especially The Senate Munitions Investigating Committee of the mid-1930's,
Senator Gerald Nye, Chairman.

predepression attitudes and policies was not likely. Howev
financial impact that seemed large at the time might now
insignificant had recovery brought with it the normal grow
real product. Substantially greater welfare benefits could
been financed at no great increase in tax rates if national inc
had continued to grow. The debt that seemed so large wo
have been a minor factor in a healthy, expanding economy. O
may conclude that it is in the realm of the intangible changes
attitudes and expectations that the greatest effects were registered

All this is emphasized by reference to the impact of World
War II; and until this period has been covered, further interpretation of the events of the 1930's must be deferred.

and the failure of World War I "to make the world safe for democracy." The failure of all countries but Finland to pay their war debts, and the general default of foreign countries on their privately floated securities, supported the generally isolationist position that had been traditional in the United States. Even many of Roosevelt's strong supporters on domestic issues considered him extreme in his Chicago speech (October 5, 1937) when he declared the interest and concern of the United States in the events in Europe and suggested a need for the quarantine of aggressors.

The impact of the European war began to grow after the fall of France in the summer of 1940. This was a shattering blow to all but the most confirmed isolationists and marked the beginning of a full scale defense effort. Immediately, Congress passed legislation authorizing a two-ocean Navy and began to build up the Army. Concern about defense production facilities led to action to increase investment in the necessary industries. The emphasis remained, however, upon defense. The draft bill passed by only one vote, and the assumption remained wide spread that protection of the North and South American continents or even the boundaries of the United States and Canada was the sole purpose of our defense expenditures.

Throughout this period, planning in Washington remained in a chaotic state, and the public tended to lag in its response to events in the world, as though failure to act would in some way protect us from the frightful results of war. Business responded only slowly to the change in conditions. Although there was a noticeable pickup in employment and production, prices remained relatively quiet, and there was little inventory accumulation or speculative buying. Consumers, with their larger incomes, increased their spending on durables and soft goods; but there was no buying spree such as was set off by the Korean war in mid-1950 or the Chinese intervention in that war in the fall of 1950.

The fact is that until the Japanese hit at Pearl Harbor on

December 7, 1941, the impact of the defense program had been
very largely to bring about the recovery that had been so eagerly
sought through the period of the 1930's. The mild upward price
movement was more than compensated for by the increase in real
product and real income among all classes, and particularly by
those who had been hardest hit during the depression.[3] The unemployed provided a large reservoir from which to draw the
needed additions to the labor force. Excess plant capacity proved
to be sufficient to increase output without serious bottlenecks developing. New investment programs could be started without
cutting into high priority end-product items. The battle of Britain
increased the concern of the average American for the fate of
Europe, but there was still general reluctance to get into the fight
and to give up the benefits of the recovery that had come at long
last and had now made the United States once more the land of
opportunity, easy spending, and the one safe spot in the free
world. Thus, in spite of the long period of warning and the gradual internal adjustments to the events in Europe, the events at
Pearl Harbor caught the nation poorly prepared for the war and
the implications of a full scale conflict in the modern world.

One of the important repercussions of the period of preparation,
prior to the outbreak of war in 1941, was the increase in prestige
it gave to the leaders of government and labor who had backed
the idea that government spending could easily bring the country
up to high levels of real income and employment. Labor consolidated the gains it had made during the depression under the
favorable auspices of the New Deal. As a result, when the real
defense program got under way, labor was on an equal footing
with industry in negotiating the terms of the stabilization program with the government.[4] The farmer also tended to consoli-

[3] The GNP rose $9.5 billion in 1940 and $25.2 billion in 1941. *Economic Report
of the President,* January, 1957, p. 126.
[4] The tripartite organization of the War Labor Board is evidence of the progress
made by labor, as was the status given to labor throughout the defense establishments.

date his strength. Supports were continued as a guarantee against
sudden changes in conditions, and his prosperity made the farmer
well disposed toward the party in power. The importance of
United States' agricultural products to her allies and potential
allies was capitalized on by the agricultural bloc in the slogan
"food will win the peace." The strength of agricultural interests
in Congress and within the executive branch gave the farmer, big
and little, a preferred position throughout the entire defense and
war period. Draft exemptions were very easy to get and later
became blanket deferments for agricultural workers. Scarce materials were channeled into agricultural implement production so
that improved equipment was generally available. Farm prices
were never placed under tight controls and eventually became
the beneficiaries of subsidy action designed to keep down the cost
of living while raising farm incomes.

After mid-1940, Congress once again delegated great authority to the executive. A Congress that had begun to revolt against
assumption of authority by the executive, but had been unable
to assume the initiative, once more found it necessary to make
sweeping grants of power to agencies and authorities subject to
only the loosest kind of control. Congress could not have avoided
such action and it was generally approved, but it definitely con-
tributed to the weakness of Congress in later years and made
more difficult the problem of fundamental reform of governmental machinery. As long as the major crises of our time can
be met with effectiveness by grants of authority and as long
as this has proved good enough to weather both the depression
and the war without loss of any obvious features of our social and
political organization, it is hard to convince many persons that
there is need for revamping of the basic structure of government
or its procedures.

Equally important is the fact that the renewed delegation of
power to the executive branch accustomed the public to look to
the executive branch for leadership. Under these conditions Con-

gressmen and Senators lost prestige. The attractiveness of service in either branch fell relatively, while the appeal of the executive office gained. The head of a government agency or even a bureau or division could exercise power greater than that commanded by the head of all but the very largest corporation. He was also in a position to learn about the operation of many of the factors most important to the future of the industry or area in which he had greatest interest. As a result, there were a large number of bright young men who entered government service and then left to take less responsible, but better paying posts in private industry.

Throughout the period of the war, Congress continued to harass the departments responsible for the defense and war program, but effective control was lost as long as the crisis continued. Congress did limit, in minor matters, the authority of the departments, but as long as the demands of the powerful pressure groups were honored the basic pattern of the controls and procedures were left to executive decision. No really strong national leaders arose in Congress during the period. The emergence of Senator Truman as a national figure depended less on his leadership than the fact that his committee investigations gained him a great deal of publicity by bringing to light the less favorable details of the progress of the defense effort. The strength of the military was greatly increased, and it was gratifying to many to find that within the Army and Navy there had been hidden leaders of the quality of Marshall, Eisenhower, King, Nimitz, Arnold, and their chief supporters. Throughout the period of the war, however, President Roosevelt continued to dominate the scene. No major decisions were made without his personal approval, and in most cases he modified these to some extent before final execution. His interest in other than major military decisions and policies lagged, but the loose organizational setup of the civilian phase of the defense program left many unresolved conflicts for final decision at the White House.

Examples could be cited without end, but it is sufficient to note that presidential intervention or decision was required to settle disputes over the allocation of steel between the Navy and the Maritime Commission. In many instances, it also took a presidential decision to determine the relative priority to be given many of the procurement programs authorized by the Joint Chiefs of Staff and presumably settled by them.

The result of these developments was not only the continued lack of congressional leadership, but also the failure of any other leader of real political strength to emerge. Strong executives were in the saddle, but their strength was limited by Roosevelt who could terminate their service at his pleasure. It is significant that Sherwood feels that Hopkins began to play a major role in the war program when he abandoned personal political ambitions and decided to devote himself entirely to the service of the President.[5] This role came easily to the military leaders but was not one that could be performed by many other aides. Thus, there was a succession of persons assuming responsibility for the major phases of the effort.

In spite of many differences with his staff, and the concern of many of his oldest admirers over specific programs or policies, the hold of Roosevelt upon the situation was remarkable. He was "the boss" and it was generally conceded that in spite of mistakes in matters of detail and some failure to realize the longer-range implications of his policies, he did not make many errors of judgment on the basic issues of the war program. In most instances his role was to encourage the timid and to set the sights of the war agencies well above the level that they would have attempted had his leadership not been so forceful. The feeling of personal loss that was so widespread after his death is a measure of the hold he had upon the men and women of the country and over the world.

A final background factor that helps to explain the manner in

[5] Robert E. Sherwood, *Roosevelt and Hopkins,* New York, 1948.

which the actual war program evolved is the fact that many former New Dealers were transferred from the emergency agencies of the depression period to key positions in the new defense agencies. Although they became the most vigorous element in the drive to gain conversion from peace to war production and to limit by direct control the production of nonessential goods to release materials and manpower for the military or our allies, they were also interested in preserving the economic and social reforms that had been achieved in the earlier period and of avoiding action that might prejudice the achievement of further gains in the post war period.

In the frequent conflict and misunderstandings between this group and the business leaders who came into the government agencies as specialists in procurement and production and assumed positions of power in these agencies, the ex-New Dealers held their own. In spite of large profits realized by business and the favorable position of many industries producing war goods or strategic materials, the lower income groups in general, and the labor and farm groups in particular, made substantial gains in real income throughout the war period.

In no place did the continued interest in preservation of the principles of the New Deal play a greater part than in the stabilization program. Staffed largely by former New Dealers or by economists with a similar viewpoint the Office of Price Administration, the Treasury, and the Budget Bureau on the purely financial side, and the War Labor Board and Department of Agriculture in their special areas, kept the achievement of reform in mind and were successful in resisting any measures that would seriously hurt the postwar position of the groups favored by them.[6] On the whole, the anti-inflation program was considered a temporary problem; and, as will be developed below, it was

---

[6] The strong Treasury opposition to a sales tax is a good example of this concern. Although it might have proved to be effective in adding to total revenues it was generally opposed on the ground that once used it would never be repealed.

generally agreed that the problem of the period after the war would be the preservation of full employment and favorable prices rather than the inflation and boom which actually developed. Thus the preponderant concern with the problem of depression led to acceptance of many policies which hindsight has shown later became major factors feeding the postwar inflation.

Direct Controls

One of the most important developments of the war period was the reliance upon direct controls. The importance of the direct-control program is found in the relative emphasis placed upon it as a stabilization device in its effect on basic attitudes and relations of groups within the economy, and in the problems which followed its collapse. Government, business, and professional economists agreed that inflation should be stopped and that whatever measures were necessary should be applied. Business groups feared the consequence of a price boom like that of World War I and the subsequent collapse in 1920 with widespread losses on inventories. Economists agreed that we should prevent such events for reasons of stability. They also stressed the inequity resulting from inflation and exorbitant profits for business, and the harmful effects of inflation upon the maximization of output for the war effort. Neither group could bring itself to the point of seriously considering a level of taxes and restriction of credit large enough to achieve price stability without direct controls. It was also generally conceded that some incentive in the form of larger cash income was needed, even though it could not be spent immediately for goods and services.

A few economists stressed the desirability of closing the inflationary gap by taxation and credit control, even though they conceded the necessity of many direct controls. An even smaller number favored the use of indirect controls exclusively. They admitted that taxation and credit control could not prevent some upward price movement in a period of mobilization, with its rapid transfer of resources from peacetime to war activity and of labor from job to job, but they were still opposed to direct control. This view never gained any real support.

The clinching argument for extensive direct controls was the strength of the major unions. The union leadership demanded price control as a *quid pro quo* for their agreement not to strike for the duration of the war and their agreement to accept wage control. Labor leaders also demanded that profits be kept within reasonable bounds and cited the war profiteers of World War I as evidence that direct controls were necessary. The alternative to some agreement with labor leadership was a labor draft—a policy not seriously considered except by a few antilabor extremists.

As a result of these developments, the United States government became the chief force determining the share of the national income going to the major segments of the economy before calculation of taxes. As a standard for determination of generally fair and equitable prices, the Office of Price Administration had to consider profits before taxes. Historical price relationships could be used only at the start, for they rapidly became obsolete. The War Labor Board granted wage increases or allowed wage adjustments to bring industries into line with the generally prevailing wage level. Adjustments for changes in the cost of living became a major factor influencing the share of the wage earner in each industry in the total national product. Rent control regulated the share going to the landlord, and also affected the purchasing power of the dollar income of the worker. Farm incomes were affected by both price controls and support policies and reflected the strength of the farm bloc in the political system. Interest income, the last major element of the total, was affected by the dominance of the capital market by the Treasury and the Federal Reserve Board. Although this control was not new, its extent and duration were greater than ever before. At no time in the previous history of the United States had government exercised such extensive control over the distribution of the national income. The direct-control program represented a politico-economic compromise among interest groups all competing for better economic position. The necessity of maintaining the compromise has been cited as one reason for the somewhat erratic course of the control program.[7] Nevertheless, the policy of trying to maintain the relative position of different groups, with an obvious bias in favor of lower-income groups, prevented a development of a much more serious problem of spiralling wages, prices, and profits.

For this study, the interest in the widespread imposition of direct controls and the assumption of governmental responsibility for the distribution of the national income lies not in the effectiveness of such measures during the war period but rather in their implications for the future. It is generally conceded that war requires the acceptance of a planned economy and that the measures taken in World War II were the minimum required. What is not so clearly understood is that the direct controls used in the war changed the basic power relationships in the United States and were an important factor in the creation of the inflationary bias of the postwar years. In spite of the great unity of the people in the United States during the war, the administration of controls greatly increased both public awareness of and emphasis upon political considerations in economic policy. Wage earners and farmers found that, in spite of the war, their gains in real income that began in 1933 under the favorable auspices of government continued. These gains were solidly based upon increased output but were guaranteed and somewhat increased by effective political action. This led to the dilemma which began to appear during the war and continued after the war: How can the political demands of powerful groups be limited to the increase in productivity once full employment levels have been

[7] Standards used in the direct control program were erratic and uneven in their effect on different sectors of the economy. In the Office of Price Administration, for example, the degree of control achieved in steel prices could not be matched in the clothing or lumber industries.

reached? The rate of progress which prevailed for so many years
in the recovery from the depths of the depression continued in
the period of tremendous expansion during the war and was
capped by the great gains of the period of reconversion after the
war. This has given a whole generation a false sense of the
rate of economic progress that can be sustained over the long run.
Add to this the possibility of one group gaining at the expense
of another by a process involving continuous inflation, and the
most serious basic issue of our day is revealed. We also find that
the past connection between inflation and rapid gains in real
income has lowered the resistance to inflation.[8]

In discussions of this issue with a member of one of the more
responsible unions, I discovered an interesting rationalization of
his position. He believes that, as labor gains increased wages,
business will find income by expanding real output so that there
is no practical limit to the rate of productivity increases possible.
This point is also accompanied by frequent references to the possibility of financing substantial wage increases out of profits.

In the face of labor's demands for higher wages industry has
not had any real incentive to resist. During the war and in the
immediate postwar period most firms found that wage demands
could be met by price increases as long as the government maintained easy credit and favorable general conditions of overall
demand. When the government is an important factor in the
market, the process may be continued indefinitely. The position
of the major groups will change slowly, with first one and then
the other gaining an advantage, while the unorganized will suffer

---

[8] A recent analysis of the relation of wages and prices indicates that one of the
greatest problems arises because of the ability of the wage earners in those industries making greatest progress to get the full benefit of their increased productivity
and thus, in a period of labor shortage to cause wages in other industries to rise
in a similar fashion without regard to productivity increases. U.S. Department of
Labor, Bureau of Labor Statistics, "Productivity, Earnings, Costs and Prices in the
Private Nonagricultural Sector of the Economy, 1947-56" (revised, May 29, 1957),
mimeographed, pp. 1-9; Joint Economic Committee, *Productivity, Prices and
Incomes,* Washington, 1957.

the brunt of the loss.[9] High rates of taxation on corporate profits also reduce the cost of granting a wage increase. If the alternative is a strike this consideration may become dominant.

The important place given direct controls also made it more difficult to develop flexibility and responsiveness of indirect-control instruments such as taxation, expenditures, and money and credit controls with which to meet rapidly changing conditions during the war and postwar period. As will be explained below, it is generally agreed that taxation should have been higher during the war. However, to many groups direct controls seemed to offer an attractive substitute to heavier taxation or credit control. This explains in part the failure to exploit both these measures to the fullest possible extent. The breakdown of the control machinery at the end of the war led to some reaction, but the dream of controls as a solution to popular demands continues to live.

An ideal price and wage control program cannot do more than suppress inflation as long as money income is increasing faster than output. This process began to create problems in the later stages of the war and was an overwhelming factor in the years immediately following the war. The result was at first a further extension of controls. Expanding incomes that could not be spent for the goods available at legal prices made it necessary to ration essential civilian products that were in short supply. This process added to the importance of political considerations in economic policy. The definition of essentiality is one that defies precise expression. The basis for sharing the limited supplies of essential and nonessential goods can either be an arbitrary equal amount per head or becomes a field where there is possibility of widespread bargaining among pressure groups. Even the per-head basis of distribution has a bias in favor of the lowest income groups if they have sufficient purchasing power to use their

[9] Edward F. Denison, "Distribution of National Income," U.S. Department of Commerce, *Survey of Current Business*, XXXII (June, 1952), 16-23.

entire ration. As mentioned above, the allocation process was not
free from political influence in the case of grants of materials for
agricultural implement production and other farm supplies. More
difficult to measure was the extent that the decisions of the War
Production Board and other agencies were influenced by the special industry interests involved in the struggle for scarce supplies.
There is no question that at the start of the war this did happen
and has been well documented by the Truman Committee.[10] The
power of the industries within the War Production Board was
such that the men controlling many aspects of materials distribution were from the industries they were controlling. It is not
surprising that they developed blind spots and maintained positions that could not be supported by disinterested investigators.
The fights that prevented the imposition of grade labeling and
the concentration of production of industry are evidence of the
extent of the concern of industry about its postwar position even
when the world situation looked blackest. It does not require a
cynic to believe that the public record of use of special influence
and position does not reveal at all fully the extent to which the
power of government controls was abused by those who exercised
it. This does not mean that outright graft was common, for
this does not appear to be the case. It was rather a much more
subtle process involving allocations, specifications, contract place-
ment and so forth.

Then there was the increase in special interest pressures
throughout the entire control system. The black market problem
is well known. It is generally agreed, that the longer controls are
imposed and the more the idle balances of cash are piled up in
consumers' hands, the greater the potential difficulties become.
A much more serious problem is the dilemma faced by the con-
troller who finds that in areas not subject to detailed allocation
of output and production control producers will vary their normal

10 U.S. Congress (Senate), Special Committee Investigating the National Defense
Program, *Annual Report,* Washington, 1942-1948.

product mix, or even abandon output of some products entirely. The obvious solution is to place such industries under production and allocation control. This can provide a logical answer to the problem but may not be practical. In any event it will greatly increase the complexity of the control job and require large increases in staff. There is no easy formula which can be used to determine the proper balance in output in a market where prices and production are controlled. The tendency in World War II was to accept some of these problems as ones that had to be lived with, and to hope that the upward price adjustments that followed would not become serious. It was a problem that grew and developed internal stresses and strains in the economy due to the imbalance between prices that were rising and those that had been more successfully controlled. Not only was there the problem of balance but the obvious injustice of such a system became more evident as time went on.

As the outcome of the war became certain, the possibility of gaining special advantage by evading or avoiding controls became more attractive. The continued and growing weakness of controls over clothing and meat production probably caused the largest reaction among consumers. Other cases in the materials field were lumber and castings. In all these areas the problem of maintaining a normal flow of the product desired by the consumer became almost impossible. Textile manufacturers and the clothing industry found that they could increase their profits by manufacturing their higher priced lines, for example, by selling only sport shirts instead of regular dress shirts. Lumber mills finding a small price advantage in 6 x 8 beams could stop cutting siding or boards until a price adjustment was made. Gray-iron foundries refused to produce a casting on which a loss might be made, in spite of a generally favorable profit position. The final blow that broke the back of price control came when the cattlemen withheld their stock and dried up the normal flow of beef into the market. The stakes were high, but the prospect of more favor-

able prices without control made the attempt to break the whole
control effort attractive. The fact that it was a farm group rather
than a business group that held up the public made success easier,
in spite of the fact that cattle raising has become a big business
and is dominated by large-scale operators.

The final result of suppressed inflation was that it provided the
means to support the postwar inflation. The idle cash and other
liquid assets built up in the war came into the market after
controls had been removed and were an important factor in the
price movements from 1946 through 1948. The chief wonder
now is that the inflation was no worse. The remainder of this
story, however, will be left for the next chapter dealing with
the postwar period. It is necessary to cite at this point only the
fact that in the years 1940 through 1946 the increase in demand
deposits, savings accounts of all types, war bond holdings, cash
value of insurance, and reduction of debt amounted to $175
billion.[11] This represented the most radical change in position of
individuals and business that can be imagined.

In addition to the financial aftermath of the direct-control program, there was the effect upon public attitudes and the thinking
of the special interest groups. There is little question but that
they further reinforced the tendency to the politicalization of
economic policy which had grown so rapidly during the depression. Industry and labor vied with each other to gain favorable
governmental action, and the farmer naturally desired to maintain
his preferred position. Labor considered the removal of controls
at the end of the war and the subsequent increase in prices
and profits as a betrayal of their no-strike and wage agreements
made at the outset of the war. Industry reacted similarly to the
rounds of wage increases which received the blessing if not the
direct support of the government. Neither labor nor industry
was too distressed, however, as long as high level employment

[11] *Economic Report of the President,* January, 1957, Table E-15, "Financial
Savings by Individuals, 1939-56," p. 138.

and a sellers' market continued. The struggle between labor and management was more vigorous in the press and in words for public consumption than it was at the conference table considering a wage increase or price policy. The wave of strikes at the end of the war proved to be too costly for both sides and soon stopped.[12] The farmers, benefiting from the world shortage of food and United States' loans and other assistance to war devastated countries, did not need to make any extraordinary demands upon government; but they did not let the basic price support machinery lapse even in the period of greatest prosperity.

The reaction of the public was mixed throughout the war and immediate postwar period. The housewife maintained her natural interest in low prices throughout and continued to demand that price control protect the consumer. But she also patronized the black market, indicated annoyance at the problems of rationing, and shared with her merchant the belief that the whole job of control was done poorly. She demanded controls to keep prices down and then denounced the measures necessary to achieve this end. Credit and monetary controls were so poorly understood that little consumer support for them could be hoped for, but on the question of taxation the use of higher levies that represented the best defense against the postwar inflation was generally opposed. At the start of the war, general public appreciation of its seriousness made possible an attempt to gain acceptance of even higher taxes than were requested, but the slowness of Congress and the emphasis of the Administration on the direct-control program prevented this opportunity from being realized.

Perhaps not the least of the long-run repercussions of the war control program was to make a large number of businessmen familiar with the ways of Washington and aware of the potentialities of government action as it affected their firm or industry for good or bad.

---

[12] The number of man-days idle time caused by work stoppages in 1946 was 116 million. In 1947 it fell to 34 million. In 1956 it was 33 million. *Economic Report of the President,* January, 1957, p. 108.

The general impact of the direct-control program of World War II was to advance further the trends in thinking and popular demands that had started in the depression. The success of controls in achieving their immediate objective—realtive price stability for the duration of the war—was a real achievement in spite of the problems that developed on their removal. In fact, many believe even to this day that if a tight direct-control program had been attempted in the postwar years the greater part of inflation could have been prevented. A further influence lessening the reaction against direct controls has been the fact that in the period of postwar inflation high-level employment and rapidly rising real income have been the rule. Thus the general reaction to the experience with a fully controlled economy has not been nearly as adverse as it might have been if it had been followed by depression. It has also been possible to contrast the recent experience with World War I, when prices moved more rapidly under relatively weak controls and then fell disastrously after general credit controls were imposed in 1920.

A more subtle consequence of our direct-control experience has been the discovery by many economists and others who were in the war agencies that the process of controlling the economy could be a fascinating occupation and an opportunity to put into actual practice their pet theories or to attain the revision of the social order that is most appealing to them. A cruder expression of this reaction is found among many individuals who enjoyed the authority and prestige of their office for its own sake, and realized that with the removal of controls fewer opportunities for such positions would be available. This group is not necessarily antidemocratic or collectivist in general philosophy but is rather without a clear concept of the basic goals of a democratic capitalism. An editorial in *The Economist* foresaw this trend in England and warned against it. They said: "The best plans are good in operation only according to the virtue and the talent of the men who mould and administer them. The end does not justify the means because it is the means which determine the end that is achieved. *There are too many clever people, so carried away by the excellence of their projects that they are prepared to risk freedom itself in order to put them into practice; there are too many experts who are so impressed by expertise that they are prepared to risk democracy itself in order to achieve the right political arithmetic; there are too many planners who would dispense equally with political and economic freedom to get a symmetrical plan.* [13]

Finally there was a group that found in the postwar experience a justification for the continuance of inflation as the only alternative to deflation. Thus the inflation that followed the removal of direct controls was not a sign of weakness but an indication of good planning which was gradually transforming the economy into a form that could continue to maintain full employment indefinitely. In this position we see again the strength of the depression psychosis that has gripped a large part of the world and cannot yet be discounted as a force influencing the basic policies and programs of the United States in a period of inflation.

[13] *The Economist*, August 29, 1942 London. (Italics mine.)

CHAPTER IV

War Finance and Transition: 1939-1946

The excellent studies of the war program now available make it possible to restrict this account to the level of an interpretation of the longer-range significance of the events of the period. Books by Blough, Chandler, Goldenweiser, Murphy, Paul,[1] and others provide an excellent coverage of the basic facts and the reasons for the policies followed during the war period. This section is an attempt to relate these events both to the previous period of depression and to attitudes affecting future policy.

The basic facts of the period can be summarized briefly. Perhaps the most important was the increase of money and other liquid assets in the hands of individuals and business. Between December, 1939 and December, 1945 the money supply increased from $36.2 billion to $102.3 billion, an increase of 2.8 times. Between 1941 and 1946 the net cash borrowing of the federal government amounted to $199,003 million of which nonbank holders bought $109,027 million, commercial banks $68,300 million and the Federal Reserve Banks $21,317 million.[2] Intergovern-

---

[1] Roy Blough, *The Federal Taxing Process*, New York, 1952; Lester V. Chandler, *Inflation in the United States, 1940-1948*, New York, 1951; E. A. Goldenweiser, *Monetary Management*, New York, 1949; Henry C. Murphy, *National Debt in War and Transition*, New York, 1950; Randolph E. Paul, *Taxation in the United States*, Boston, 1954.

[2] "Adjusted demand deposits and currency outside banks," *Federal Reserve Bulletin*, May, 1957, p. 538.

mental transactions, the largest involving the Old-Age and Survivors Insurance trust fund, increased the federal debt, even more. In June, 1940, the debt was $48.5 billion and in June, 1946, $269.9 billion.[3]

Although much has been made of the public's spectacular rate of savings, it is pointed out by Chandler that "it was the size of the cash deficit, which was roughly equal to the amount borrowed outside the government, that largely determined the total amount of private savings. And the savings generated by deficit spending were in the first instance received by individuals and business firms in the form of money."[4] Saving took place because, under a system of direct controls—including the rationing and allocation of goods and materials in short supply—there was no other legal outlet for the increased income generated by new money creation.

The debt-management policies pursued by the Treasury and the Federal Reserve System furnished an additional incentive for individuals and business firms to hold large sums in the form of government obligations. At the outset of the war period the Federal Reserve System abandoned any attempt to maintain its initiative in controlling the money supply or to relate the cost of credit to general economic conditions. The Federal Reserve assured the Treasury that the government could be certain of all the money it needed. As Chandler puts it, the Federal Reserve became a slot machine that would always pay off. The maintenance of low rates of interest by Federal Reserve purchases, which monetized a large part of the debt, leads Chandler to suggest that we went on a "low yield government security standard" for the duration of the war.[5] The Open Market Committee of the Federal Reserve maintained for the duration of the war the pattern of interest rates prevailing at its start. These rates ranged from $\frac{3}{8}$ of 1 per-

---

[3] Joint Committee on the Economic Report, *Historical and Descriptive Supplement to Economic Indicators,* Washington, 1953, p. 61.

[4] Chandler, *op. cit.,* p. 132.

[5] *Ibid.,* pp. 191-192.

cent for the short-term bills to 2.5 percent for long-term bonds.
They bore no resemblance to the rates that should have been
maintained if credit policy had been used as one of the weapons
to fight inflation after the earliest stages of the war. As long as
the Federal Reserve continued to support the market for government securities, the reserve position of the commercial banks
could never be tightened. In addition to direct purchases of government bonds by the Federal Reserve from the Treasury, which
led to increased reserve balances of member banks, the Federal
Reserve bought large blocks of governments in the open market
whenever the banks or other holders of governments felt the need
for more funds. Although it took some time for the financial
community to learn to accept the facts of this situation, it eventually became the practice for business and financial institutions
to unload their short-term low-yield obligations and to hold or
purchase the more profitable longer-term obligations.[6] Under
the policy followed, the risk of holding long-term bonds was
reduced to the point where they were almost as good as cash. It
is not surprising therefore that long-term issues eventually sold
at a substantial premium. By the end of the war, the Federal
Reserve found that it had to sell government bonds to keep the
premium from rising to levels that would eliminate most of the
differential between long- and short-term issues.

A final factor of significance in this area of credit policy was
the experiment in the use of selective credit controls by the
Federal Reserve. The most important was Regulation W dealing
with the terms of consumer installment credit. The evaluation of
the success of this measure is difficult in view of the fact that
most of the goods normally sold on the installment plan were
not available and that the continued increase in money income
gave consumers more ready cash than usual. Its greatest sig-

6 By the end of 1945, Federal Reserve holdings were distributed as follows: 66
percent had maturities within 90 days; 90 percent had maturities of less than a
year, and less than 3 percent had maturities beyond 5 years. L. V. Chandler, *op. cit.*,
p. 196.

nificance, however, was that it was a new *selective* instrument of control. The reaction of the industries which were regulated again suggests that controls greatly stimulate political action by the groups affected.

Tax Policy

The history and significance of tax legislation and developments in the period deserves a book in itself. The highlights were:

1. The individual income tax was transformed from a tax bearing only upon the relatively rich into a tax paid on a current basis by all classes of the population, thus making it a highly productive and sensitive instrument. The progressive element of the tax remained strong and the rates on the upper brackets went to the highest levels ever imposed, but the payment by 42 million persons in 1944 [7] as opposed to 4 million in 1939 represented the most important tax change made during the war.[8]

2. The second major tax change was the great increase in the impact of the corporation income and excess-profits taxes. Along with price control, and the development of contract renegotiation, this move reflected the popular desire to prevent anyone from making excessive profits during the war. Debate over the incidence of the corporation income tax did not affect the popular belief that this tax was taken out of profits and largely from the relatively wealthy stockholder. Contract renegotiation had the same goal as the excess-profits tax. Both were attempts to prevent profiteering and to use selective means to achieve this end. The importance of the Renegotiation Act was that those administering the act were left with considerably more discretion in the determination of what represented a fair return to business. A stronger excess-profits tax administered by the Treasury

[7] U.S. Treasury Department, *Statistics of Income for 1953, Part 1*, Washington, p. 232.

[8] U.S. Treasury Department, *Statistics of Income for 1942, Part 1*, Washington, p. 232.

might have been a wiser policy, but renegotiation recovered large sums in the war period.

3. Rejection of the sales tax was a major instrument of war finance. Opposition was based partly upon administrative grounds, but more important was the reaction against the regressive features of a sales tax. The belief that once imposed it would continue in the postwar period was also important. It was objected to on the ground that it would threaten the maintenance of full employment in the postwar period and adversely affect the gains achieved by the low-income groups during the war.

In general, the relatively mild tax policies followed during this period were a result of an early emphasis upon expansionist policies and of fear of a postwar depression that led to the underestimation of the danger of a post-war inflation. Perhaps the abortive attempt of the Treasury to impose a spendings tax reveals as clearly as anything the underlying thinking of the period. This proposal, and the proposal to use compulsory loans, were supported both as attractive substitutes for heavier taxation and as a means of assuring high-level consumer expenditures in the postwar period when depression was expected.

The history of congressional action on tax bills during the war revealed clearly the difficulty of getting legislative action upon measures required by rapidly changing events. Tax bills introduced at the opening of Congress in January were debated and subject to exhaustive hearings in the traditional manner. Thus the 1942 tax proposals of the administration were not acted upon until October, and the action requested in January, 1943 did not result in law until February, 1944.[9] Congress found it easy to delegate power to administer the economy in most particulars, but in the field of tax policy tight congressional controls were maintained, and all groups or even individuals who might object to any aspect of a tax bill were encouraged to state their views. Even such an obvious measure as the simplification of the individual income

[9] Chandler, *op. cit.*, pp. 116-117.

tax so that a short form could be used, and the average wage earner not be required to be a public accountant, was delayed in passage until 1944. This failure of Congress to step up its pace in considering tax legislation, even in a period of extreme danger suggests that the optimists who think of fiscal policy as a device of great sensitivity must either find some solution to the political problem or lower their estimate of the practicality of using taxation as a means of correcting short-run swings in the cycle. Although all tax increases were opposed by interest groups and much concern was expressed about the adverse effects of taxation upon incentives, the growth of liquid assets in the war period is evidence of the capacity of the public to have paid more.

Government Contracts

Another feature of the finance of the war period was the sheer magnitude of government contracts and payments. At the peak of the war effort approximately 50 percent of the total product of the economy was diverted directly or indirectly into war output. This means that 50 percent of the business done in the country depended on the policies pursued by the government. It is also obvious that the remaining 50 percent, subject to direct controls, was almost as dependent on government policy. The general prejudice of businessmen against the government did not deter them from using whatever means were available to gain the coveted contracts that could mean more or less profit to them. In addition to the concentration of sales to the government, plant expansion and investment were controlled, and largely financed by government either directly or indirectly. In many cases business interests risking hardly any of their own capital became major producers of war goods and recipients of returns which, although they were small in relation to sales, were extraordinary in terms of capital or risk involved. The case of the expansion of the Kaiser interests is an example of an extremely successful operation of this type.

Both during and after the war the building of Kaiser plants and
the expansion of Kaiser interests into new fields were either directly or indirectly sanctioned and financed by the government.
Kaiser represented a new type of entrepreneur. His financial base
was Washington, D.C., and his promotional activities concentrated
upon government officials. Congressional relations became more
important than friendship with the financiers on Wall Street, and
the support of the White House could prove to be a source of
riches and influence greater than that offered by the largest financial institutions in the country. The ultimate in the politicalization
of economic policy will be reached if this type of enterpriser becomes dominant and if it is generally accepted that the path of
business success depends upon access to government contracts and
financial assistance. Aircraft and shipbuilding have long been in
this status; housing may soon achieve it. All companies producing
primary aluminum, including Kaiser, depend on governmental
favors. States and whole regions are also involved in attempts to
secure government contracts. Witness the efforts of New England
to achieve a steel plant, and its more recent efforts to gain favor
from Washington as a means of improving employment and
income in the region.

The agency responsible for the allotment of government funds
for most of the capital expansion during the war was the Reconstruction Finance Corporation. Conceived in the depression as a
means of preventing the bankruptcy of business and financial institutions pressed for cash, it became, through its subsidiary the
Defense Plant Corporation and others, the source of capital for
entirely new companies and activities in the war period. Its budget
was not subject to any real supervision by Congress or the executive branch, and it found that frequent requests for assistance to
particular companies came from Congressmen and Senators. It is
a wonder that it did not become even more corrupt than has been
revealed in the recent congressional investigations of its prac-

tices.[10] The failures of these investigations to find more evidence of outright graft involving transfers of large sums of money for special favor does not mean that there were no deals where the payment for services received took a less crude form. The stakes were power and influence, and the consequences of corruption of a less direct type could be fully as disastrous as outright transfers of cash. In the war period, the government could not avoid many of the invasions into the field of financing and controlling investment, but the experience should make clear the dangers involved in the process.

The experience of the Commodity Credit Corporation, is similar to that of the Reconstruction Finance Corporation. In addition to its activities in the field of agricultural price support programs, it or its subsidiaries became the chief agent of the government in the purchase and sale of internationally traded commodities. The results were less conspicuous because the public generally lacked knowledge of this area, but the results proved to be similar. Importers, exporters, consumers, and producers of the commodities involved found that they could do business best if their contacts with the government official involved were maintained on the most friendly basis or if they could get the assistance of some helpful congressman. Prices were affected by political pressures and often became major issues in diplomatic relations.[11]

Still another area where discretion was mixed with a chance to grant special favor was in the determination of eligibility for special relief under the excess-profits tax, and in the granting of certificates of necessity making the firms receiving them eligible for accelerated amortization of new investment. No investigation such as that made of the Reconstruction Finance Corporation or the Commodity Credit Corporation has been made in these areas, but, whether abused or not, the same negotiations between busi-

[10] U.S. Congress (Senate), Committee on Banking and Currency, *Study of Reconstruction Finance Corporation, Hearings,* Washington, 1950.
[11] U.S. Department of Agriculture, *Report of the President of the Commodity Credit Corporation, 1940-1946,* Washington.

ness and government officials took place with the consequent emphasis upon the importance of political processes as a means to financial gain or survival. Frequent hearings and several changes in the basic legislation revealed the extensive interest of the parties involved. Even within the government there were interest groups advocating more or less strict interpretation of the features of the law. Once the decision had been made that equity or the pressures of the immediate situation required such discretionary laws, the problem of reasonable interpretation was bound to arise and the conflict between different groups was accentuated.

An attempt to appraise the general impact of the World War II period leads to three general conclusions. First, although the tax program of the government was less than could have been desired and increases in rates and coverage lagged badly, the transformation of the individual income tax into a mass tax collected on a current basis is one of the major financial achievements of recent times. It has given the country in the postwar period a chance to maintain both a reasonably equitable and sound basic tax structure in face of increasing demands upon the government. Second, the money and credit policies followed during the war period of spectacular increase in the public debt created a new set of vested interests and have seriously weakened the ability of the government or Congress to maintain stable prices and free markets. Third, more and more groups and individuals found that the government either directly or indirectly determined their business future, level of income, and chances of improving both. Thus the politicalization of economic policy that had begun during the depression continued throughout the war period. The net impact of these somewhat conflicting results is the story that must be told in the next section.

Transition Period: 1945–1946

The period of transition from war to peace, or reconversion, cannot be defined with precision. For the purpose of this study it will be defined as the period from the collapse of Germany to the end of 1946. After the last German offensive that led to the Ardennes Bulge in December, 1944 had been repulsed, the pace of the allied march into Germany increased, and before V-E Day, May 7, 1945, we had begun to shift forces to the Pacific in preparation for the final assault on Japan. As a consequence, planners in Washington began to prepare for the termination of contracts and the eventual demobilization of the largest part of the armed forces early in 1945. By V-E Day many modifications had already been made and the cutbacks in program increased rapidly after that time. The unexpectedly rapid termination of the Japanese war (formal surrender September 2, 1945) with the dropping of the first atomic bombs hastened the demobilization. By the end of 1946, both military and civilian demobilization had been fairly well accomplished.

The dominant trend in the thinking of government officials and the public was the danger of a period of widespread unemployment and depression following the end of the war. In the public mind this was a rather vague fear that was based on the memory of the post-World War I depression and a rule of thumb adage "that what goes up must come down." Support was also given the public's pessimism by the pronouncements of professional economists and others in government. An interesting feature of the public's expectations, however, was that most individuals did not believe that their own affairs would be so severely hit as that of others.

The predictions of both government and the most articulate private economists agreed in their pessimism about the transition period.[12] Model building, based upon estimated projections of the various components of the Gross National Product, led to the conclusion that in no way could aggregate spending be maintained at

---

[12] For an excellent review of these forecasts see Michael Sapir, "Review of Economic Forecasts for the Transition Period," Conference on Research in Income and Wealth, *Studies in Income and Wealth*, XI (1949), 275-367.

a level sufficient to absorb all those seeking work. A common estimate was that there would be as many as 8 million unemployed within a year after the war. The dissenters who did not believe that depression would be the rule and who feared inflation were in a minority. Their views suffered because their interpretations of events did not have the superficial precision of the model builders, and because they relied more upon monetary theory which had been previously abandoned by many of the more influential economists.

Two major influences grew out of the fears of the majority. One was that it was immediately necessary to consider legislation to deal with depression both in the short and long run. Second, all steps possible were taken to see that the measures adopted in the reconversion period were favorable to maintenance of high levels of demand. The first point led to the debate over the terms of the Employment Act of 1946. The second is responsible for the generally easy money, credit, and debt-management policies of the period as well as for generous terms on contract settlement, and for government influence favoring higher wages. Few could object to an act defining the policy and procedures of the government in attempting to stabilize the economy, but it is of interest to note that, both in the hearings and in the wording of the version of the Act which finally passed, the emphasis was upon depression and not inflation.

On the question of reconversion policies covering contract settlement and wages and prices there was much greater conflict. The policies finally adopted represented more the resolution of the conflicting pressures brought to bear upon the government than a reasoned policy. However, the general climate established by the government was favorable to the upward push of basic costs and led to the spiralling of wages and prices. The end of general price control was officially recorded on November 9, 1946; but the failure of Congress to act on the extension of the Price Control Act or to break the strike of the cattlemen who held their beef on the range meant that effective control was over in July.

The problems of characterizing the period are revealed, however, when the total budget position of the government is reviewed. In spite of the widespread fear of a transition depression, the cutbacks in the war program were not only rapid but more severe than many believed desirable. On the other hand, the tax program of the federal government was sustained and the prospect of a substantial budget surplus did not deter the administration from requesting the maintenance of high war-time tax rates. Demobilization of men in service also was pursued at a rate that was more rapid and less favorable to orderly transition into civilian employment than a somewhat slower rate would have been. The major concession to the needs of the civilian economy for assistance in the transition period was the contract settlement program and the repeal and rebate program under the excess-profits tax. The generous terms and relatively rapid settlement of war contracts, the favorable financial position of most firms during the war period, and the rebate of 10 percent of the excess-profits tax all combined to place the business community in a favorable position of great liquidity. The final factor leading to the inflationary pressure in the reconversion was found in the intensity of the demand of both consumers and industry. Need for consumers' goods, housing, and investment in machinery and equipment had been held in check, first by the depression, and then by the war. With the relaxation of controls and the means of financing assured the demands of the public proved to be insatiable.

The less favorable aspects of the period are found in the breakdown of all controls and the initiation of a series of upward price adjustments that continued into the post-transition period. How much of the rise in price level can be blamed upon the policies followed and how much merely reflects the inflation that had been built into the system during the war and then suppressed is a matter of debate. It is certain that the index of consumer prices that prevailed at the end of hostilities could not have been maintained without severe deflation and unemployment. Basic prices under the Office of Price Administration did not reflect normal cost-price relationships, and some of the major cost-of-living items were held down by a subsidy program which disappeared with the end of controls. The expansion of the money supply also tended to call for an increase in relative prices after controls had been removed and free markets once more prevailed. The belief of some economists that the large cash and other liquid balances built up during the war would remain idle was based on depression experience, not on a more reasonable relationship of past behavior in prosperity. However, even the most foresighted were surprised at the potency of the demand and the tendency for the average consumer to draw heavily upon his assets, so that savings in the transition reached the unheard of level of less than 1 percent of personal income in 1947.[13]

This experience cannot become the basis for generalizations about the future, however, as the combination of the depression and war had left the consumer particularly short of durable goods and housing. An additional source of strength was the remarkable reversal in the rate of family formation and the baby boom which set in during the war and the transition period. Demographers are still debating whether this is a permanent reversal, or a temporary change in the timing of family formation and births which will be corrected at some future date. The final result is of little consequence in the short run, however, as the immediate impact of the baby boom has already greatly affected the economy.

Perhaps the most remarkable feature of the period was the fact that there never developed the sort of bottleneck problems that had been widely anticipated as a cause of substantial difficulties in reconversion. Shortages of basic materials were wide-

13 U.S. Department of Commerce, *National Income, 1954 Edition,* Washington, 1954, p. 227.

, spread; and plant capacity could not be fully utilized in many areas, such as auto production, because of such shortages. But there was little sectional or special industry unemployment and in most lines there were more jobs than men able to fill them. Thus the widely feared problem of temporary unemployment due to the technical problems of plant reconversion never materialized. The genius of management in its ability to make do and find means of rapidly getting some products in the hands of the hungry consumers must be recognized. Both the remarkable record of the war plants and this reconversion record emphasize the flexibility of our complex industrial system as long as there is an assured market for its product, in spite of its growing emphasis upon specialized equipment and highly intricate processes.

We are still too close to this period to see fully its implications, but one problem stands out. The favorable market conditions that accompanied inflation make one wonder if an equally favorable record could have been achieved had a less inflationary policy been followed. The constant tendency for the spread between costs and sales price to widen, the inventory profits realized, and the decline in the burden of debt all combined to create a favorable profit outlook and high expectations for the future. The fictitious nature of the dollar profits has been emphasized by many business analysts. This is only partially true, however, as an appraisal of the deflated profit figures will reveal. It is also true, probably, that even fictitious profits can help create a more optimistic business attitude. The reverse is also true—namely, the fear that any attempt to check the inflationary tendencies would precipitate a depression. Here again the extreme importance given to the maintenance of full employment at whatever price reveals the heritage of the depression. More disturbing is the query in the minds of many: Can inflation of a relatively mild variety be sustained and serve as an instrument of policy for a full employment capitalism? No attempt will be made to answer this question at this point; but the transition experience

has made it a major issue and it cannot be ignored. Its most
sophisticated adherents suggest that the worst inequities of a mild
inflation can be offset by escalator clauses and other adjustments
to reflect the decline in purchasing power.

In this period of transition, Congress began to reassert itself—
mostly by acting in a negative fashion. It could deny the executive
power to continue effective wartime controls, but it could not
or did not assume a positive role. The fall election bringing in a
Republican majority made the trend toward an impasse more
pronounced, but did not radically alter the situation. Uninterested
in the subtleties of economic analysis or in long-range institutional
reforms and, at the same time, interested in establishing himself
as a President free from the dominance of the Roosevelt cabinet
and tradition, Truman gave birth to the Fair Deal—a strange
mixture of social welfare program and small-town political favoritism. Opportunism and stubborn insistence upon certain planks
in his program were equally mixed. The field of foreign affairs
and policy was completely separated from domestic policy and
the idealistic side of Truman gave full support to Marshall,
Acheson, and their chief lieutenants. Firm loyalties to old friends
led to the selection and support of rather weak personalities in
most domestic offices. Thus the new postwar domestic responsibilities of government were assumed by relatively weak executives and executive staff, and further checked by a resurgence of
congressional spirit.

Conclusions

The entire war and transition period reflected both the growth
in strength of the formerly weak interests of labor and agriculture
and the growth of concern among all groups in the role of government as it could help them achieve a larger share of the total
product. The remarkable efforts of industry and the spectacular
achievements of the productive forces of the nation characterized

the entire war and postwar period. The growth in the feeling of economic well-being by all but the top income groups increased the public's faith that government had aided in the process. For others than members of the armed forces, the rise in real income was pronounced, and the war was fought without demanding any substantial economic sacrifices from the bulk of the people.

In the financial realm, the failure to follow tough policies in the field of taxation or credit controls, the tendency for strong pressure groups to attain advantage for their constituents, and the increase in liquid assets made this a period of unusual prosperity for the great bulk of the populace. The dominant fear at the end of the war was that of another depression—the rush to pass the Employment Act revealed the strength of this fear. Fortunately the original version of this Act, calling for projection of total demand over a year in advance and the use of government powers to fill in any deficiencies or to remove any excesses, did not pass. There is now general agreement that such a proposal would have been doomed to failure if not worse. The version that did pass was more temperate and called upon the government to use all practicable means to maintain favorable employment conditions without limiting it in any particular.

The war and transition periods completed what the depression had started—commitment of government to assume a new role in the affairs of the nation and growth in the realization that government was a factor that could radically affect both the distribution of income and the shares going to different segments of the economy.

CHAPTER V

Between Wars, and the Impact of the Korean War: 1947–1951

The transition from all-out war production to an equally impressive output of civilian goods, housing, and industrial plant and equipment continued without interruption throughout 1947 and 1948. The recession of 1949 began in the last months of 1948, but by the latter part of 1949 recovery had started. By June, 1950 the economy was back at its old level and the administration was congratulating itself that it had planned it that way. Thus the return to peace was accomplished without any real depression, and in June, 1950 the country could look back over a period of ten years of almost constant high-level employment and rising real income. Although the inflation of 1946 continued through 1947 and 1948, the levelling of retail prices and the decline in agricultural and many wholesale prices in 1949 restricted concern about inflation to the few who had not been able to keep up the pace and ride the escalator. The chief characteristic of the period was the fact that the largest relative gains in real income went to those in the lower income brackets (except for the small number of pensioners, teachers, and others who did not share in the general upward wage movements).[1] The pros-

[1] Average family personal income increased from $4130 in 1947 to $4440 in 1955 current prices before tax, and the family income groups with incomes above $5000 increased from 10.8 percent in 1947 to 13.8 percent. *Economic Report of the President*, January, 1957, p. 106.

perity was broadly based; agriculture, labor, and even the relatively poorer sections of the south all shared with business the
good times that were in such sharp contrast to the prewar decade
of low incomes and depressed agriculture, labor, and business.

The one flaw was the continued need for high taxes. The
heritage of the war debt, international commitments, pension
requirements, and the expanded welfare commitments of the
federal government made necessary a revenue that could be obtained only by levels of taxation greatly in excess of anything
known in the prewar period. The revision of the income tax
system achieved during the war assured the direct taxation of
the mass of the public, but the highly progressive rates that were
maintained furthered the general trend toward more equal income
distribution. There was even a small group of highly paid executives that could complain that their net income after taxes was
steadily falling as the result of taxation and inflation that continued its upward course faster than their salary adjustments.[2]
Low interest rates and conservative dividend policies made the
recipient of investment income another laggard in the rising
income picture, although the generally favorable business conditions assured sustained returns on almost all securities. The most
important method of sustaining the higher-income groups in
something like their accustomed position was the favorable treatment of capital gains under the income tax. With inflation and
good business this became an important source of income which
was taxed at a maximum rate of only 25 percent. Other loopholes
became attractive under the generally high tax levels that prevailed but discussion of them will be deferred.

Still another force tending to equalize real income was the
shift in relative prices of services in face of sustained full employment. The generally favorable labor market continued to

[2] Simon Kuznets, *Shares of Upper Income Groups in Income and Savings*, New
York, 1953.

draw persons from the lower-paid service trades into manufacturing and the building industry. Thus the higher-income groups could not get the personal services to which they were accustomed without a much greater outlay and in many cases could not find any satisfactory servants at any price. It can be generally observed that even with equal remuneration the lower status given domestic servants made it attractive for many to move into other occupations even at the same or slightly lower pay scales.

The consequence of this state of affairs was to sustain or to aggravate the feeling of class and political differences that the relatively wealthy had developed under the Roosevelt administration. The Fair Deal became as much of anathema to the rich as the New Deal. The one offsetting political development was the fact, so well pointed out by Lubell, that the rise of the lower income groups had brought many of them within reach of the top so that they identified their interests with those of the traditional conservatives.[3]

In the field of stabilization policy the experience of this period is most instructive and discouraging. The two major fields of control, fiscal and monetary policy, had become more important because of the large budget, high taxes, and the large federal debt. The declaration of policy as stated by the Employment Act of 1946 gave the administration a mandate to attempt to bring the full force of the government to bear upon the problem of full employment. The rather general terms of the Act gave no really new powers, but they were not needed unless the revenue-raising and appropriation functions of Congress were to be delegated to the executive. Although this point is of great interest and raises many questions that will be discussed later, it seems clear that the main powers required in the postwar period were available and no excuse can be given by the administration for the relative weakness of the policies pursued. If the full powers

[3] Samuel Lubell, *The Future of American Politics,* New York, 1951.

available had been exercised and failure had been the result, a stronger case for new controls could be made.

In the field of fiscal policy, two facts stand out. First, the amazing surplus realized in 1948 and second, the rapid transition from this surplus position to one of deficit.[4] As will be indicated later, the timing of the transition proved to be fortuitous. It was, however, in the right direction and of approximately the right magnitude. In the field of monetary policy, the continuance of Treasury domination of the Federal Reserve and the generally easy-money policy which prevailed throughout the period as a consequence of Federal Reserve support of government bonds at par is the most significant fact.

One of the most controversial issues of the period arose because the Council of Economic Advisers, which assumed office at the end of 1946, chose to ignore largely the role of monetary policy as an instrument of stabilization policy or to positively assert that credit must always be easy. This issue reflects the sharp differences which still exist in the field of economics and the political strength of an easy-money program. It is also a reflection of the particular characteristics of the original members of the Council. Dr. Nourse, the Chairman throughout this period, was a believer in the exhortative approach to stabilization; and, as an economic analyst, was committed to the strategic role of wage-price relationships as the main determinants of economic trends. Keyserling was committed to the ever-expanding economy and to a social welfare program which he thought was threatened by every suggestion of a need for tightening credit or otherwise restraining the boom. Clark was equally committed to the easy-money philosophy of the depression period and reluctant to take responsibility for a restraining policy. The record of the Council as revealed in Council and presidential reports may be referred

[4] In 1948, cash receipts from the public exceeded cash payments by $8 billion. In 1949, a cash deficit of $1.3 billion was realized by the federal government. *Economic Report of the President,* January, 1957, p. 175. The figures are for calendar years.

to as support for this contention.[5] Although the Council did encourage the administration's wish for maintenance of taxes at maximum levels, this position was offset by its willingness to go along with many of the more expansive spending and credit programs that were proposed to meet certain social needs or merely because they were in line with the expansive trend of the period.[6] No adequate analysis of monetary developments appeared in the Council reports of that period, and whatever was said was in line with the Treasury bias for low rates and continued par support by the Federal Reserve.

To return to the budget developments of the period, the change in the net budget position of the federal government between the fiscal years 1948 and 1949 stands out. The following table summarizes the changes in both the regular budget and the Treasury

	(in millions of dollars)				
	1946	1947	1948	1949	1950
Net budget receipts	40,027	40,043	42,211	38,246	37,045
Total budget expenditures	60,703	39,289	33,791	40,057	40,167
Budget surplus or deficit (—)	—20,676	754	8,419	—1,811	—3,122
Total cash operating incl. (Cash budget receipts and cash trust accounts)	43,839	43,591	45,400	41,628	40,970
Cash operating outgo (Cash budget expenditures and cash trust account expenditures, exchange stabilization fund, clearing account)	61,738	36,931	36,496	40,576	43,155
Net cash operating income or outgo (—)	—17,899	6,659	8,903	1,051	—2,185

SOURCE: Treasury Bulletin, June, 1953, pp. 5, 12.

cash income and outgo budget for the fiscal years 1946-1950. The sharp cut in total expenditures at the end of the war and the retention of the high tax rates through fiscal 1948 brought the budget into balance in 1947 and produced the remarkable

[5] Even after the Korean inflation, the Council of Economic Advisers in the Midyear report to the President, July, 1951, favored selective rather than general credit controls.
[6] Paul J. Strayer, "The Council of Economic Advisers: Political Economy on Trial," *American Economic Review*, Supplement, XL (1950), 144-154.

$8 billion surplus of fiscal 1948. The cash figures are even more significant, as they represent, more accurately, the influence of the Treasury on the market and money supply. Thus, the cash surplus of 1947 of $6.5 billion represents the extent to which the Treasury was able to reduce the purchasing power in the hands of the public by its budgetary operations. The extent of the difference between the cash and regular budgets for the years 1947 and 1948 is distorted by the effects of the payment of the armed forces leave bonds and the issuance of notes to the International Bank and International Monetary Fund. The more normal relation of the two budgets is determined by the influence of trust account transactions and intragovernmental payments that tend to be more stable over the years.

The tax cut of 1948, the increased foreign aid program (started with the "Truman Doctrine" of aid to Greece and Turkey, and the declaration of the Marshall Plan in June of 1947, which was really backed by an operating program in 1948), the reversal of the downward defense expenditure trend, and the large increase in agricultural support payments operated on both sides of the budget so that a steady trend set in, changing the fiscal policy of the Treasury from that of exercising a restrictive force to that of making a net contribution to the national income which was realized in the cash deficit of over $2 billion in fiscal 1950. A part of this result is due to the much discussed built-in flexibility of the highly progressive tax system and the commitments of the federal government to increase agricultural payments and other welfare payments in the event of an economic decline. However, the tax cut is what made the shift so extensive and can be justified by hindsight as a wise move in face of the failure of business to expand. For our purposes, the lesson to be learned is the difficulty of knowing when such a major change in fiscal policy should be initiated. The author, along with most other economists, was strongly opposed to the tax cut of 1948 and applauded the President's veto of the bill. Although there were other reasons to be less than enthusiastic about the 1948 bill, the fiscal policy was correct and the economists were wrong.

The difficulty of policy formulation is further revealed by the abortive attempt of the administration to launch a new anti-inflation program in January, 1949 with special emphasis upon additional revenue.[7] Although the request of the administration was ignored by Congress on general political grounds, not on economic policy, the repeated attempts of the administration to gain its tax increase program stand out as a horrible example of the inflexibility of executive policy in a period of transition. The record of the Federal Reserve in reversing its policies insofar as it had the power, specifically the easing of its restraints on consumer credit and housing credit, suggests that the economic indicators were sufficiently clear by early 1949 to guide the policy formulators had they been free from political commitments.

The record of the entire period is one that raises many more questions than it answers. The reason for the mildness of the recession of 1949 has been argued at great length, but it is still difficult to be certain why what might have been a substantial adjustment proved to be a mild inventory recession of relatively short duration.[8] The continued emphasis of the Council on the temporary props which sustained full employment and rising real income prior to 1949, in spite of inflation, represents another source of confusion. What would the record have been had there not been a succession of measures such as the armed forces leave bonds, the European recovery and mutual assistance program, the revival of defense expenditures, a remarkably sustained demand for new housing, and a very favorable agricultural price situation and good crops? The significant result of the temporary or uncertain nature of many sources of effective demand was the unwillingness of those who had either the power or influence to act with force to try to stem the inflation. If this is a fair

---

[7] See *Economic Report of the President,* January, 1949.

[8] Benjamin Caplan, "A Case Study: The 1948-1949 Recession," National Bureau of Economic Research, *Policies to Combat Depression,* Princeton, 1956.

explanation of the reason for the timidity shown, it is significant for the future, in that it undoubtedly indicates a bias against restraint, and the arguments pointing out the dangers of too restrictive a policy always tend to appear more persuasive than those favoring restrictions. It is this tendency backed by the interest group pressure opposing specific acts against their immediate interest, that threatens a perpetual inflation much more than the force of organized labor.

This period also revealed the inadequacy of a program that is not internally consistent. In the years 1947 and 1948 the large cash surpluses would seem to have been a significant force in preventing an inflation. They were, however, offset to a large extent by the easy-money policy which permitted the expansion of credit and the monetization of the outstanding debt so that there was never any real money or credit stringency.[9] A further source of inflationary pressure came from the rise in the velocity of circulation of the money supply.[10] Thus, if one lesson can be drawn from the record of these years, it is the need for a much more highly integrated policy, with full awareness of the various means of escape from restraint that can be exploited in periods of boom.

One final point has to be made with regard to the Tax Reduction Act of 1948. This act is the first of a series of acts that have greatly lowered the severity of the progression of the individual income tax without clearly indicating that this was the intention of Congress. The key device used in the 1948 revision was that of extending to all taxpayers the privilege of joint returns once restricted to the states with community property laws. Thus, the salaried man with an income of $50,000 who could split his income with his wife (assuming she had no income) paid at

[9] Total bank loans and investments increased from $114 billion in 1946 to $120.2 billion in 1949, while bank holdings of government obligations fell from $74.8 billion to $67.0 billion. *Economic Report of the President,* January, 1957, p. 166.

[10] Turnover of demand deposits increased from 25.2 in 1946 to 32.1 in December 1948 in New York and from 16.5 to 21.0 in other leading cities. *Federal Reserve Bulletin,* XXXV (1949), 1465.

rates applicable to a $25,000 income although, of course, he had to pay on the entire $50,000. Similar rules were applied to the estate tax with equally beneficial results to the top bracket group. This point is made, not to argue for or against any particular pattern of progression, but to point out that the major reduction accomplished in 1948 was done in a manner calculated to conceal the true nature of the action.

All the trends noted in the earlier sections were accentuated and some new forces set to work. The expectations of the mass of the voters were further increased. The recession was too brief to more than dampen the spirits of the public; and the inflation, although troublesome to many, was overshadowed by the high levels of income and employment. It even became possible to think of the inflation as a good thing if the coincidence of inflation and prosperity were believed to be interrelated in some causal manner. If this interpretation is correct the result was to make the public believe that nothing much more need be done at the moment to assure the continuance of prosperity. Demands for action or basic reforms must await the first signs of real distress.

Throughout this period the dominant political trend was conservative in spite of the remarkable Truman victory in the fall of 1948. The problems of a Republican Congress and a Democratic President which were troublesome and frustrating to the administrator and politician alike did not end with the election of 1948, for a coalition of southern Democrats and northern Republicans operated effectively to prevent any major changes in domestic policy. The substantial achievement in the foreign field was made possible more by the poorly timed Russian moves of aggression than by a conversion of the conservatives to a new sense of American responsibility.

It seemed throughout this period that the forces leading to a relatively enlightened foreign policy were working in the opposite direction domestically. Fear of Russia, disillusionment over China, the failure of all attempts to find a basis for a settlement between Russia and the West, and the revelation of the penetration of Communists into the government and their acquisition of some atomic secrets all worked to increase the trend against government and reform.

The spectacular implications of the Hiss indictment in December, 1948 caught the public's imagination and excited their interest much more than basic political or economic reforms. The Hoover Commission Report gained some attention, and in June, 1949 Congress granted power to the executive branch to follow the report's major recommendations on reorganiztaion. But the popular hope that the Hoover recommendations would lead to government economy, and thus tax reduction, far outweighed, the public's interest in improving the basic machinery of government so it could do a better job with the same money.

The Impact of the Korean War: June, 1950–June, 1951

The unexpected outbreak of the Korean war and the United Nations' decision to intervene at the instigation of the United States occurred under vastly different circumstances than the outbreak of the European war only a little over ten years earlier. Recovery from the 1949 recession had progressed so that there was little slack in the labor market. Plant capacity was practically fully utilized and investment expenditures were at a high level. Consumer demand was strong, especially for durable consumers goods; and at the beginning of the summer building season a new record for building starts was established.[11] Taxes were at a peace-time peak much above the level prevailing in September, 1939. The public debt was approximately $256.7 billion instead of $47.6 billion.[12] States and municipal budgets were expanding rapidly as states and local governments sought to meet needs which had been deferred during the long period of depression

[11] $28.5 billion of new construction activity was put in place in 1950 in contrast to $22.8 billion in 1949. *Economic Report of the President,* January, 1957, p. 155.
[12] *Economic Report of the President,* January, 1957, p. 174.

and war when less than normal capital expenditures had been made. New demands for local government services arose out of the shifts in population and industry which had occurred during the war and as the result of the continued "baby boom" and high rate of family formation which continued the startling reversal of population trends begun in the war period. Consumers and businessmen had recently experienced a long period of serious inflation and the problems of living under the direct controls required by a war economy. Liquid-asset holdings were large and net indebtedness was low relative to income.

All this was in sharp contrast to the conditions that prevailed at the start of the previous war. At the start of World War II, when the slack in the economy permitted a large increase in output of war materials and also an increase in available civilian goods, the tendency of consumers and businessmen accustomed to depression was to respond conservatively to the new situation. A further difference was the lack of ready cash in the earlier period.

The result of these differences was fully as great as one might expect. As soon as it became evident that a serious disturbance was possible, consumers and businessmen reacted alike. Memories of shortages and price increases which had been characteristic of the later stages of the past war drove them to buy ahead and in large amounts. Price was a secondary consideration. This was possible without the government running a deficit as there were large cash holdings available and credit continued easy due to the rigid bond support policies of the government. Inventories started to climb and sales of durables rose to extraordinary levels. Some claimed that they had to buy ahead to "get the products before they were all taken by the hoarders." Others were frank to admit that they were following what they believed to be the lessons of recent experience and were going to do their best to hedge against the sacrifices that they had suffered before. The trader saw a favorable market and could not resist marking up goods even before they rose at an earlier level of production.

The buying spree was encouraged by the uncertainty of the nature of the war in which the country was involved and the frequent and alarming reports coming from Washington about the need for full mobilization. Thus conditions that did not prevail in the earlier war until well into 1942 or 1943 were immediately brought to the mind of the public with the consequent stimulus of inflation in the worst possible manner from the point of view of the stabilizer. Additional difficulties arose because of the debate which started almost immediately over the need and appropriateness of direct price and wage controls. The dangers of being caught with a low price or a low wage rate in the event of a price "freeze" also served as a stimulus to rapid price and wage advance.

The importance of the psychological basis for the buying wave is revealed by the drop in purchases after MacArthur started driving the North Koreans back up the peninsula. The lag between planned expansion of military goods and actual output also served to allay the fears of the public, who believed at the outset that the shortages of civilian goods that might be expected at the peak would be miraculously realized within the first months. Although it has been alleged that some of the military budget requests called for levels of production that were as high or higher than those achieved in World War II, actual contracts placed and firm orders received by producers were disappointing to all concerned. The Bureau of the Budget and the President cut the requests of the more eager military with the aid of the Department of Defense top civilian staff. Even given the authority, contracting officials found that weapon designs had not been agreed upon and that the actual composition of the additional arms required by the new situation was still being debated with acrimony among the armed services. By November, the speculation of July and August had subsided; and with MacArthur on his way to the Yalu, the public was relaxing and conditions were returning to normal. In the brief flurry set off by the outbreak of the war, prices had risen and wage rates had continued their post-World War II climb. The indices of wholesale prices rose from 157.3 in June to 171.7 in November.

Throughout this period the budget was in balance and net government expenditures were slow to rise. But the effect of the new obligational authority extended by Congress was felt well in advance of even completed contracts and far in advance of any cash payments by the government. Another way of saying the same thing is to say that in face of expectations of new orders business added to inventories and investments. Business wanted goods rather than money.

The sudden reversal of the course of the war following Chinese intervention on November 26, 1950 and the retreat of the American and United Nations' forces back down the peninsula renewed the speculation of midsummer with even greater force. A state of national emergency was declared on December 16. Again the stories emanating from Washington were alarming and the public began to fear the outbreak of World War III. The knowledge that Russia had created an atomic explosion in the fall of 1950 added to the public's fears. Stories of a plan for an 8 million-man army with appropriate equipment were circulated. Although again the actual orders for equipment and the drafting of men did not keep pace with the expectations of the press, the delays were discounted and the full fever of a war situation led the economy on and upward.

This speculative discounting of the impact of the war took place in spite of various steps taken by Congress and the administration to check the inflation. Soon after the start of the war, in June, Congress considered legislation requesting additional powers of a discretionary type to impose direct price, wage, and materials control. New revenue legislation was requested with the goal of maintaining a balanced budget. On all fronts the administration was rather more successful in getting additional powers than

might have been expected in a situation short of a major war.
New revenues of almost $10 billion were provided by the first
Revenue Act of 1950 and the Excess Profits Act of 1950.[13] The
Defense Production Act of 1950, signed on September 8, gave
the administration powers to impose virtually all the controls used
at the peak of World War II. The one flaw in the policies followed was the continued commitment of the Treasury to the low
interest rate policy and the continued support of the long-term
interest rate by the Federal Reserve. Even in this area, however,
new trends were foreshadowed by the rise in short-term rates
and the sharp break between the Federal Reserve and the Treasury (August 18, 1950) over refinancing, when the public first
had knowledge of the extent of the differences of the two agencies.[14] Little more could have been asked in the short period since
the war began. The response was probably as good as it was because of the widespread fear that the war would develop rapidly
and might even open up into a major conflict with Russia.

As the procurement program lagged, so did the control program. As long as we were not in a full scale war it was difficult
to get the personnel to man the control jobs. It is alleged that
many men turned down the directorship of the Economic Stabilization Agency before the President was able to get Alan Valentine
to take the job. Once established, the Economic Stabilization
Agency had difficulty in getting any staff; an equally difficult
period followed before Mike DeSalle came to head the Office of
Price Stabilization. Even more confusing was the general lack of
precision in thinking on the issue of the nature of the job ahead.
Few wanted to impose direct controls if they were not absolutely
necessary. On the other hand, given the power to do so and the
public belief that they should be imposed, there was danger in
delay which played into the hands of the speculators. Also the

---

[13] Donald C. Miller, "The Revenue Act of 1951: A General Survey," *National
Tax Journal,* V (March, 1952), 40-52.

[14] C. C. Abbott, *The Federal Debt,* New York, 1953, pp. 96-100.

vital question of who was to administer the control program served to check those who wished them but could not willingly start a program without an adequate staff.

The general easing of the situation up until November made the question of a thoroughgoing control program an academic one, unless some bold spirit was going to attempt the impossible job of rolling back all prices and wages to levels that prevailed in June of 1950. Although there was some public pressure to do this, it was never seriously considered in view of the magnitude of the job and the lack of organization. Thus, when the situation once more started to get out of hand after the reversals of late November, the government lacked the basic staff and information necessary to place the economy under full-scale controls. The growing seriousness of the situation began to help in recruiting personnel for key posts in the control agencies, but as late as January the total personnel of the Economic Stabilization Agency (including the Office of Price Stabilization) was well below that necessary to do the job of price control. No field staff existed and basic organizational structure was still being debated.

The rapidity of the renewed price rises brought increasing pressure for action to halt the movement which at some points began to take on the quality of a German type inflationary panic. The story of the final events leading up to the decision to impose a general price freeze on January 26, 1951 has been told elsewhere, but it is of interest to note that the chief proponent of control was Mike DeSalle, a politician with an ear to the ground.[15] It is also worth noticing that organization of the office, and especially the field organization with which to cope with the control problem became the function of the professional politician rather than the professional administrator.

The fiscal program of the administration received new impetus from the turn of events, and the 1951 request of the administra-

---

[15] G. G. Johnson, "Reflections on a Year of Price Controls," *American Economic Review, Proceedings,* XLII (1952), 289-300.

tion for an immediate $10 billion and another $5 billion later should be applauded as more vigorous and much more timely than the record of the Treasury at the outset of World War II. Although there was resistance on the part of Congress to so large an increase, the 1951 Act did add $7.2 billion to the annual revenue and permitted the Treasury to balance its cash budget in fiscal 1952, although the conventional budget showed a $4 billion deficit.

The general strength of the overall fiscal action taken in both 1950 and 1951 can be attributed to a greater appreciation of the need for a strong policy by both Congress and the administration. This was aided by the widespread belief that there was danger of an even greater war than had yet been faced. In other words, the need to plan our defense to protect the country in the event of a full-scale war tended to work to our adantage. Much less favorable was the renewal in the 1950 and 1951 acts of the trend noted in connection with the 1948 legislation. This was the opening of loopholes for special-interest groups and the failure to tighten up some devices of avoidance that became increasingly attractive in the face of the higher tax rates. Among the worst of these actions were the extension of of percentage depletion allowances to almost all the extractive industries (including such products as sand and gravel, clay, and coal), opening up of the family partnership device of tax avoidance, extending the capital gains treatment to income from cattle raising and coal mining, and the increase in the rate on long-term capital gains only 1 point (from 25 percent to 26 percent), when other rates rose much more sharply. As a result, by use of all or some of these devices, almost anyone with a diversified income or funds to invest could avoid the severe rates of taxation that were nominally required of large-income groups.

Another tendency that had serious implications was the growth of outright evasion as evidenced by audit of returns and the scandals in the Bureau of Internal Revenue. Self-employed, including

professional men, farmers, and casual workers, were major offend-
ers, and the records all show a widespread underreporting of dividend income.[16] Attempts of the Bureau of Internal Revenue to
obtain additional staff to make a more complete audit were not
successful—Congress refused to grant the necessary appropriations to hire the men in spite of the evidence that a dollar spent
on additional enforcement would return several dollars in additional revenue. The result of this situation has been to place at a
substantial disadvantage the worker or white-collar employee who
has his income tax deducted at the source and raises an issue di-
viding the country along lines that roughly conform to class interests. This feeling has been accentuated by the extensive publicity
given the abuse of expense accounts as a means of realizing tax-
free income. Together with wasteful advertising outlays and
other business expense charges this problem has probably been
exaggerated in importance, but the testimony of many businessmen who have sought to strengthen their case against the excess-
profits tax by making wild statements about their free spending
of a 10- or 20-cent dollar has confirmed the public's belief that
there are many who are able to defeat the true intent of Congress
and avoid the impact of the progressive tax system. Add the
growth of insurance and pension plans designed as tax avoidance
devices, and the popular conviction that the whole revenue system
is a racket is substantiated.

One must conclude that the net gain in revenue achieved in a
remarkably short period was gratifying. However, the growth in
the differential impact of our tax laws was discouraging and offset
the feeling of progress in management of our fiscal policy. If
the tax system is further modified to open additional avenues of
escape it will not be long before it will be intolerable.

[16] Selma Goldsmith, "Appraisal of Basic Data Available for Constructing Income
Size Distributions," *Studies in Income and Wealth,* vol. 13, New York, 1951, pp.
266-327.

George Garvey, "Functional and Size Distributions of Income and Their Meaning," *American Economic Review, Proceedings,* XLIV (1954), 236-253.

The field of monetary policy represents a much clearer picture in this period. Starting with a rigid government-debt-support policy and the extensive monetization of the debt, the period ended with the freeing of the Federal Reserve and the general tightening of the money and credit markets over the country. The story of the various steps involved in the transition cannot be covered in this review, but the importance of the Treasury-Federal Reserve accord of March, 1951 cannot be exaggerated. Not only did monetary policy once more come to play a role in the general stabilization program, but the forces of "expansion at any price" were defeated in the first major engagement since the beginning of World War II. It is still too early to tell how permanent the victory may be, but the influence of the inflationists has at least been offset to some extent. The political implications of the new policy make it difficult to anticipate how reactions will work themselves out. The recession of late 1953 and early 1954 was cited by the inflationists as the inevitable result of the tightening of credit. If such an interpretation is accepted, the public may begin to believe that a return to a perpetual easy-money policy is required. This issue is strategic, as it is but another aspect of the overfull employment bias which is the basis of the fear of many economists that there is an underlying inflationary current in the United States today.

The story of the use of direct controls in this period is instructive for a variety of reasons. It is important to study this period in order to emphasize the difficulties of planning a direct-control program in a period of rapid transition when the objectives being sought are not clear and the basic conditions affecting the achievement of any objective keep changing all the time.

Perhaps the main reason why the direct-control program did not make much difference was the fact that it was not imposed soon enough. It is difficult to see how this could have been avoided, for even if the most confirmed advocate of controls had been in power he would have had qualms about their imposition prior to December, 1950 and in this event he would have gained a few weeks at the most. Even an elaborate stand-by control organization offers little hope for improvement due to the difficulty of getting adequate staff for such an agency.

A second reason was the writing into the law of various exceptions or limitations on the control powers—limitations which proved to be inconsistent with tight control. Most difficult and almost inevitable were the various concessions that were made to agriculture in the name of parity. Once granted, similar adjustment clauses had to be given labor, and it was not long before industry gained similar treatment. These concessions interacted; it is even claimed by some students of the recent period that controls accelerated the pace of upward wage adjustments by rapidly generalizing the concessions made to the major unions by granting increases to the smaller unions and the unorganized. The Wage Stabilization Board started to weaken as early as February, 1951, when it permitted the United Mine Workers to get a raise negotiated just prior to the wage freeze of January. It may be claimed that the bureaucracy slowed up the pace of increases even when no real standards prevailed, but this assumes that the pace would have been rapid without controls.

A third reason for the ineffectiveness of controls was the necessity for many upward price adjustments to permit rapid increases in certain military products and to reflect the sharp rise in the prices of basic materials traded in world markets and not subject to full domestic control. Price stability could be achieved only if compensating downward adjustments were forced in other sectors. This is now generally conceded to be impossible in view of the rigidities which prevail throughout the economy. The price lid can be held on only so tightly and in a situation short of full-scale war this cannot be very firm. Combine this failing with those mentioned above, and the difficulties of price control are clearly indicated.

The second major lesson mentioned above, that of the difficulty of planning or controlling an economy in a period of rapid transition when objectives keep changing, is one that is not yet as widely understood as it should be. In its simplest terms the lesson of 1950-1951 is that we have not yet learned how to formulate policies and programs so that they are internally consistent and so that their full implications can be transmitted to those who have the job of interpreting the impact of program upon the economy. One reason for this failure is the difficulty of setting objectives when the initiative is in the hands of a foreign power.

One of the greatest sources of difficulty was the uncertainty of departmental and congressional leaders as well as the public about the nature of the Russian threat and the best means of combating it. The reasons for the sharp differences among responsible officials in their estimation of the immediacy of the Russian threat cannot be generally known at this time because of security restrictions on the basic intelligence reports that were the basis for differences in view. The fact that does stand out is that, for various and sometimes obvious reasons, the original program for full mobilization was cut back and postponed several different times during the period 1950-1951. To those who still believed that we were in immediate danger this was a frustrating experience, but to those who were attempting to design the control program the frustration was increased by a lag of several weeks or longer between the cutback and the translation of new programs into meaningful schedules of production and therefore materials availability.

For example, during the first half of 1951, the Economic Stabilization Agency had to work on the assumption that steel, copper, and other strategic materials would be in such short supply that a sharp cut in civilian output of durable goods would be required. When, in March, the pressure on prices was reduced and goods seemed once more to be in ample supply, the official conclusion that this was merely a temporary respite was forced by both the public statements of production officials and the internal schedules of military production then available. Actually, durable goods and car output were cut only moderately and in many cases no more than would have been the case without controls, since the market surge of 1950 had weakened demand for such items as refrigerators and television sets in the subsequent period. Car and truck output, for example, reached 8 million units in 1950 and was still at the 6.8 million level in 1951 and 5.5 million in 1952. The conclusions of the Economic Stabilization Agency were not wrong because of poor analysis but simply because the official production data given as basic material for analysis was grossly exaggerated. The author, working in the Economic Stabilization Agency at the time, began to attempt to make some allowance for the lag in program but found it impossible to get verification of his suspicions from official sources. It was not until he had spent an evening with financial analyst Joe Livingston that he became convinced of the extent of the difference between projected and realizable military output.

The implications of this failure of economic intelligence to be correctly transmitted within the government are far reaching. Not only did it lead to an attempt to impose a type of direct control that was not required but it could have caused serious market difficulties had the tax program of the government been passed as requested by the administration in January. One of the features of this program was the use of selective excises at high rates on durable goods that were scheduled to be cut back sharply within the year. Had these rates been approved, unnecessary hardships would have been imposed upon consumers and industry. A similar problem arose in connection with selective credit controls. The extent of the necessary or desirable tightening of credit to consumers is relative to the availability of goods. In addition, the very selectivity of both the excise tax and "Regulation W" program made the impact of wrong intelligence bear heavily upon only certain sectors of the economy and raised the question of the justice of such action.

To conclude this section it can be said that while the psychological gain from the imposition of direct controls in January may have been considerable, the continuance of controls after mid-1951 may have done more harm than good. The only qualification necessary is the fact that the existence of a control agency with a staff gave some protection against a rapid change in the situation and a renewal of the sort of speculative fever which had been set off by the Chinese intervention. This point has such strength that even the most hardened opponent of controls could not deny its cogency, but it suggests that some concessions might have been made during the summer of 1951 instead of claiming that the direct-control program was essential at the moment.

Still another suggestion, frequently made, has attracted considerable attention. This was to maintain a truly selective control program. Galbraith has given this theory its most persuasive presentation, but again political realities make it difficult to see how the program could be expected to receive the necessary support without being so weak that it would be ineffective. It is also true that in a modern complex economy problems have a way of multiplying beyond the original point of impact, and a selective program might well be forced to become a comprehensive one in a short period after its inception.

To date, nothing has been said about the materials-control program and the various controls and subsidies for investment in defense plants and equipment. The material-control program suffered from the same problems mentioned above in connection with price and wage control. Assuming a rate of defense output that was grossly exaggerated, the full array of materials scheduling and allocations developed in World War II was attempted. The consequence of this type of program was probably to slow up rather than speed up the achievement of the defense effort. Here, however, the relation of materials and price control raises an important issue. If the above analysis is correct, it follows that the slower pace of the defense effort made the problem of inflation control easier.

In both areas of direct control another fact must be mentioned. This is the difficulty of judging accurately the true capacity of the economy as a whole or any particular sector of the total. In World War II this lesson was never fully learned and many emergency programs were superimposed on a fully controlled economy without cutbacks in previously authorized programs. Overestimation of objective and underestimating of ability to do it both indicated much greater strains on the civilian sector than later proved to be the case. Expansion in gross national product during the last half of 1950 and first half of 1951 proves that even generally accepted standards of full employment do not measure some theoretical maximum but more nearly a practical operational maximum until pressure for further advance is felt.[17] The problem of measurement of our real capacity remains one of the most difficult problems we face.

In spite of the rather unpredictable events in the area of planning and control the most important area where unforeseen events took place was in the field of consumer spending habits. The end of World War II brought out the importance of large liquid assets and deferred demands as a basis for a temporary spending spree, sharply reducing the level of net saving out of current income. The Korean outbreak indicated that a similar spree could still be set off as long as asset holdings were relatively high and credit easy. What was added in 1951 was the fact that after a spree of major proportions it was possible for the shift in buying habits to be reversed suddenly and lead to a rate of net saving completely unprecedented in a period of relative freedom and general availability of goods. Thus the hope of economists that the consumption of individuals would remain in some stable relation to income has been doomed, at least as far as the short

[17] GNP increased from $329.9 billion in 1950 to $354.2 billion in 1951 in prices of 1956 value. In current prices the increase was from $285.1 billion to $328.2 billion. *Economic Report of the President*, January, 1957, p. 123.

run is concerned. The spending habits of consumers have proved to be volatile and especially sensitive to shifts in consumer expectations. This fact combined with the tremendous leverage that can be exerted by changes in the inventory segment of net investment makes the possibility of rapid and frequent changes in the direction of the economy seem rather more formidable than has been generally conceded in recent years. In any event, the machinery to meet quickly such changes does not exist, and the lessons of the period just studied do not help much in instructing the planner how to devise such machinery.

It is enough to note that as of June, 1951 inflationary pressures were slight in spite of the Economic Stabilization Agency and Office of Price Stabilization predictions. The request of the administration for an extension of the Defense Production Act with additional powers was rejected by Congress which generally weakened the control sections by insisting that every group be permitted to get on the escalator and enjoy the benefits of normal markups above any price or wage change. Consumers, told that price inflation would be renewed in full force by fall, still "sat on their hands" and spent less than a normal part of their current incomes. Construction and investment subject to special restrictions continued at new, high levels; but predicted shortages did not materialize, so that an increase in both civilian and military output continued simultaneously. Some cynics began to worry about the effect of peace on the economy and as one put it, "what we have to fear is not the fear of peace but peace itself."

Hoping to stave off some of the worst amendments to direct controls, the President asked the new session of Congress for an extension of the Defense Production Act without seriously attempting to tighten the terms that already made it difficult to hold the line. Instead of accomplishing this objective, the new fiscal year was started off with the passage of a seriously weakened control act. In the one instance where the President sought additional power, that is, the authority to control livestock slaughtering by license, he met a resounding defeat and consequently had to withdraw the promised rollback of meat prices in the later months of the year. Margins of business profit were further protected by the addition of a clause in the new act requiring the Office of Price Stabilization to adjust prices without question to reflect the increase in costs since the outbreak of the war. In spite of the general prosperity which prevailed, the government became increasingly unpopular and confidence in it was seriously reduced. The war was unpopular, controls unpopular, and even President Truman lost some of the widespread popular support that had given him the election in 1948. Party lines were badly split and some of the stronger Democrats such as Paul Douglas became almost as far removed from the President as the opposition. Within the executive staff, the strong bid for power and influence of Leon Keyserling was doomed by his resounding defeat on the bond support issue, and the Council generally fell to low estate and could exercise little influence within the government. The restoration of the Federal Reserve to a position of greater influence was qualified by the withdrawal of its power to control consumer mortgage credit. It was fortunate that the fiscal year 1952 was to be one of relative ease, as it is doubtful if the government was in a position to exercise the leadership that would have been required in the event of a new crisis of major proportions.

CHAPTER VI

1951-1958

The recovery of the United Nations forces in Korea from their setback in late 1950 led to a general relaxation of the tempo of the defense program, in spite of all protestations to the contrary by the administration. Although spending continued to increase, the rate of increase was not as rapid as projected and the capacity of the economy was not placed under severe strain. Consumers continued to spend somewhat less than normal proportions of their current incomes; and, although business investment continued at extraordinarily high levels, no repetition of the speculative boom of the later part of 1950 and early part of 1951 reappeared. In some lines, such as television, inventories were too large and manufacturers had to cut output until they were reduced. The period as a whole was, however, one of sustained boom, plentiful job opportunities, and high incomes. The upward movement of prices was limited and the serious inflationary pressures that had been predicted in early 1951 did not appear.

The new policies of the Federal Reserve continued in force without any of the dire effects so widely expected by the opposition prior to the March accord. Although auto and durable goods production were cut again slightly from 1950 levels, the cut was not sharp and few persons had to do without any product that was needed. By 1952 some of the new plant capacity for the output of basic materials began to come into production and thus ease the basic materials problem. Men were still fighting and being killed on the mountains of Korea, but the country was once more congratulating itself on the high level of prosperity, living standards, and full employment.

The tempo of the election campaign increased up until November of 1952. Communism, corruption, and Korea were played upon with mounting fury; and a combination of the great personal prestige of General Eisenhower and the low estate of President Truman made the campaign focus less on the issues of the future than the errors of the past. How much the victory of the Republicans represented a belief on the part of the people "that it is time for a change" and how much it represented a personal vote of confidence in Eisenhower can be debated at length. There is little question, however, that the vote for the Republican side was a vote motivated in part by a hope that the Republicans could reduce the cost of government, stop the war, and in some way sustain the prosperity of recent years without demanding as many taxes from the people as had been required in the past. That the sacrifices of the past were purely relative, with the real income after taxes rising throughout the postwar period, made little difference. The attempt of Stevenson to assume the initiative and stress in general terms the need for new measures of social economic reform in the tradition of the New Deal brought the enthusiastic response of those already convinced but seemed to have little vote-getting power. The social gains of the past were so firmly established that the Republicans could not fight them, and they were not subject to question. Apparently additional measures were not in great demand so long as prosperity continued.

Perhaps the most significant development in the political and administrative area was the growth of internal differences within the two major parties. The loose coalition that had kept the Democrats in power over a period of 20 years began to fall apart. The solid South was in opposition to civil rights legislation. And from the time of the convention, when segregation became a major issue, many southern leaders withdrew their support for the Democratic candidate. The industrial workers in the cities of the North could be counted on to support the party but without the same enthusiasm as when they were dependent upon government relief or assistance for their livelihood. The war and Communism issue also led many workers to oppose the party in power. The agricultural states which had been responsible for the margin that led to the remarkable Truman victory in 1948 had so established their economic claims upon government that they had little to fear from the election of an opposition party and proved to be susceptible to the personal appeal of Eisenhower and their natural hope that a change would bring an end to the war. Stevenson's nomination represented less a consensus of the major elements of the party on candidate or program than the rather desperate hope of the feuding factions within the party that he had the best chance of any tolerable candidate of winning. His ability stood out in the campaign, but throughout he was handicapped because he was so little known to the public at large.

On the Republican side, the wave of popular sentiment for Ike swept him into the nomination with the aid of those in the party who saw the possibility of winning the election made almost certain by the choice of so popular a figure. He did not win the nomination, however, without the strong opposition of the old guard regulars who were bitter in their opposition to a political upstart who also was tarred with the stick of internationalism and coöperation with the previous Democratic administration. Leading the opposition was Senator Taft, the recognized leader of the Senate, and the most forceful exponent of old-fashioned Republicanism in the party.

The result of these battles was to make less likely than ever the consolidation and unification of the party machinery in either camp, and to continue the system of divided powers, with greater emphasis upon the congressional branch than had been the case in many years of crisis government and delegation of power to the executive. It also tended to bring out into the open the different goals and beliefs of sectional groups within the country. All things were promised to all sections and the possibility of increasing the internal consistency of government economic policy was lessened substantially. The popular identification of Communism and government planning also tended to make the parties hesitant to spell out any real program of action for fear of losing support. Both parties promised to continue to do what had been done; but even Stevenson's reform program was mostly generalities and no bold new programs were advanced for the consideration of the voters.

One of the major difficulties of the period was the uncertainty of the international situation. In July, 1951, truce negotiations with the Communist forces, which were to last for over a year, began. In Europe, both the friendly Western powers and the Communists waxed hot and cold so that the defense program was never pushed with the force that many on this side of the Atlantic believed necessary.

After July, 1951, when the President once more requested Congress to increase revenues to $10 billion rather than $7.2 billion and to strengthen rather than weaken the direct-controls section of the Defense Production Act, no major policy changes were sought or achieved. Placed upon the defensive by events and the countless series of investigations, the administration had to concentrate on the maintenance of past gains. Even in the foreign field the continued attacks on the State Department made it difficult to achieve our objectives, and little could be accomplished other than to continue previous policy. Prices continued to be relatively quiet—employment was high and production rose throughout the period. The result of the election was a surprise only in the margin of victory for Eisenhower. Relief was felt because the new administration was expected to be able to deal with pressing issues relieved of the timidity required in an election year. It was also hoped that new blood would find new approaches to the world impasse that continued the cold war without prospect of early solution.

The Republican Administration

The advent of a Republican administration after a period of 20 years of Democratic rule has not yet led to many substantial changes in the policies and programs of the government. The policies of the new administration reveal how deep seated are the changes that occurred in the previous administration. The record so far tends to confirm the basic thesis of this analysis, namely, that certain fundamental changes have occurred in the viewpoint of the public, and that any government will have to respect these new viewpoints or soon lose its power.

As Professor Viner predicted, the basic postulates of the New Deal have been only slightly modified by the Eisenhower team in Washington.[1] The area of greatest difference in party view, international policy, does show some signs of change, but the White House is much closer to the policies of the Truman regime than it is to the Republican party in Congress; thus the longer-run developments in this field will be determined by the relative strength of executive and legislative branches rather than by a clear change in party viewpoint.

Following Viner's basic postulates, we find that there has been little change in the commitment of the federal government to assume responsibility for the proper functioning of the entire economy. Second, we find that in spite of much talk there is as yet no sign that the demand for the use of government taxation, subsidies, and transfer payments as devices for income equaliza-

[1] Jacob Viner, "The New Deal under Republican Management," *The Yale Review*, XLII (March, 1953), 324-325.

tion has been substantially diminished. The choice of the administration to continue the excess-profits tax had many justifications, but not least was the unwillingness of either the Treasury or Congress to suggest the replacement of the excess-profits tax receipts by additional tax burdens upon the mass of the lower-income voters. The third basic plank of the earlier period, favoritism to agriculture continues in spite of some qualifications under the leadership of Secretary Benson. Agricultural support policy is still related to the "great god parity" and the cry for assistance has been met without any real effort to return the land to its proper use.

Viner's fourth postulate, that of the New Deal's moderate readiness to extend the area of direct government production even when it encroached upon areas traditionally reserved for private enterprise, is the one that so far has been most radically altered. The administration's support of the action giving the tidelands oil rights to the states was a step in this direction, as was the return of the government rubber plants to private companies, and the developing policy toward public lands and such activities as the Reconstruction Finance Corporation, the Rural Electrification Administration, and housing. The President's description of the Tennessee Valley Authority as creeping socialism, however, did bring immediate reaction and suggests that even a conservative government cannot undo what has been done in the past.

The fifth postulate, that the government under Roosevelt and Truman was skeptical of the operations of the free markets as evidenced by the attempt to set up the cartel system under the National Recovery Administration, the Agricultural Adjustment Agency, the Guffy Coal Act, and "fair price" legislation as yet has not been really tested. But the dominance of the larger-corporation executive familiar with price leadership and nonprice competition within the government suggests that little change can be looked for in this area.

Viner's sixth point, the failure of government to check price inflation—failure due to fear of ending full employment, seems to have been overcome by the Republicans. The refusal of the Council of Economic Advisers and administration to push for a major fiscal program to offset the recession of 1953-1954 can be cited as evidence of a real change in attitude.

Viner's final proposition is that social security has become a sacred cow and that little change can be expected in the future. The extension of Old-Age and Survivors Insurance to cover 10 million more citizens was one of the first proposals that the administration asked the Congress to consider when it convened in January, 1954.

The facts seem to indicate that the extent of the change in basic orientation of the new regime is less than campaign oratory would have the voter believe. This means that the success or failure of governmental policies depends on an increase in the internal consistency of governmental programs in the economic sphere. This in turn depends upon internal organization, operations within the executive and legislative branches, and relations between the executive and legislative branches. The record to date seems to suggest that the situation has remained much the same, and that individual leaders in Congress are slow to see the value of integrated programs and policies. The widespread abuses of the investigatory powers of Congress have caused much critical comment, but little has been done to provide for fundamental reform of procedure. The seniority system still flourishes and the great personal power of committee chairmen continues without fundamental modification.

Devices continue to be developed for taking action in the economic area without accepting responsibility for the acts committed. A good example is the periodic conflict between the administration and the Senate over the limit of the national debt. The need for the increase rose because of tax and appropriation legislation passed by both houses of Congress, and yet a small group within the Senate attempted to offset the previous decisions of the same body by their insistence upon a low debt limit.

Another development of long-run significance, in terms of the efficiency and ability with which the government can discharge its responsibilities, is in the general field of executive department personnel. With the New Deal and the rapid expansion of the federal departments in the late 1930's, the possibilities of a career in the federal service began to appeal to many young men with professional qualifications. Economists, lawyers, specialists in public administration, and natural scientists were brought to Washington and to field offices of the government in large numbers. Advancement was relatively rapid and, although top salaries were limited, the salary scale in the lower ranks compared favorably with industry and was considerably better than the average teacher's or professor's salary.

Interest and responsibility offered by many posts were very much greater than could be found in comparable positions in private business. There was also a growing stress on the idealistic side. Government offered a chance to serve one's country and help make a better world. Universities began to train many men for government service and a considerable number of special programs were established for just this purpose.

The problem that now arises is just where the line should be drawn by the new administration in determining who should be kept on as a career worker and who should be replaced because it is necessary to have the policy-maker sympathetic and coöperative with the aims of the new administration. Complications have arisen also because of the stress placed upon security and loyalty arising out of the fear of Russia and the knowledge that some Communists had been able to get important or strategic government posts. Not the least of these complications has been the reaction of professional men and women to the extreme vulnerability of a government employee to a charge of disloyalty or that of being a security risk. Moreover, for every case that has been brought to the public's attention because of some charge and consequent public hearing, there are hundreds where the employee in question has been denied advancement or a new post because of some blot or supposed blot on a record that literally includes his entire lifetime. Denial of a new job or promotion into a higher rank involves economic discrimination only less painful to the employee than actual discharge as a loyalty or security risk. A similar risk is involved in any case where a department is involved in a reduction of force. In such cases those who have some derogatory comment on their record are the first to be severed from the agency. This can be done without a hearing or clear-cut finding of fact, although government procedure requires a hearing for discharge on loyalty grounds when no reduction in force is taking place.

The fear of many today is that the interpretation of the new administration of the level where it is necessary to draw the line to asssure execution of administration policy will be so far down that the whole idea of a professional civil service career will be destroyed, leaving in permanent government service only clerks and others in equally routine jobs. If this is the case, there is little question that the quality of the government departments will suffer and the public will pay the consequences. Big government with second-rate government employees is a mixture that can do immeasurable harm. A government department is not an agency that can be run well by political hacks or, on the other hand, by some partially committed businessmen who come to serve their country on a temporary basis. As many a businessman has come to know to his grief, government operates in ways very different from the large corporation. As almost any government employee knows, the government is a most complex structure, and many of the jobs that government does are larger and even more demanding of skillful personnel than anything in the corporate world. Our ability to solve this problem of personnel will do much to determine the future course of the country.

The paragraphs above are clearly critical of the rather sweeping discharge of government employees in many departments and agencies of government. It should be admitted, however, that the fault lay in part with the experts who were not content to serve their agency as resource personnel or administrators of previously worked out policies but who began to shape policy directly and indirectly in their own image. In these cases, and where the commitment to policy of their own creation had been made in the past, the protection of civil service tenure would be an impossible impediment to the new government. This was too often the case, and the number of young men who rose to high position by playing internal politics was considerable in the years of rapidly expanding federal agencies and departments. Few contributions could be made that would help the country more in the future than that of solving this problem in a manner that would raise rather than lower the quality of those seeking government jobs and that would keep able men on the job.

In the end a solution will require a revision of the relationships between the executive departments and the Congress. Under the present appropriation procedures, detailed hearings of the operation of an agency or department are generally conducted by the appropriate committees in both the House and Senate. In such hearings the committee may call upon departmental personnel down the line as far as a minor section chief to explain some action of the past or to justify some request for the future. Under such a system political questioning forces the expert to take what seems to be political stands. Knowledge that an appropriation may be modified so that the particular section or branch may be drastically affected in both personnel and function also leads to the political involvement of the persons concerned. In this area practice varies widely, with the Treasury Department standing out in my mind as an agency that has been successful in establishing precedents which protect the lower-level personnel in the department, and yet satisfy Congress on the basic issues for tax legislation. Perhaps one of the greatest gains in this area has been the existence of the staff of the Joint Committee on Internal Revenue which has usually worked with Treasury personnel before new legislation has been submitted to Congress formally. It should also be noted that all the difficulty does not arise from Congress. In many cases the executive department personnel, dissatisfied with the budget or authority approved by the President, will seek indirectly to get a special hearing before Congress so that they can bypass executive restraint. This problem has been acute from time to time in connection with the allocation of funds and program determination in the military area. Strong Navy, Air Force, or Army groups have often modified the program of the civilian heads of the Department of Defense and the President by, in effect, appealing over their heads directly to Congress.

A final issue, that of patronage, cannot be ignored when the question of government personnel is discussed. As long as the party system in the United States depends upon so-called volunteer workers, some sort of patronage must be allowed as a reward for their efforts. It must be remembered, however, that the total number of state and local employees is still larger than that of federal government, and that many of these jobs can be filled better by party organization than can the more complex federal jobs. It is also true that it is the quality of the leadership that is critical, and if professional personnel can be established at the top, the bottom can be kept in line.

We conclude this section with the statement that after 20 or 30 years we have the same problems of political economy with which we started. The increase in the relative magnitude of government makes it more and more difficult to tolerate the old weaknesses in government organization. The new administration seems no more willing or able to tackle directly the issue of basic governmental organization and relationships than the old. Perhaps the main difference is that it is dedicated to the belief that the pace at which government assumes new responsibilities should be slowed up. This is a palliative, not a cure, and if the basic analysis above is correct, the best that can be accomplished will be too little and we will still be forced to consider more fundamental reforms.

CHAPTER VII

The United States Economy: 1958

An attempt to summarize the total impact of the events broadly outlined in the previous chapters is required if a true perspective is to be achieved. First the basic facts will be summarized, second the basic commitments, and third the basic direction that seems to be indicated by recent trends and beliefs.

The most important fact is that the federal budget has become one of the most important single forces affecting the contemporary social, political, and economic life of the country. Taxes, expenditures, and debt-management policies are now major determinants of the economic health of the nation. Second, the public at large has enjoyed a growth in real income over the past 20 years. People have come to expect future progress at the same rate, as well as the possibility of achieving a minimum standard of living for all equal to that required for health and decency. Many now enjoy luxuries that previously were restricted to the relatively few in the upper income brackets. More Americans hope to achieve this position soon. If defense expenditures could be significantly reduced, the achievement of almost utopian conditions would be within our grasp. An important fact is that the gains in real income have been greatest for those who were formerly in the lower income brackets.

At the same time that these basic economic gains were being

achieved the most difficult public policy issue became the restraint
or prevention of inflation. This is in sharp contrast to the almost
exclusive concentration in the earlier part of the period on the
problem of depression and its related evils. In this battle, experience was gained in the application of direct controls over prices,
wages, and rationing. Although controls over production were
also used twice in the period, the public connects them much
more directly with the requirements of a war economy than they
do controls that have affected the cost of living or price received
for goods and services.

Changes in political and economic relationships have also been
significant. The growth in real income and political power of
both farmer and labor groups placed business in an entirely different relative position than it had been in the 1920's and earlier.
Within the business sector the dominance of large corporations
continued, but increased power of labor and agriculture helped
create a better balance on both sides of the market. This development has been given the appealing title of the "Concept of Countervailing Power." A workable balance of power has been evolving
as the government has given new strength to the former under-
dogs, labor and agriculture. This gain can probably be retained
by labor without further underwriting by the government. In the
case of agriculture, the continued support of government is required. Of great importance has been the greatly increased consciousness of labor, agriculture, and business of the efficacy of
political power in achieving economic gains. They may tend to
exaggerate the advance possible in the future, as past improvements were measured from the depths of the depression and were
accompanied by a shift in income distribution in favor of the
lowest-income groups. Governments of the future will never be
able to ignore the interests of either labor or agriculture as was
possible in the 1920's. The greatest danger is that the new power
balance or system of countervailing power will prove to have an
inflationary bias. This is feared primarily because of the appeal

of boom employment levels, sellers markets, and labor shortages. If government does intervene to sustain a perpetual boom, the struggle for shares of the total product among the major interest groups will be intensified.

Both the relative and absolute increase in the role of government has had the effect of making all members of the community increasingly conscious of the impact of government policies and programs upon them. The level of taxation, the growth of government employment, the growth of government purchases from private industry, and the increase in the size of transfer payments make the government a positive influence determining the level of income, profit potentials, and even the investment decisions of private industry. Much of the perpetual viewing with alarm that is found in public statements of conservative leaders stresses the dangers of the growth of government influence. But, too often, fears are expressed about the influence of government that seems to give advantage to another group and ignores the influence that is favorable to the speaker. As corporation executives are opposed to government provisions favorable to labor, so labor leaders oppose the acts of government seeming to favor business. In many cases both labor and business and even agriculture may join in condemning a given governmental policy or even requesting some particular form of government support. Once granted, however, the question of the form it will take and the relative gain to each major interest group will be likely to arise and the more normal struggle for position will be renewed.

It is in the realm of political and administrative institutions that the least change has been seen over the past 30 years. The basic structure of government remains the same, and the modifications that have been introduced to cope with the tremendous growth of governmental responsibility are in the realm of minor rearrangements to meet specific difficulties rather than major revisions designed to increase the power of government or its capacity to act with greater flexibility. The greatest gain has been in the staff available to the President, but he still must sell to Congress the basic legislation he desires. There still remains a basic distrust of government in the minds of the voters. This condition has made necessary the delegation of power to the executive branch in periods of national emergency, but has led to sharp conflicts between different branches of government in more normal times. The importance of executive leadership is recognized only grudgingly, and the legislative rules that have preserved the personal power of committee chairmen and others with seniority have led to delay and indecision growing out of the inevitable conflicts between the two branches of government. The growth in the size and complexity of governmental functions has aggravated this situation, and the minor irritations that might have been passed off as inconsequential some years ago now loom large on the horizon. On the other hand, the danger of judicial restriction upon effective discharge of governmental responsibilities has been slight since the early period of the New Deal, and today, the judiciary is primarily relied upon to protect individuals from the excesses of the legislature.

The biggest shift in governmental institutions has been the relative growth of the federal and state governments at the expense of local governments. Federal growth is primarily due to the war and defense requirements of recent years, although the absolute increase in federal employees and expenditures would have been large in any event. In the case of the state governments, however, the relative increase in state budgets and employment have been caused by the need for the states to assume directly many of the functions that had been previously left to local government or private institutions. With the addition of grants-in-aid and other devices to share with the local government the financing of local services, the state level is assuming more and more direct responsibility for the day-to-day services required by the public in an industrialized economy with high standards of welfare. The result of this trend is to remove government and

government officials further from the people at the same time
that the people are making greater demands upon them. The
town-meeting ideal of democracy is dead for all practical intents
and purposes. It has been replaced by a representative form of
democracy that increases the opportunity for lobbyists and others
to seek special favor at the expense of the national interest. It
is an impressive testament to the level of public morality to note
that in spite of these trends the level of honesty and morals among
government employees and government departments is certainly
no worse than it has been in the past and is, in many respects,
substantially above that which prevailed in simpler days when
there were fewer opportunities for abuse. Outright graft and corruption at the federal level are the exception, and even at the
states and local level are relatively less than at many times in the
past. The new problem is not outright graft but the influencing
of policy in more subtle ways so that the same purposes are
accomplished without the same risks of eventual retribution.

The problem of public understanding and debate of policy
issues remains one of the most difficult problems of the day. This
is true in spite of the rapid strides in provision of educational
opportunity to all. The lack of a strong party system, the strength
of regionalism, and the rise of the interest groups make it increasingly difficult to take most of the issues of national importance directly to the people. Add to this the great complexity
of most economic issues, and the magnitude of the problem can
be seen. Public opinion polls can reveal the extent of the ignorance
that prevails but can do little to offset it. It is even to be feared
that the statesman interested in leadership of opinion will become
increasingly rare in face of the opposition of the opportunist who
keeps an ear to the ground and shifts with the winds of public
opinion scientifically measured by the public opinion expert. It
may even be that the difficulties of the pollsters in predicting
elections are in part the result of each candidate using public
opinion polls to avoid treading upon any toes or raising any

issues of substance on which there is a clearly recorded opposition.

A final change is the increase in the ability of the federal government to measure economic conditions and rates of change. In large measure this is the result of needs realized in World War I and the depression of 1929. The analytical framework necessary to give significance to raw data has grown at the same time so that the current national-income accounts, while not explaining why we are as we are, can be relied upon to give a reasonably satisfactory picture of past and current conditions. Add to this the great improvement in knowledge about the composition and detailed operation of industry and the labor force, and the possibilities of more intelligent management of national economic policy are revealed. Although the tools of analysis are still crude, they are not lacking as much as the means to put them to effective use.

The upshot of this attempt to record the most significant factual developments of the period is to emphasize the lag between the governmental assumption of responsibility for economic life and the machinery with which to discharge this responsibility effectively. When we add the disturbing element of instability in the international realm to the normal adjustments that must be made because of changes in public attitudes, in technology, in population, and in natural resources, the need for greater flexibility, wisdom, and leadership on the part of public officials and representatives becomes obvious. The fact is that, except for periods of crisis, this improvement has not been realized. The danger of really serious mistakes in the area of the public economy increases each year.

Basic Commitments

The basic commitments made by government in the period since the Great Depression are largely related to the public's demand for individual security. Government is now responsible for em-

ployment, agricultural support policies, and social security legislation. The commitment, however, may be substantially greater
than even these acts suggest, for the patterns of welfare payments
and subsidies for families and lower-income groups established
in various European countries and Canada may foreshadow similar developments in the United States. The public demands that
means be found to prevent individual want from arising from
the increasing dependence of the worker upon general economic
conditions. The level of tolerance of the public for economic
fluctuations is low. There is also a trend toward equalitarianism
as an expression of the ideal of equal opportunity for all.

The other major commitment is to a much more conscious
pursuit of the objective of economic progress. This has always
been a goal in modern Western countries, but the important
change in recent years is government acceptance of responsibility
for this achievement and its attempts to accelerate the process.

The combination of these trends and commitments, if un-
checked, is to create an unstable system with a strong bias toward
inflation. The countervailing power thesis is again of interest
as it indicates the vulnerability of the system to inflationary conditions. Galbraith admits that the system will break down in a
period of sellers' markets and that a continuous inflation cannot
be sustained.[1] What he fails to admit is that his system will tend
to produce inflationary conditions. Power aggregates find that
they must be on their guard continuously to prevent their relative
position from being adversely affected by rivals. When the government has accepted the role of a mediator among groups and
a supporter of the interests of major segments of the economy,
it is difficult to see how any sector can accept a cut in its relative
share of the total national income without feeling it to be a
defeat caused by either the neglect or hostility of the government.
Thus changes in the relative distribution of the national income
that were necessary in the past to bring about the reallocation of

[1] J. K. Galbraith, *American Capitalism,* Boston, 1952. See chap. XIV.

labor and resources become the concern of the government, and the political resistance by all segments to a cut in wages or profits will tend to encourage an inflationary policy to conceal the real process of change. No major power group can afford to accept a cut in dollar income, and all are certain to use their power to seek government intervention in order to raise their absolute and relative share of the total. Thus the downward flexibility of the system will be reduced, and all pressure will be in the upward direction.

A second reason for the inflationary bias of contemporary economic life is that most of the power aggregates are equally concerned about the volume of employment in their respective sectors. Thus they become strong advocates of an overfull employment situation that keeps labor in short supply. There is no other way in the short run of preventing periodic changes in economic conditions from leading to fairly large-scale unemployment in certain industries or sectors of the economy. This would not be bad if there were a chance that full employment could be maintained over the long run. The danger is that inflation is used as a means of temporarily avoiding the issue. Inflation is a tax more discriminatory than any that could be devised by man—a fact which makes the acceptance of inflation as a means of sustaining full employment intolerable.

There has been much discussion of the possibility of finding means of compensating for inflation so that the social costs and inequities could be reduced to negligible proportions. Such a system has little to offer, inasmuch as the very force that makes inflation a stimulating influence for a short period would be reduced by compensating adjustments. Thus, if holders of dollar securities or pensioners were given some compensation for the change in the value of the dollar in inflation, profit margins that seem so attractive as the result of the lightening of debt burdens, and the fictitious profits resulting from accounting conventions for depreciation and inventories, would be lost. If such a system were perfected the apparent advantages of inflation would be lost completely, and the only result would be the complication of the monetary system and a vast increase in bookkeeping required by the government and business community.

A more optimistic interpretation of the current outlook is that the forces seeking inflation are a benevolent influence as they offset the natural tendency for the economy to follow a deflationary course. This argument stresses the need for a continuous increase in the money supply to match the increases in real output resulting from population increases and increasing productivity. It is further argued that there is a long-run tendency for the volume of saving out of current income to exceed the investment outlets for such saving and that the stagnation or depression threatened by this tendency must be warded off by a government deficit. Thus it is argued that only as pressure is brought to bear on the government to run a deficit financed by new money creation can we prevent deflation and unemployment from being more typical than inflation. The relatively stable price trend from mid-1951 through 1954 in spite of federal deficits is cited in support of this position.

This optimistic position is weakened by the fact that there is as yet no evidence that the Keynesian analysis of short-term saving and investment propensities will hold in the long run. If there is not, as alleged, a longrun tendency for saving to exceed investment at full employment levels but rather a tendency for investment spending to exceed the current rates of saving, then policies appropriate for a deflationary period will prove to be inflationary in the future.[2] Even if this is a cyclical phenomenon and inflationary pressures recede, the economy will be subject to a periodic inflation with irregular upward movements not offset by compensating downward adjustments. The difficulty of getting substantial downward price movements is now widely accepted. This

[2] One factor which may make a great difference in the future is the large sums currently being spent for basic research and product development by industry.

is the case because there have been built into the system so many
rigidities and pressures against deflation as to make any substantial decline in prices unlikely. Even if the government attempted
to force such an adjustment it would immediately face the fact
that it could be achieved only at the price of an intolerable level
of unemployment.

Perhaps an even more cogent reason for pessimism about the
future trend of prices is that it is in an inflation that the interest
groups seem to find their efforts to gain advantage for their
members most certainly rewarded. Thus they have a tendency to
bring pressure upon the government to follow policies that will
sustain this condition. If this is true, the assumption of the
optimists that the natural policies of government will be deflationary is wrong and reflects conditions that no longer prevail. Reference to the history of prices in most countries of the world, and
the recent experience in England and France, support the conclusion that it is abnormal, not normal, for government to follow
fiscal and monetary policies with a deflationary impact. A subtle
method of accomplishing inflation without need for even conscious action about the particulars is for the pressure groups to
make demands that either specific or general government support
be granted every time any sign of market weakness is felt in any
sector. As time goes on, standards of what constitutes a period of
incipient depression change and government may begin to overcompensate. Thereby, conditions are prepared for a wage-price
spiral that can only end in a substantial inflation. Much has been
written about the menace of big unions, but it is appropriate to
point out that little could be done by unions to force up wages and
prices if industry were not operating in such an extraordinarily
favorable market that the cost of increasing wages can be met
without difficulty. It may well be that industry in its advocacy
of policies that foster favorable profits has done more to
strengthen union demands than any act passed by government.

A final point must be made with regard to the inflationary

implications of the current international situation. The United States is still uncomfortable and divided, in the new role forced upon it by world events. Recognizing the need for defense expenditures, and aid to her allies, and forced to use economic assistance to prevent the further extension of Communism into the poorer countries of the world, there is nevertheless great reluctance to pay the price of such commitments. This, with the burdens still remaining as the result of World War II, makes any increased budget for defense or aid difficult.

We may conclude that unless inflation is recognized more commonly as a serious reflection of internal weakness, the country will be forced into positions that are detrimental to the preservation of both economic and political freedom and economic progress. One of the difficulties in changing popular opinion on this subject is the negative emphasis that has to be maintained. If inflation is to be checked, taxation, credit control, and price policies have to be restrictive. This is in sharp contrast to the positive and pleasant sound of measures appropriate to stimulating greater economic activity, such as tax reduction, credit expansion, and price and wage supports. No one can be against full employment, but those who wish to prevent inflation can easily be accused of being willing to risk unemployment. Many groups believe that they stand to gain substantially by inflation, if only in the short run. The state of world affairs makes concern about the longer run less attractive than in more stable times.

The question remains, therefore, how can the revolutionary developments of the past 30 years be used to gain a better balanced economic and political system? It is my firm belief that this is within our grasp if only the means of gaining a public consensus of means and ends can be found.

CHAPTER VIII

The Political and Economic Framework

Many of the differences about governmental financial policy arise because there is an inadequate framework for analysis of the issues involved. This is not surprising, as the field is not neatly confined to a precise area well designed for purposes of theoretical analysis but has ramifications that often force the investigator to abandon systematic theory for the sake of clarity and completeness in his analysis of particular issues. In no area of economics are the limitations of the basic theoretical framework more noticeable. The lack of the market test for most government actions and the intrusion of clearly noneconomic motives require the complete abandonment of formal value theory in many cases. It must be noted, however, that there is a continuing relation between the field of government finance and traditional value theory. For example, the effects of government tax and expenditure policies, however motivated, will make the decisions of the private entrepreneur other than they would have been without such actions. In some cases the change in environment caused by government action is more important than any other variable that can possibly enter into the judgment of the businessman.

What can be said with some certainty about the economic effects of government finance will fall within an area covered by a few reasonably simple propositions. It is proposed to list these points rather dogmatically and then to discuss their implications at somewhat greater length.

1. Government employment of land, labor, or capital makes less available for the private economy (assuming full employment). It is this act rather than taxation or borrowing that is the best measure of the burden of government or the size of government operations. If there is unemployment of land, labor, or capital, this proposition still holds if it is assumed that government can find means of stimulating the private sector in other ways than direct employment.

2. Government purchase of the product of private industry will significantly affect the forces that control the decisions made by private management and thus the product that is turned out by the private sector and its distribution.

From points 1 and 2 above, it follows that the differences between direct production by government and government purchase from the private sector are less important than often alleged. While managerial procedures and rewards may be different in the two cases, the effect on the allocation of scarce productive factors may be similar. The important point is that even in the case of government purchase the basic decisions as to the volume and character of the product and its distribution are in the hands of political forces rather than market forces.

3. Two types of government spending must be distinguished. First is spending to hire land, labor, or capital or to purchase the product of private industry as indicated above. Second is the spending generally included in the category of transfer expenditures including such items as social security benefits, unemployment insurance, and relief. Transfer expenditures affect income distribution, but their repercussions upon the character of the real output of the economy are uncertain. Once the recipient has received his transfer expenditure he is free to act as he sees fit with no more government control of such income than that received from wage, profits, rent, or interest. Exceptions to this rule are

found in the case where eligibility for transfer payments may be made conditional upon some act or agreement on the part of the recipient. An example is the restriction of certain agricultural payments to those who agree to limit their output of specified crops, but even in this case the farmer is free to spend his cash as he pleases.

4. In addition to their immediate effects upon prices, upon income distribution, and upon the character of production, government financial transactions have direct effects upon the purchasing power and money supply of the private economy. Taxing, borrowing, and selling are all acts that reduce the supply of money in the hands of the public and increase the holdings of the government. Spending, lending, and buying have the opposite effect.[1] It does *not* follow from this statement that an increase in private purchasing power will assure an increase in private spending or that a contraction will assure a reduction in private spending by an equivalent amount. The response of the public to a change in government financial operations will be determined by many considerations other than the direct impact of government finance, and requires an analysis of the specific effects and secondary repercussions as well as the aggregative effects visible in terms of national income models.

5. Some of the most important repercussions of government finance arise out of the manner in which revenues are obtained. Government borrowing may dominate the capital markets and become the primary determinant of the availability of credit and interest rates. Taxation often has repercussions upon prices, profits, and other returns, and thus may significantly change the market's decision as to product composition and income distribution. For example, an excise tax may make it unprofitable to produce a given product or require a substantial reduction in output. The existence of a tax exemption or differential in tax burden

---

[1] A. P. Lerner, "Functional Finance and the Public Debt," *Social Research,* V (1943), 38-51.

may become the basis for a substantial shift in the direction of investment and economic activity. The greater the differential the more certain will be the response.

These five general propositions represent the areas in which we must attempt to make an analysis of the economic effects of government finance. They carry no implications as to the most desirable system of finance.

When policy issues are faced, the analysis must become more inclusive. The critical issues facing the policy-maker can be discussed under four main headings: (1) maximization of economic product in short and long run, (2) maximization of social welfare, (3) maximization of political welfare, (4) achievement of administrative efficiency. In seeking to solve the issues raised under these headings several basic issues may arise and certain fundamental assumptions must be made. Most difficult is the fact that there cannot be a single solution equally compatible with all four objectives. Compromise is required. With this in mind let us consider each in turn.

Maximization of Economic Product

The traditional approach to public finance has held that the basic principles of economics, including marginal analysis, should be applied to an analysis of the proper role of government in the economy. Thus, it has been held that the expenditures of government should be carried to the point where the value of the last unit of all governmentally produced goods and services is equal; and the value of the last unit produced for the government sector is equal to the value of the last unit produced for the private sector of the economy. Others have held that the government should spend until the value of the sums lost by taxation is equal to the value of the last unit bought by the government.

Several difficulties arise when one attempts to apply these theoretical rules. First, there is little possibility of measuring the

value of government product or making a valid comparison with
the value of the product of the private economy.[2] It is only in
the rare case of a government product which is sold on the free
market that a basis for comparison exists in the form of price.
Second, it is often the conscious intent of government to provide a
product that would not have high value in the market for the
express purpose of substituting a political or social judgment for
that which would result from the free play of individual choice.
Many governmental services can be justified because collective
action can produce values impossible to achieve if each individual
were left to his own devices. The example of the control of flood
waters along a river shows that on occasion everyone can benefit
from a governmental action which no one would find profitable
to undertake as an individual.[3]

Still another source of difficulty is the conscious educational
purpose of many governmental activities. Government finds it
desirable to create a demand for its product when none has previously existed. Further complications arise because of the remote
and often nonexistent connection between the availability of
government goods and services and an individual's contribution in
the form of taxes or loans. Except in time of war, few individuals
are aware of the limitation of the output of the private sector of
the economy as the result of government output. In other words,
the choice between government product and private product could
lead to an erroneous judgment because the government benefits
are visible and tangible and the sacrificed private product is
intangible and unspecified. In other cases the government product
often yields values of an extremely general nature, such as national defense, police, or fire protection. Measurement of the
value of such services is difficult. These issues are familiar ones
and have become the source of sharp debate in the field of welfare

[2] National income-accounting values government product at factor cost but this
begs the real issue.

[3] William Baumol, *Welfare Economics and the Theory of the State,* Cambridge,
1952.

economics and also in the field of national income measurement. The conventional valuation of government product as equal to cost really begs the question.

Familiarity with the political process which actually determines the pattern of government expenditures suggests that the economic calculus of traditional theory is seldom followed. At best, we can say that there seems to be a tendency for the public to increase its valuation of governmental services over time, which suggests that some conscious process of weighing public against private product does take place. It would be misleading, however, to suggest that this is based upon other than the crudest calculations. It is more often the result of the growing awareness of unmet needs due to changes in the economic, social, and political environment than to a popular weighing of the issue. The tendency is for governmental services to lag rather than lead.[4]

To further complicate the process of evaluating the success of governments in achieving their goal of maximizing the economic product is the growing emphasis upon the necessity of governmental action to assure the full use of available resources and continued economic expansion. Focus on these issues brings out the limitations of much formal economic analysis as well as the limitation of much of the recent theoretical analysis of employment stabilization. What has been achieved is a general acceptance of the fact that government financial policies are one of the most important determinants of the health of the economy. Theoretical knowledge has progressed to the point where it can tell us what *not* to do and can sometimes tell us when it is necessary to reverse the direction of policy. It still, however, cannot tell the policy-maker when he should act to prevent a change in economic conditions; what the response to a given act by government will be; or which course, among the many possible, is the most desirable at a given time. The confidence generated when the Keynesian

[4] Solomon Fabricant, *Trends of Government Activity Since 1900*, New York, 1952.

system of autonomous and dependent variables was first developed has long since been lost, and a reappraisal of the whole system of relationships is needed in view of the uncertainties which still abound. Such a reappraisal is now taking place and is being subject to much more intensive testing than ever before.

So little is known about the determinants of economic growth that only broad generalizations are possible. The need for innovation, product development, and continued investment is obvious; but the sensitivity of these forces to changes in governmental policy is still in the realm of speculation and assertion. Much of the current thinking in this field is so dominated by popular clichés that very little serious attention has been given to the question of determining the most desirable rate of economic growth.

In recent analysis, more emphasis is being placed upon the interdependence among the components of the nation's economic budget. For example, when estimates suggest that private investment will be insufficient to assure full employment, it is now realized that the size of the gap cannot be measured without taking into account the repercussions of a government program upon private investment and consumption. As was illustrated so vividly at the time of the Korean crisis, the consumption function is sometimes drastically affected by the *prospect* of government spending and private investment on a large scale. Changes in excise taxes anticipated or discounted prior to becoming effective can shift demand temporarily so that for a year or more normal relationships will be disturbed.

Although our ability to predict either the course of business or the response of individuals and business firms to government acts is less precise than would be desirable, recent theoretical developments have increased the general awareness of how government policy can be a major determinant of employment, income, and prices. As a result, there should never be any surprise if, under conditions of full employment, inflationary tendencies result from an increase in aggregate demand of government not offset by appropriate reduction in effective demand in the private sector, or vice versa. It is now possible to justify government programs consciously designed to offset known deviations from the ideal of stability, without slavish adherence to some rule such as the annually balanced budget. Uncertainty about the response to governmental actions suggests, however, that the best that can be hoped for is a policy of reaction to known deviations from the normal rather than a policy designed to prevent such deviations from occurring in the first place. This would then be a policy requiring frequent changes as events dictate and would make a virtue of reversal of policies if the reversals were in response to observed departures from previously established norms. In this respect the use of fiscal policy is becoming more like monetary policy.[5]

Several dangers appear in the application of this theoretical analysis to specific situations. One is that changes in government finance designed to stabilize the economy should not be so frequent or so drastic as to result in a government-initiated cycle. Later chapters will consider more practical limitations in detail, but it is necessary to note here that there is no satisfactory theoretical guide to the problems arising if there is inflation at the same time that unemployment reaches a high level.[6] Closely linked with this problem is the danger that in seeking the end of stabilization through government finance the limitations of some of the possible means may be obscured. Although most of these limitations are of a political variety, the result of a singleminded pursuit of stability of employment at any cost could well be the loss of efficiency and the reduction in both the current value of output

---

[5] Jacob Viner, "The President's Economic Program," *Current Business Studies*, III (1949), 32-43.

[6] A. G. Hart, "The Problem of Full Employment, Facts, Issues and Policies," *American Economic Review, Proceedings*, XXXVI (1946), 280-290.

and long-range economic growth.[7] Some of the reasons for this fear will be made clearer when the political and administrative aspects of the problem are discussed.

Maximization of Social Welfare

Formal analysis of the determinants of welfare has gone through a radical reappraisal in recent years; the results of this analysis have been largely negative. Inability to make interpersonal comparisons, awareness of the inadequacy of the traditional concept of the economic man, and the equally valid claim of many measures of human welfare have sharply limited the conclusions of neoclassical welfare economists.[8]

In the end, it is a personal judgment that justifies the imposition of such welfare-motivated acts as a progressive income tax; the exemption of income tax below a certain level; the payment of public assistance to the dependent aged, blind, or to widowed mothers. Basic social and political value judgment, not value theory, is the basis for action and for the construction of a welfare program. For example, a basic judgment that a high value should be placed upon equality of opportunity can justify a whole set of related propositions about taxation, expenditures, and the type of economic institutions most favorable to the achievement of this objective.[9] Recent attempts to prove the need for more equal income distribution in order to assure income and employment stability are as yet inconclusive.

A review of the most important prevailing value judgments is, therefore, the most useful means of indicating the basic forces controlling public policy in the welfare field today. Such a review

[7] Jacob Viner's criticism of the United Nations' report on stabilization. Jacob Viner, "Full Employment at Whatever Cost," *Quarterly Journal of Economics*, August, 1950, pp. 385-407.

[8] Tibor Scitovsky, "The State of Welfare Economics," *American Economic Review*, XLI (1951), 303-315; Kenneth J. Arrow, "Little's Critique of Welfare Economics," *American Economic Review*, XLI (1951), 923-934.

[9] Frank D. Graham, *Social Goals and Economic Institutions*, Princeton, 1942.

is bound to be arbitrary and to reflect the writer's personal judgments and some of his own biases. This is freely acknowledged, and no claim for scientific objectivity is advanced. Nevertheless, I have attempted to record accurately the forces at work, whether they conform to my own prejudices or not. The following list is therefore presented as suggestive of those basic ideas that underlie the acts of legislators and others responsible for policy in this field of welfare legislation and administration.

1. A fundamental belief in the dignity of the individual has been associated over the years with the principles of democratic liberalism and the concept of a free society. Under this general heading come the related and ever-evolving concepts of equality of opportunity and a general bias in favor of egalitarianism. It is from these concepts that we derive our support for public education, health, housing, and other similar programs to make possible the minimization of the differential barriers facing individuals of equal potential and to approach that ideal state of affairs when all citizens will have an equal start in the race and the winner can be said to be the most capable. However, complications begin to develop at once out of the conflict between the principle of equality of opportunity and the bias toward equality in a material sense. If the material rewards for excellence are minimized and the incentives for successful application of one's talents are restricted to prestige and power, motivation to excel in the economic world may be substantially reduced at the cost of the total product. There is also danger that such action would tend to encourage the search for power for its own sake and thus endanger preservation of the basic principles of individualism. These arguments are usually met by the counter-arguments that as long as there are marked differentials in income and wealth there can be no meaningful equality of opportunity. Although seldom debated in these terms, the existence of this conflict creates a situation where there must be sharp differences about a policy favoring equality of material goods at any cost. A compromise bound to be unsatis-

factory to all but a very few is the inevitable result. It can be further argued that in the process of attempting to remove all material differentials, the resulting loss of individual freedom would more than offset any gain from the reduction in differentials.

A recent expression of this general line of thinking is found in the belief that governments are responsible for the provision of a minimum subsistence for all citizens without regard to age or their individual contribution to society. This minimum should be related to family size and circumstances.[10] This can be achieved by widespread provision of free services and goods or can be pursued by establishing a system of family allowances and other cash contributions for all. Although this idea has gained strength in England, the western European countries, and Canada more rapidly than in the United States it has grown in influence in this country and may be expected to continue to do so in the years to come. Possible only in a country relatively wealthy and with a strong central government, democratic conscience and moral judgments are bound to focus on such issues for many years to come. Fair shares for all may become the next basic issue in the welfare field in the United States.[11]

2. The second basic principle that controls action and policy in the field of social welfare is that of equity in the sense of equal treatment of all in equal circumstances. Honored in the breach rather than the observance, it is nevertheless a basic principle that can be invoked to correct injustices that are too flagrant to tolerate and is the basis for appeals to extend to all special grants awarded to a few. Basic legal principles can be appealed to as well as a sense of fair play growing out of the fundamental belief in the dignity of man and the equality of all men before God.

3. The third principle is that the chances of promotion of the

[10] A. H. Hansen and Harvey S. Perloff, *State and Local Finance in the National Economy*, New York, 1944.

[11] An interesting exposition of this viewpoint is found in Lady Rhys-Williams, *Taxation and Incentive*, New York, 1953.

general welfare are greater under a system of private property and modified capitalism than under a system of complete socialization. Although a substantial minority holds views in sharp opposition to this position on one side or another, there is no current indication that either a return to unregulated capitalism and extreme laissez faire or to the other extreme of detailed and persuasive social controls is acceptable to the people of the United States.[12] In the event of war or other national disaster, however, it is generally conceded that a high degree of state planning would be required. Debate has largely disappeared regarding use of the market and market price as the fundamental determinant of the allocation of resources, character of output for civilian consumption, and preliminary pattern of income distribution—even socialists will concede the value of the market mechanism for this purpose. However, the debate continues over the issue of the degree of control required over investment as it relates to the maintenance of full employment. Although there seems to be no general disposition to support the socialization of investment, the logic of much of general stabilization theory suggests that the extent and severity of the controls and actions that may be required to assure the maintenance of a stable economy is such that the differences between the socialist- and capitalist-minded may be diminishing over the years. The commitment to maintain full employment will be controlling over the years to come. If private investment fails to be sustained at adequate levels no commitment to the sanctity of capitalism will prevent a substantial degree of intervention to stimulate the volume required.

The implications of current commitments for the achievement of welfare objectives upon the structure of economic institutions are highly uncertain and are among the most controversial issues of the day. Some of the most troublesome problems arise

[12] Even in Britain the trend is away from socialization. See P. T. Homan, "Socialist Thought in Great Britain," *American Economic Review,* XLVII (1957), 350-362.

out of the growth of large corporate organizations for both the production and distribution of goods and services and for investment of the increasing volume of individual savings made possible by a higher standard of living and growth in real income at the lowest levels. It is apparent that we have created a structure that many believe cannot be allowed to be subject to the normal test of the market—failure. The failure and general liquidation of a single large institution may have serious repercussions. As a result, it is exceedingly difficult to decide when the public interests require intervention. It is suggested that the tendency will be gradually to increase the commitment of government to take the necessary action to prevent or offset the consequences of any large corporate failure. In this event, there is an interesting question about the social obligation to preserve in full the profit which is the primary compensation of traditional capitalism for the undertaking of risks. It may turn out to be true that in an attempt to protect the welfare of individuals, communities, and others directly affected by the possible failure of some of our giant corporations, the corporation acquires the full support of government without becoming fully accountable to the public for its acts or subject to the possible price of failure. Some growth of consciousness of this new status is found in the more advanced corporate leadership, and it has been suggested by Berle that there may evolve over the years a sort of common law which will formally bring to account the large aggregates of power that are the modern corporation.[13]

Another approach to this problem of maintaining the welfare responsibilities of the large impersonal corporate entity is by direct legislation on such matters as wages, hours, and conditions of employment. This can be effective in raising minimum standards but can do little more unless the controls expand to the point where the power of decision is largely assumed by government.

[13] A. A. Berle, Jr., *The 20th Century Capitalist Revolution*, New York, 1954.

At the present time, the forces most certainly operating to assure the discharge of corporate power in the public interest are the fear of adverse legislation, the competitive pressures exerted by the giants among themselves as buyers and sellers of both labor and their own products, and the existence of well-organized labor unions. The competition among the large buyers and sellers and the pressures exerted by unions are the basis for the generally optimistic theory of countervailing power. By appealing to government to assist in cases where there is an inadequate balance of power, Galbraith assures us that the greater technical resources of the giant corporation can be enjoyed without the fear of exploitation of the consumer or wage earner. This system is vulnerable, however, in a period of inflation where the large aggregates of power can and in fact seem to have worked together to preserve a preferred position leaving the unorganized minority in the lurch. There is also always danger of the growth of a conspiracy among the power blocs to exploit the unorganized.

No discussion of this issue can end without reference to the popular view that the general welfare will be protected by the growth of a greater sense of public responsibility by the large aggregates of power. This view, developed most fully by Nourse and Clark, is disturbing for two reasons.[14] First, this view neglects the possibility of institutional changes which should be considered. Second, is the distaste with which many, including myself, view an economy where basic decisions affecting the welfare of the public are made by an elite or by any group which is neither directly responsible to the public for their tenure in office nor subject to democratic controls. That managers and administrative officials must inevitably make many of the most important day-to-day decisions affecting the people is inevitable in today's complex society, but the existence of the power of legislative bodies and of directly elected executives serves as a healthy check upon those

[14] E. G. Nourse, *Price Making in a Democracy,* Washington, 1944; J. M. Clark, *Alternative to Serfdom,* New York, 1948. See especially chap. V.

responsible for day-to-day administrative decisions. Finally, it seems likely that a society ruled by the most benevolent dictator or corporate management would soon stagnate. In the process, those in power would become corrupt, or at best, cynical in their discharge of power.

The elusive nature of the public welfare is going to continue to baffle those who seek to define it with precision and attempt to develop an airtight system guaranteed to achieve it. In fact, the greatest danger is that someone will attempt to force upon the unsuspecting public his particular brand of welfare at the cost of the very basic principles of democratic individualism. The best that the economist can do at the moment is to make certain that the alternatives open to the public are made known and that the obvious economic implications of alternative courses of action are suggested, and then to hope that if the democratic process is followed with consistency the long run results will prove to be desirable.

Maximization of Political Welfare

Although the economic theorist can avoid the field of politics, anyone who is seriously concerned with the formulation of governmental policy must be fully conscious of political objectives and procedures. Political forces will determine the practicability of many suggested financial policies. In addition, the choice between alternative courses of action may be determined by the effects of those courses upon the political framework.

The power of the purse is one of the most jealously guarded powers of democratic government. Much of the time and effort of all legislative bodies is spent in the discharge of their duties in this field. Most legislative policies cost money to implement. Many an executive office or department has been eliminated by failure to renew its appropriation.

In the United States the budget process requires action by the legislature on each appropriation and tax bill. This process is duplicated, as all bills have to pass both the House of Representatives and the Senate. In parliamentary systems the process of budget legislation is in sharp contrast procedurally: The executive presents the budget as a whole for approval or rejection without each major item coming before the legislature for separate action. Nevertheless, there is no less popular concern over the detail of the budget or political sensitivity to it. In fact, it is often alleged that the parliamentary system as administered in Britain, at least, has the advantage of focusing the public's attention upon the big issues and avoiding the danger that it will be diverted by minor issues.

The danger of loss of popular control over the budget is remote as long as current legislative procedures are preserved. On the other hand, the sort of flexibility in expenditures and taxation that is implied in much modern fiscal theory is impossible to achieve under current procedures. It is not unreasonable for the economist to protest that the traditional practices are outdated, but unless he can assure the public and its representatives that his alternative to existing procedure is guaranteed to maintain the same degree of popular control over the purse he is not likely to make much headway. Unfortunately the area most likely to be effective for purposes of income stabilization, the revenue side of the budget, is the side least likely to be turned over to the executive for control, even under the sort of restrictions that would protect the ultimate power of Congress. Although the process of delegation of congressional authority over the expenditure side of the budget has increased of necessity over the years, there is no general disposition to give any more than is essential; there may even be a trend toward the return of more detailed congressional controls. We are left then with a dilemma common in the area of democratic policy making: concentration upon a single objective may place in jeopardy other equally important objectives.[15]

This problem is not one that can be ignored without grave danger to the preservation of a healthy democracy. Although it might seem that the object of a public expenditure or tax is of little consequence, and therefore wide discretion should be given the executive, there would be an almost certain deterioration in public responsibility if such a policy were followed. This may become acute in the event of a depression, when any policy which will provide employment may seem better than none and thus justify in the minds of some an uncritical attitude toward the purpose being served. A change in range and scope of governmental action may well be justified, but in such an event it is even more important than in a period of stability to make certain that the new responsibilities of government reflect the public's desires. There can be no substitute for the democratic process. The results may seem short-sighted or positively perverse. Nevertheless, any abandonment of its principles would probably lead to much graver abuses.

Effective democracy requires, however, a fair hearing of conflicting viewpoints and debate of them within the legislative assembly. As currently organized, congressional machinery for consideration of budgetary matters is not well designed to assure such hearing and debate. Immense power is given to the committees considering taxes and expenditures and a large part of that power is often exercised by the committee chairman. Selection of chairmen by seniority and the application of this same rule in the assignment of membership on these preferred committees has caused serious difficulties. A review of the hearings of the appropriations subcommittees and Ways and Means Committee of the House and the parallel committees in the Senate suggests that the level of the debate leaves much to be desired and that

[15] The revival of public interest in tax reduction in 1957 was a good example of the sort of public attitude which prevails. There is little interest in the reason for high taxes—just a demand that they be cut.

there is a disproportionate representation of interest groups with an axe to grind.[16] The result has been to establish the executive branch of the government as the primary defender of the public interest in hearings held by the people's own direct representatives. In periods of emergency the process has almost completely broken down; and the executive has had, in fact, a freedom of action inconsistent with the basic principles so hotly defended by Congress in more normal times.

No simple solutions to these problems are suggested, but it is well to keep in mind that there are grave dangers in a continuation of the present system. No reform can be seriously considered, however, if there is a tendency to take lightly the essential principles on which the whole democratic structure rests. A common suggestion that all would be well if a system of party responsibility were to be instituted is impractical, and it is far from certain that such a system would assure the results desired. At the same time that the public is growing more conscious of the necessity for controlling governmental policies in the general interest, the stakes available for the spoils-minded operator have been increased. At the present time we are in a state of uneasy suspense. Improvements in governmental procedures can help assure the sort of responsible public policy desired, but this will be the case only if there is a level of public morality and understanding that is substantially greater than that which prevails at the present time. There are no sure-fire panaceas. The greatest hope for improvement is based upon strong executive leadership.

At this moment one must conclude that a realistic appraisal of the limitations of the democratic process suggests that it is unwise to place too many burdens upon it and that a relatively slow rate of growth in governmental responsibilities should be favored if this is humanly possible. R. M. MacIver has properly stressed the point that the great advantage of a capitalistic system of production is that it provides an area in which individuals may

[16] Roy Blough, *The Federal Taxing Process*, New York, 1952.

seek advantage and power separate from the political arena.[17] I share his belief that if control of production and distribution were centered in the state the danger to individualistic democracy would be greatly increased.

The rather pessimistic views expressed above do not suggest that there can or should be a return to an extreme of laissez faire. The tendency for a higher valuation of those goods and services that government can provide collectively has been noted above. The place for government intervention to provide a basic living standard for all has been conceded. No government can refuse to accept some responsibility for the general state of employment and future growth of the economy. The demands of national defense have increased enormously in recent years. Although it is hoped that the demands for defense can be reduced in the years to come, the chance that they may increase is equally good. Whatever the course of defense expenditures, there is little reason to believe that the trend toward a higher level of governmentally provided services relative to those provided by the private sectors will be reversed. This is due in no small measure to the growth in the complexity of our economy and a growth in the public's consciousness of the possibility of collectively abolishing many of the most common sources of want and misery.

The conclusion that is advanced is that moderation is essential. It is difficult enough for a democracy to work out satisfactory plans for the solution of the problems it now faces without having entirely new ones thrust upon it.

Federal Structure of Government

Another set of problems in the political sphere relates to the federal structure of the United States government. The advantages of a federal system are generally conceded by anyone who gives thought to the immensely complex and differentiated problems of

---

[17] Robert M. MacIver, *Democracy and the Economic Challenge*, New York, 1952.

the different regions of the United States. In addition, there can be no question of the importance the states place upon a high degree of independence. In view of the fact that the states have the basic political party organizations and thus the ultimate control of political power, there can be no realistic financial program that ignores the demands of the states.

Unfortunately, the problems of the federal system are increasing with the growth in the relative importance of government. Whereas the modest federal role of defense and regulation left the bulk of the revenue sources to the states over the period up to the 1930's, except in the case of war, the states now face extreme difficulty in raising revenues from the taxpayer so heavily burdened by the federal government. Not only has this resulted in sharp debate between the states and the federal government over questions of tax policy and the obligation of the federal government to assist in the financing of locally administered functions, but, in addition, high taxes have tended to increase the rivalry among the states and to lessen the ability of each state to pursue its own tax policies independently of others. These tendencies have greatly hampered the states which might wish to experiment and innovate in the field of governmental policy. Although few states have done much experimentation, the few which did have had a disproportionate influence, e.g., Wisconsin.

A new balance is in the process of being worked out between the states and the federal government. It is certain that a larger role will continue to be assumed by the central government at the expense of the states and localities. This trend, feared by the states, can, in fact, help preserve the strength of the federal system. Properly administered grants and a fiscal policy successful in tempering, if not preventing, wide fluctuations in business can help the states a great deal. The most certain way to assure the demise of strong state government is for the federal government to retire from the scene and wait for the pressures to mount. Incapacity to finance any major countercyclical program and the substantial differentials in the capacity of the states to pay for basic governmental programs plus the rivalry already mentioned as a force limiting the ability of an individual state to go it alone, are all important reasons why the new relationships in the federal structure of government are here to stay and are likely to favor a still larger relative role for the central government.

Underlying much of the more basic thinking in this field is the growing realization that improvements in transportation, communication, and specialization in production have developed to a point where the most isolated region in the United States is now more closely involved in events taking place thousands of miles away than it would have been in events in the locality of its nearest neighbor only a hundred years ago. Even in rural areas the specialization of production for the market has made the successful and efficient farmer a capitalist who is even more sensitive to market conditions and to fluctuations in income and employment than the manufacturer or distributor. A new sort of federalism is bound to evolve as new responsibilities are assumed by government. However, the basic essentials of the problem are preservation of those advantages that derive from a federal system and avoidance of the extremes of centralization and its resulting loss of sensitivity to local problems. Where the line must be drawn cannot be established in the abstract, but that there is a line between acceptable and unacceptable centralization of government authority is basic to public policy.

Among the long-range problems are those which arise within the structure of states and local government, because the states or local powers are often too limited to cope with problems of a type that include more than one jurisdiction. With the rapid growth in population and the growing mobility of population, the area of regional planning will require increasing attention. Some control can be exercised by state governments, but many of the problems are peculiarly local in scope and should be solved at a local level. The multiplication of "authorities" and other types of governmentally sanctioned independent corporations to deal with these problems is a sign of the times. Although many of these governmental corporations have done a good job and may have been reasonably successful, there is a growing danger that they will seriously weaken the responsibility of local and state government. Of greatest concern to this analysis is the fact that "authorities" are isolated from the normal democratic process and have often been given a high degree of financial autonomy. Although necessary in some few cases, the independent government corporation has been abused as a result of a desire to find an easy answer to some of the pressing problems of finance faced by the states and local governments.

We may conclude this section on the political aspects of government finance with the generalization that it is important to remember that the means are often more important than the ends and that a good end cannot justify the use of methods contrary to the basic principles of democratic control of the budget.

Administrative Aspects

It is a trite but nevertheless a true axiom that, however well worked out the economic, social, and political objectives of government policy, administrative competence will determine success or failure. In general, it should be easier to administer a program that conforms to prevailing judgments and values of the majority, but it can also be true that refinements which might be desired and well worth achieving for the sake of democratic principles or welfare objectives cannot be adopted for purely administrative reasons.

One element that can give an objective basis for judgment is the administrative cost of a given program. Although high costs can be justified in some cases, there is obvious gain to be realized if the same job can be done at a lower cost. In view of the fact that one out of seven or eight of all persons gainfully employed are employed by federal, states, or local governments the possibilities of substantial savings in real terms cannot be discounted. Where the problem becomes difficult is in the determination of the point where costs become so high that an objective generally approved becomes too expensive. The inadequacy of economic analysis in answering this question has been pointed out above. We may conclude that some subjective measurement must be made through the political process and hope that it reflects the changes in basic values that are continuously occurring.

A much less conspicuous cost, but nonetheless a real drain upon the economy, is the cost incurred by the private sector of the economy in complying with government regulations and programs. Attention must be given these costs as well as those directly incurred by government if the objective of maximization of economic product is to be achieved. An illustration of the basis for decision can be found in tax administration. If a refinement in the tax law designed to remove some inequity costs those who are to benefit from it as much as the possible reduction in tax burden, the question of the desirability of the refinement can well be raised. On the other hand, the fact that some taxpayer may incur additional costs without any benefit does not automatically lead to the conclusion that the policy is bad, as there well may be many others who receive a deserved and important adjustment in their liability. As in the case above, the line can only be drawn roughly and on the basis of judgements which reflect social and political as well as economic considerations.

Perhaps the most important administrative standard is that the application of governmental policy be certain and free from arbitrariness. No democracy can tolerate laws that in application are grossly discriminatory or taxes that are capricious in their incidence. The guiding principle is that those in equal economic circumstances should be treated equally, except as some clear social or economic objective justifies an exception, as in the case of family allowances or a subsidy or penalty to achieve a specific economic purpose. Although this principle is impossible to apply precisely, it can be and is appealed to in objecting to abuses that are clearly unjustified. It is a rule which serves to temper the tendency to find easy solutions to difficult administrative problems at the price of equity.

It is clear then that there must always be an uneasy compromise between the objective of minimum costs and maximum equity. But it must be remembered that in the long run compliance with government laws depends upon public acceptance of their fairness, and thus if equity is slighted costs may well rise.

In the area of direct government operations involving the employment of labor and capital by government agencies, well established rules of administration should be applied. There is, however, need for a much stricter accounting and reporting procedure than is commonly found in the field of private business. Without regard to the merits of the practices used in the private sector, it is clear that there must be full disclosure of public operations and a full accounting for all monies spent. This may sometimes seem to involve the maintenance of costly records and unnecessary red tape, but there can be no compromise with these principles so long as public funds are involved.

The final issue of importance in the administrative field is that of policy coördination. Too often governments act as though the right hand does not know what the left hand is doing. If this is the result of conflicting or contradictory demands of the public, only a campaign of long-run education can resolve it. If, on the other hand, it is the result of a failure of the executive or the legislative branch to realize the need for coördination of policies, administrative reforms can be of value. It is clear that there are many instances where administrative reorganization can help; and it is necessary therefore to keep this in mind continually as financial policy is being formulated.

One of the most serious barriers to policy coördination is the tendency for the conflict between the executive and legislative branches of government to perpetuate the existing decentralization of authority and policy. The strong executive required, if consistency is to be achieved, is often an anathema to the legislature. Pressure groups are always at work in national as well as state and local governments. Officials in government departments acquire vested interests in both their jobs and in the policies which they have instituted and are currently administering. Finally, and it cannot be stressed too much, the magnitudes involved in government operations today are so large as to defy comprehension. This problem has become acute in the case of the federal government, where defense outlays have become so dominant and the necessity of secrecy and the general lack of standards for appraisal make this part of the budget one that is taken largely upon faith. Long tenure in office can give an elected official who served an apprenticeship on a single committee a high degree of competence but in not more than a field or two. Those congressmen and senators who attempt to take a broad view and focus upon the interrelationships of policy are few and far between and, however competent, find it difficult to stand in opposition to their fellows who are willing to concentrate upon a single program or area.

Within the executive branch substantial obstacles to coördination of policy are presented by the departmentalization of the executive offices and the strong liaison between the major departments and their congressional sponsors. The Department of Agriculture, for example, can rely upon the farm bloc for aid in opposition to any of the other departments or even the President. The Budget Bureau, established as a staff agency to aid the President in coördination of policy, has to operate within narrow limits established by executive fiat, which is usually based upon the political realities rather than some well-integrated plan or program. The Council of Economic Advisers, established to provide guidance for coördination of economic policy, is also a staff arm of the President and cannot be expected publicly to oppose inconsistencies that are endorsed by the party in power and given tacit, if not full approval, of the President.

In the realm of economic policy, one of the realities that must be faced is that there has not been a President in recent years who has been sophisticated in the field of economics. Most of them have been bored by the complications of economic analysis, even in the most elementary terms. Although life might be simpler if this were not the case, there is no reason to believe that the Presidency is going to be filled in the future by men of a different persuasion. Improved staff work in the Budget Bureau, the Council of Economic Advisers, and the congressional committees has done much to raise the level of economic policy discussions in the federal government, but it is not realistic to expect perfection and complete consistency.[18]

At the state and local level there is little chance that coördination can be improved without the use of subsidies, grants, or other means of making the state and local governments find it financially attractive to pursue a coördinated policy. This means that state government will grow more rapidly than local and the federal government if nationwide or statewide programs are attempted. This principle is illustrated by the social security program where unemployment insurance was adopted by all the states only after the imposition of a federal tax with a credit for adoption of a state program. However, it was found desirable to institute a federally subsidized and administered program of old-age assistance. Barriers stand in the way of coördination of state and local government programs with federal programs designed to stabilize the economy. The limited financial powers of the states and local governments and the proper but limited concern of these governments with matters of local welfare and

---

[18] One of the greatest improvements in recent years has been the growing significance of the Joint Economic Committee (formerly the Joint Committee on the Economic Report). Its studies have been at a high level and have done much to raise the level of congressional understanding of economic issues.

service make it certain that without federal financial incentives
there will be no major countercyclical program at the state level.
Real progress will have been made if, even with federal assistance,
the states can be prevented from acting perversely over the
business cycle.

Conclusions

There is a growing consciousness of the pervasive influence of
government finance. Its strategic importance in the determination
of not only purely economic conditions but also social welfare
and the political health of the country has led to the development
of new approaches to the analysis of policy issues. Attempts to
give precise answers to the major questions in the policy field
have proved to be inadequate, and in many cases even the partial
analysis possible is expressed in terms that cannot be applied to
achieve measurable results. Nevertheless, the gains in the form
of greater sophistication in approach and avoidance of simple-
minded or dogmatic statements about the eternal verities have
been substantial. It is now clear to most students of the problem
how important basic assumptions and objectives may be. It is
also generally agreed that it is necessary to consider the effects
of government financial transactions upon the general level of
employment and income. There are a great variety of means
available to influence income, employment, and prices. The choice
among the means used cannot be based upon purely economic
considerations. Perhaps the greatest change in attitude that has
resulted is the growth in the realization that it is vital to take
a positive attitude toward governmental financial policies and
to pursue aggressively the public interest in its broadest sense
rather than attempt to keep government in the background. Even
those who would favor the minimum role for government and
the maximum for the private sector of the economy have come
to realize that there is danger in continuing to maintain a neg-

ative attitude toward government. A government which fails to relate its financial policy to the state of the economy, and popular demands for basic services, and guarantees of minimal security and opportunity, will eventually cause popular resentment. Negative attitudes are likely to lead to an extreme reliance upon government in the event of a decline in business because of the general disillusionment which will set in. Private enterprise will be popular only so long as the results do not offend the moral and political aspirations of the majority.

Some of the greatest gains in our understanding of the impact of government upon the economy have come as the result of the development of national income analysis and national income measurement in the form of national income accounting. These developments have made possible the recording, after the fact, of the relationship between the public and private sectors of the economy. Although there has been some disappointment at the abortive attempts to project the national income components into the future, the possibility of giving concrete expression to alternative assumptions about the future in terms of national income accounts has real advantages.

We must continually remind ourselves of the subjective nature of policy judgments; of the internal conflicts and inconsistencies that may arise among policies that seem equally attractive; and finally, of the controlling nature of the assumptions that underlie all policy positions. One of the basic values of our society is that of democratic individualism. This leads to emphasis upon the maintenance of democratic procedures and controls over the government. The expert may often become intolerant of government economic policy and give vent to his frustration by seeking to impose his will in spite of public opinion. This position cannot be tolerated. We must conclude, therefore, that there are real limitations upon the power of democratic capitalism to guarantee economic order and stability. From this conclusion follows the position that false claims of governmental omniscience should be avoided like the plague and realistic limits be assigned to the responsibilities that it assumes. A government that attempts too much is almost as certainly damned as one that attempts too little.

Our problem today is still to adjust to the new responsibilities that have been thrust upon government in recent years. A period of adjustment to these new demands is needed so that the basic attitudes toward government and basic machinery of government can be adapted to the new circumstances. It is not too strong a statement to say that we are living in a period of revolution in the role of government. If this revolution can be accomplished without a radical change in basic democratic procedures and values, it will be one of the really great achievements of democracy. We will achieve success if we can avoid either a negative view toward government, which lessens our capacity to govern ourselves, or a view of the potential of government that exaggerates its role and leads to either disillusionment in the event of failure or to the politicalization of the economic process destructive to future economic growth. Such extremes can be avoided only by devoting attention to political and administrative considerations as well as purely economic ones.

CHAPTER IX

....

Stabilization Theory as a Policy Guide

....

In no area of economic policy have attitudes changed more rapidly than in the field of economic stabilization. As recently as the 1930's the role assigned to government was a minor one, and the necessity of government intervention of any sort to alleviate the consequences of depression was viewed with alarm. This view was shared by economists as well as the public at large.

The use of governmental policy for stabilization of income, employment, and prices has been the result of the events described in earlier chapters. The impact of the Great Depression has made everyone realize that the equilibrating forces of the market may not work quickly enough to prevent widespread distress and substantial declines in real income. A significantly large group of economists also denied the validity of the basic theory of self-equilibrating forces by emphasizing the adverse effects of the income repercussions of the price adjustments assumed to play a major role by traditional theory.[1] This view coupled with a pessimistic view of the investment outlook led Hansen and others

---

[1] This is still one of the basic points of difference between Keynesians and others. For example, Viner believes that "wage-reduction, if made across the board and once-for-all, would promote and not reduce employment during a depression." Jacob Viner, "The Role of Costs in a System of Economic Liberalism," Chamber of Commerce of the United States, *Wage Determination and the Economics of Liberalism*, Washington, January 11, 1947, p. 32.

to develop the stagnation thesis. Although the extreme pessimism of the stagnationists has been proven wrong by events, the need for positive government direction of the economy is now widely accepted.

A second reason for changing views about government's role is the realization that the federal government is likely to continue to be a much more important factor in the economy in the future than in the past. It is impossible to ignore the influence of governments when they are taxing, spending, and borrowing at the rate required by current conditions.

A third factor has been the growth of both better theory and better data. The theoretical developments stimulated by the Great Depression are most frequently associated with the name of the late Lord Keynes, but equally important has been the development of the theory of national income accounting and measurement and the availability of current national income data. It is interesting to note that the latter development was initiated by the National Bureau of Economic Research under the general direction of Kuznets and occurred in spite of a rather hostile attitude of the National Bureau toward Keynesian economics.

Finally, the importance of public attitudes must be emphasized. This change has been covered above. Popular demand for a more aggressive public policy to relieve the worker, investor, and others, from the extreme insecurity caused by violent depressions came at a time when it became possible to develop a public policy with which to temper the extremes of economic fluctuations without making too many radical changes in either the economic or political structure of the country.

Granting the change in attitude and the new commitments of government to act to prevent or to offset the effects of economic fluctuations, there remains the question of the power of government to achieve its objective. We must analyze the capacity of the federal government to take preventive action in order to assure the maintenance of stable conditions at all times. We must also consider the extent to which governments may expect to find that, in spite of attempts to develop preventive measures, they will periodically have to take corrective action to offset or compensate for inevitable, if unwanted, deviations from their objective. In each case it is assumed that there will be continued growth with an accompanying set of internal adjustments required as a result of changing tastes, changing technology, and changing resources, including changes in the labor force.

Ideally, government action to preserve stability should be preventive in character. Any deviation from the normal that can be prevented is to be desired if it does not require the sacrifice of some basic political or social objective. Much has been accomplished by such measures; the strengthening of the financial system by improved banking legislation, closer supervision of the securities markets, radical reform of mortgage lending practices, insurance of bank deposits and mortgage loans, agricultural price support programs, and finally, the development of the social security program granting to those suffering temporary loss of earning capacity unemployment benefits, and to the retired pensions or public assistance. The recent extension of social security in four states to provide for disability cases is a major advance. When one realizes the stabilizing influence of larger government budgets and more orderly financial practices, the extent of the preventive measures adopted in recent years may be appreciated. These measures should prevent the sort of cumulative fluctuations so common in the past. However, these measures can do little to prevent a serious depression or inflation from developing as the result of a sharp decline or increase in investment spending or shifts in consumer spending in either direction. When both investment and consumption move together some marked repercussions are bound to occur.

Preventive action to avoid all fluctuations would necessitate governmental ability to predict the event before it happened, and enough knowledge to act in such a manner that its preventive

action would be perfectly designed to bring about just the degree
of response desired. In spite of the progress in both our understanding of the theory of fluctuations and our change in attitude,
we cannot claim that either of these conditions can be fulfilled.
The capacity of economists to predict events in the future is
subject to debate—the record of recent years indicates that prediction is more of an art than a science. Although many fore-
casters may have a good record in recent years, the critical
question is their ability to predict major shifts in economic conditions.[2] We are equally limited in our capacity to anticipate the
reaction to a specific governmental action.

Before turning to the question of the corrective measures available, a few more words on the subject of prediction are in order.
The reasons for the failure of recent "crystal-ball gazers" is not
hard to find. It is largely the result of the fact that in each critical
turning point some element has been ignored or wrongly estimated. For example, at the end of World War II the predictions
of depression and unemployment were in error because the influence of the improved net asset position of the consumer was
largely ignored, because the rapidity with which the business firms
of the country could reconvert their plants from military to
civilian production was underestimated, and because the strength
of investment demand was not realized. The extent of foreign
demand and the degree of foreign assistance offered by the United
States were also unexpected.

Prediction is also complicated by the impact of external events
upon the expectations of the business and consumer sector of the
economy. The outbreak of the Korean war is a perfect example
of this sort of development causing a sharp inflationary development which could never have been predicted in advance. Even in
more normal situations the significance of psychological influences
is such that the critical question of timing is bound to be beyond

[2] National Bureau of Economic Research, *Studies in Income and Wealth,* Princeton, vol. 16, *Long-Range Economic Projection,* 1954; vol. 17, *Short-Term Economic
Forecasting,* 1955.

the capacity of formal scientific analysis. In certain instances there may be advance warning given by some indicators more sensitive than the economy as a whole, but even these do not act with consistency.

One final word is required on this subject. Assuming a negative position on the possibility of predicting events to come, how can any action be taken either to prevent or correct for a deviation from ideal conditions? The answer is found in the rule of basing policy actions on the conditions known to be in effect at the moment. This is, in other words, a policy of predicting for the future the continuation of current conditions. As economic indicators change, an adequate basis for changes in policy is developed. This position still leaves the issue of degree of action and response to a given action in the field of the unknown. To cover this deficiency two policies are required. First, action in small steps and second, quick reversal of policies that are in either the wrong amount or in the wrong direction.

The need for primary emphasis upon corrective action is clear. If the analysis is right, the type of action required must be flexible. This does not deny that there can arise situations such as wars or particularly violent depressions when bolder action will be in order, but in so far as good preventive policies have been pursued and successful application of a flexible policy has been followed in normal times, there will be few instances when more drastic action is required.

In appraising the techniques available for corrective action, attention must also be directed to their consistency with the basic political principles desired, and their susceptibility to the inflationary bias earlier described. The latter point may become critical, as there is a strong possibility that from time to time situations may arise when a moderate amount of unemployment may be unavoidable if inflation is to be prevented or a moderate amount of inflation may be required to assure the maintenance of the desired level of employment.

In the event that either unemployment or inflation must be tolerated, there is no hope for a perfect solution in the field of general controls. Price and wage relations, power complexes, and monopoly are all to be investigated as possible means of finding a way of avoiding the conflict. The best that fiscal or monetary policy can do is to avoid underwriting the tendencies that have become matters of concern. In other words, it must be admitted that the general financial controls upon which so much faith has been placed are of limited value if there are underlying forces leading to inflation or, to prevent inflation, some unemployment is required. This forces one to the conclusion that a consistent position is one admitting the limited nature of governmental powers.

In the case where either unemployment or inflation is likely, there remains one other possibility—the use of extensive direct controls. In a period of emergency or war, this is the only practical alternative, but short of a crisis of major proportions there is no possibility of using controls effectively and at the same time maintaining the political and economic principles that are basic to the maintenance of a free society. The same forces that make for the underlying trouble are likely to be equally effective in manipulating a control program to their own advantage. The problem of compliance in a period other than crisis is practically insuperable so long as the ultimate power remains in the hands of the people and their elected representatives. Even in a period of war, the record of the past suggests that there is danger of abuse of direct controls by power blocs and grave distortion of the use of governmental power to the advantage of the well-organized groups.

The limitations of direct controls are economic as well as political in character. The economic problem relates to the determination of the specific prices, quantities, and relationships that are most desirable. The problem of making a rational solution of the complex price and output relationships in the economy becomes impossible if any other than a war situation prevails. Even in the latter situation, not all problems can be solved. During World War II, emergency programs were frequently superimposed upon the existing programs, and materials and manpower surpluses were found in what was supposed to be an already fully allocated and regulated economy. Reasons for this limitation are not hard to find. First, the estimates of schedules and material requirements for the output of goods are made by individuals who are trying to do the best job possible but who maintain a limited outlook. There is a tendency for those responsible for procurement of equipment to overestimate the speed with which their particular program will get ahead. Those in charge of aircraft procurement are not going to be damned as much if they slightly overestimate requirements than as if they underestimate them. Even if a bill-of-materials approach or input-output grids are used, the critical question is the speed with which each of the many programs are going ahead. Another source of difficulty is the dynamic nature of the economy. Relationships which may have held for some years will suddenly change either because of technological developments or as the result of economies and diseconomies of scale following a shift in the product mix. For example, a ship that took 100,000 man-hours to complete when first built, may, by the time the twentieth has been made, require only 50,000 man-hours.

In the field of price and wage controls, the problems are even more complex. No standard of price and wage determination has yet been devised that can be applied equitably and rationally to all prices and wages. The pricing of new goods presents a special problem, as does the maintenance of the proper price relationship among different products in the case of a multiproduct industry. Price and wage incentives are also sources of difficulty since there is danger that the substitution of directives for the accustomed role of the market will lessen output. Not the least of the problems involved is that of allocating the extensive manpower to the job of administering the controls, gathering the necessary data for the job, and enforcing the regulations. These same individuals might better add to the total output of the economy in other ways than by the administration of controls.

Necessary in a period of war, direct controls are no solution to the problem of stabilization in a period of peace. The dangers of political abuse, economic inadequacy, and administrative waste all argue against their use. This suggests, therefore, that the requirements of stabilization policy are going to be met, if at all, by the wise use of the sort of general controls now familiar to the government and the public. It is to this question that we must now turn.

Two major instruments of corrective action are available at the present time. These are monetary (credit and debt-management policy) on the one hand, and fiscal (taxation, spending, and debt operations) on the other. The inclusion of debt management in both cases was done advisedly as it is in this area that the two policies most frequently overlap. In general, it is my conviction that little can be accomplished unless monetary and fiscal policies are well coördinated and each policy used to back up the other. Although it is conceivable that either monetary or fiscal policy could stabilize the economy alone, such a policy would require such vigorous measures that popular reaction would set in before stabilization was achieved. Although each instrument of stabilization policy will be discussed separately the necessary interrelationships will be noted as the discussion develops.

Fiscal Policy

The basic theory of fiscal policy is derived from the basic national income concept $Y = C + I + G$. This is: Income equals consumption spending plus investment spending plus government spending. From this, we can derive the conclusion that if there is a deficiency or excess in spending in the private sector of the economy, resulting in either a decline in effective demand below that sufficient to clear the market or in an excess of demand leading to inflation, all that is required is for the government to make the necessary adjustment to restore equilibrium. What is not so obvious is that the government has a great variety of ways of exercising its influence. Besides varying its rate of spending, creating either a deficit or a surplus, the government can directly encourage or discourage spending on private account by budgeting outlays at constant levels and lowering or raising taxes. Endless combinations of these techniques are also possible. Further means of affecting the economy are offered by the use of subsidies or penalties to private groups which can cause total spending to vary by large amounts with the minimum change in budget totals.

The necessary relationship of monetary policy to these fiscal actions should be clear. If stimulation of total spending is desired and fiscal means are used as the primary instrument, a generally easy or at least nonrestrictive money policy is required. If restraint of spending is the goal, a tight money and credit policy is a necessary condition to success. Little will be accomplished, on the other hand, if expansion of the monetary supply through credit expansion is permitted to offset the beneficial effects of a cash surplus in the budget.

The gravest difficulties in management of fiscal policy arise, however, from the fact that the extent of the action required to bring about the results desired cannot be estimated with any degree of accuracy. For example, it is possible for tax remission to be of great or little value depending upon the response of consumers and investors. If leakages occur through an increase in idle balances, repayment of consumer and commercial debt, or the bidding up of prices, the stimulation of real output will fall short of that expected from a given tax cut. If, on the other hand, tax remission stimulates consumers to spend more than the amount of relief, by encouraging them to increase their indebtedness or to draw down idle balances, and a similar pattern is followed by investors, a greater than anticipated effect may occur. As these responses will be largely the result of expectations of consumers and investors, there is little hope of predicting accurately in advance the results that will follow from any given action. Further complications may arise as the result of changes in the international situation and changes in such factors as rate of population growth and new family formation. Also, changes in technology may lead to variations in new investment volume. In a period of extremely rapid change such as that characterized by a full mobilization of the economy, bottlenecks, and the regulation of the pattern of production to eliminate certain goods from the market, may produce unpredictable results. Experience in World War II suggests that money earmarked for purchases of durable goods and housing may not be spent for nondurables or services if the period of the restricted availability of a normal supply of goods is expected to be of relatively short duration.

Add to these complications those expounded by White in his analysis of the lags in response to a change in level of individual income tax, and the problem of the policy-maker in deciding to request action is fully revealed.[3] The extent of the deficiency in employment, income, prices, or the size of the inflationary excess is impossible to determine with accuracy, but the extent and timing of fiscal action in order to affect a deficiency or to curb an excess is even more difficult except as the most arbitrary assumptions are made.

The conclusions that follow from this analysis are clear. Any action taken of a corrective nature must be tentative in both amount and in direction. The more rapidly the government responds, the more often it will have to reverse its policy. If government lags in its response, the direction of its action may remain clear over a much greater period of time, but the question

[3] Melvin I. White, *Personal Income Tax Reduction in a Business Contraction,* New York, 1951.

of the amount will still bother those responsible for policy making. In general, we may say that the more successful we become in keeping the economy at full employment levels the more frequent will be the cases when we do not have clear guides to policy.

Equally serious problems arise when considering the issue of the best instrument with which to do the required job. Assuming that the amount of stimulus or restraint required has been decided, there still remains the troublesome choice among the various means of stimulating or restraining the economy as a whole. Too much of what passes for stabilization policy considers the aggregate models only and passes lightly over the problems of the secondary repercussions of the alternative means of bringing about the change required. For example, a decision to increase government spending by a certain amount will have quite definite effects upon those benefiting both directly and indirectly from the increased government outlays. Industries, regions, and individuals all have a stake in the way the government distributes its increased outlay. Opportunities for political favor arise, and the decision made will have some influence upon the distribution of income among income classes. The military, welfare, and general service agencies of government will all compete for a larger share of the total. Distress areas or underdeveloped areas within the country will make a strong plea for a greater part of the total. Even the structure of government may be affected as the larger outlays are used to strengthen state and local governments or are used exclusively for federal programs. As the decision to spend and where to spend is made by the various appropriation committees of Congress, political forces will have their influence. This suggests that the result will reflect the influence of the pressure groups, the locus of political power in the Congress as determined by the power of committee chairmen, and the activities of logrolling more than it will the economic forces assumed by economic analysis. Still another factor must

be appreciated. Almost any increase in expenditures will be difficult to reverse when the need for stimulus is removed. Thus, a
program of stimulation by expenditure increase may later cause
trouble or require an offsetting use of tax powers to prevent
government policy from proving to be a force causing inflationary
tendencies.

The possibility of restraining the economy by expenditure cuts
in a period of boom offers even more difficulties. After the automatic cutbacks which will result from the built-in flexibility of
budget outlays for certain items such as unemployment insurance,
old-age assistance, and agricultural supports, the problem becomes
really difficult. Who is to bear the brunt of the cutbacks? How
will this affect interest groups? Will some regions fare better than
others? How should the cuts be distributed among all beneficiaries
of government outlays? Again the decision will be difficult and
largely determined on the basis of political forces and power blocs
rather than on the basis of economic principles. In fact, it is quite
unlikely that in a period of strong inflationary pressure adequate
cuts can be made. As mentioned above, periods of boom are often
periods requiring a larger volume of government expenditures.

Further complications arise, moreover, as the degree of stimulus
or restraint will be affected by the distribution of the expenditures
among sectors of the economy. In other words, the assumption
that the amount could be taken for granted is not valid; and if
the knowledge of the differences of response to each distribution
of expenditures or changes in tax rates were available, the total
required in each case would be different. Not knowing in advance
what the differences will be, there is little to be said other than
that a policy of trial and error will be required.

A policy of revenue variation as a means of taking corrective
action presents many of the same difficulties but involves somewhat fewer decisions about the possible effects of the action taken
upon different sectors of the economy. Although certain taxes
have specific effects upon industries and regions, the sort of

revenue variation assumed can be accomplished without using such levies. By restricting the changes to such broadly based taxes as the personal and corporate income tax, their selective impact will be reduced. In spite of this possibility, the problem of distribution of the tax burden remains. If there is to be an increase in taxation each group will try to avoid it. If there is to be a decrease all wish to get the lion's share. Arguments about equity, incentive, and even national defense will be used to plead each case. Maneuvering to gain a long-run advantage will be particularly strong in a period when the tax cuts are in order. A recent example is found in the argument over the relative desirability of stimulating the economy by a cut in the lower bracket tax rates or in the upper. Both sides pleaded their case on the ground of maximization of stimulus. Those favoring the cut at the bottom argued the necessity of stimulating consumer demand. Those favoring cuts in the upper bracket rates claimed the need to stimulate investment incentives and risk-taking both for the recovery of the economy and to assure continued economic growth. Both arguments have merit, but it is surprising how few voices were heard suggesting that cuts across the board would be desirable.

When tax increases are required there is the equally difficult problem of the distribution of the increase. Any increase will tend to meet resistance. The practical problem of gaining an equitable distribution of the heavier taxes is complicated by the possibility that technicalities in the law will be used as avenues for escape—particularly in the upper income brackets where the possibilities of manipulation of income are somewhat greater than in the lower brackets. Even the wage earner has found the possibilities of escape open to him and has become the beneficiary of such features of the law as the exemption of pension contributions by his employer and other fringe benefits.

The quantitative response to a change in the level of taxation is even less certain than in the case of expenditure variation. The uncertainty of response of those persons and companies subject to changes in their tax burdens is much like the uncertainty of response to a change in expenditures. But the psychology of the consumer and investor is even more a factor in the case of tax variation than in the case of expenditure variation. In the latter case there is at least the actual payment for goods or services and the secondary effect on materials suppliers of the prime contractor. Tax variation is more like variation in transfer payments where the effects depend upon what the individual decides to do after government has taken action.

One new complication in the case of tax variation is the possibility of offsets to a change in tax levels. This is most likely in the case of tax increases when they cause an increase in the consumer price index. If this is the case, there will be some automatic wage increases; and when the increase is not automatic, there will be agitation for a wage increase to offset the rise in the cost of living. The automatic increases will take place when there are escalator clauses in the wage contract. Thus, the imposition of a federal sales tax reflected in the cost-of-living index would be offset to a substantial degree by the rise in incomes and costs resulting from wage increases. Even in the case of an increase in income tax there is danger of a demand for a compensating wage increase to maintain take-home-pay. A corporation income tax rise in a period of inflation might have similar repercussions if the corporations were successful in passing on a large part of the rise in the form of higher prices which again might be reflected in the cost-of-living index. This possibility is most likely in the event of a boom accompanied by rising prices.[4]

Tax remission is not so likely to be offset by wage cuts, but there is always the danger that the primary effect of tax relief is first to satisfy a newly enhanced desire for liquid assets by both business and consumers. If this is the case, the amount and

[4] L. V. Chandler, "Taxation as an Instrument for Inflation Control," Tax Institute, *Limits of Taxable Capacity*, Princeton, 1953.

duration of the tax cut will have to be much greater than would be assumed in most simple models. The consequence of these conclusions is clear. Again there is need to realize that the uncertainties of response leave the field wide open when the issue of amount is raised.

Debt Management

. The final area which must be covered is that of debt management. Although this is the area which requires a combination of monetary and fiscal theory there are many occasions when the initiative is with the Treasury. Depending upon the state of the economy, the Treasury can merely divert funds that would have been idle to government use, or force a decline in investment or consumer spending in the private sector as the government sale of bonds absorbs funds which would have found other use. In the first instance the net effect may be siimlar to that resulting from sale of debt to the banks. In the latter case the net effects will be more nearly like those resulting from taxation. The major difference in the latter case is that there remains in the hands of the lender the net asset of a government bond rather than a tax receipt. This might somewhat reduce the contractive influence of borrowing.

There is little reason for government borrowing from the public in periods of depression, as the uncertainties of response are even greater than would be the case in the event of borrowing from the banks or from the direct issue of money. Borrowing from the banks has the advantage of adding to the supply of money in the system, offsetting the decline caused by the contraction of private credit, and thus tending to satisfy the enhanced desire of the community for greater liquidity. There remains a danger that borrowing will so disturb the confidence of the public in the policies of government that it will adversely affect the rate of spending in the private sector.

Other repercussions of the management of the debt may arise as a result of the terms and rates prevailing on the public debt. When the volume of debt is as great as it is at the present time there is no possibility of leaving the terms to the determination of the free market. In the case of long-term debt the concern of the authorities will be with the variations in market value reflecting changes in the rate of interest rather than the immediate changes in the costs of government debt service. Concern about the terms of the debt is essential, inasmuch as the government cannot escape responsibility for the consequences of its debt-management policies upon the general credit situation. If, for example, the Treasury tries to place either a short- or long-term issue at a very low rate, it must realize that this requires the Federal Reserve Board and the Treasury to take action to create conditions favorable to a low rate. If the Treasury, on the other hand, issues debt at a high yield, this will be done only as it believes, and is supported in this belief by the Federal Reserve Board, that a policy of restraint is required and generally tight credit should prevail. In addition to the action assumed by the Federal Reserve Board, the Treasury itself can vary the size of its balances, the use of trust fund receipts, and the policies it follows in deposit of tax receipts, to make for easier or tighter credit. Still additional powers are reserved by the Treasury as a result of its powers to monetize gold and silver and its policy when gold is flowing into the United States.[5] There is always the possibility of offsetting the expansive effects of gold inflow by borrowing directly from the public.

In addition to the repercussions which will result from a Treasury decision to vary the length of the debt, the market will tend to absorb more or less government debt of a given term and rate depending upon the economic outlook and the demand from the private sector. For example, in a period of inflation and credit restraint, investors may show a natural reluctance to purchase

[5] See G. G. Johnson, Jr., *op. cit.*

long-term debt for fear of a sharp decline in market values in the event of a further rise in interest rates. The favorable opportunities for private investment also make government bonds unattractive. On the other hand, some long-term investors will find the opportunity to purchase long-term governments at high yields an attractive proposition if they expect a later decline in interest rates and do not desire liquidity. If rates are expected to go down in the future, a strong market for long-term issues can develop, based upon the expectation of a quick capital gain. In each case the repercussion of changes in the outlook for government debt will have an influence upon the general credit situation and the availability of credit in the private sector of the market.

One of the more foolish policies recently advanced has been the insistence of the Federal Reserve Board upon the restriction of its open-market operations to bills only, or what is popularly known as the "bills-only doctrine." Although advocated as a means of freeing the government bond market from government interference and leaving the determination of rates to the market, the consequence of this position has been to restrict unduly the Federal Reserve in its open-market operations. It has also raised the question of the adequacy of the supply of bills when a restrictive policy is being administered. This came out in the early summer of 1956 when the newspapers reported that the Federal Reserve desired the Treasury to refinance some of the maturing debt in bills to add to the depleted supply. In view of the need for large amounts of bills and other short-term issues for tax accruals and other similar purposes, the doctrine can only cause trouble. In addition there is always the possibility that economic conditions will tend to put special pressure upon one segment of the bond market; and if the Federal Reserve Board restricts its operations to bills alone, it will have to bring more general pressure or create a situation of more general ease than it would if it could be more selective in its operations.

To give the Board its due, the case for the bills-only doctrine is based on the recent and unhappy experience of the Federal Reserve when it was forced to support the entire bond market at par. To free themselves from any action suggesting a renewal of such a policy in the future, the bills-only doctrine makes some sense. But there is little reason to believe that a doctrine that may require more violent action in the long run can help make more popular the exercise of credit control.

  Other influences can be exercised by the government as it uses its power to vary the terms and extent of its guarantees of loans made by private lenders. An important area is that of housing finance where the Federal Housing Administration, and veterans loan guarantees and terms can have a profound effect upon the availability of mortgage credit and thus the volume of investment in this important area. Three variables are involved—the amount of the down payment, the duration of the loan, and the rate of interest. To the average home buyer the important fact is the size of his monthly payment and the amount of his down payment. Many will be affected by the size of the cash payment required. Others will be affected by the size of the monthly payment. If the amount of downpayment is increased, while the rate of interest rises and the length of time required to pay is shortened, there is little question that the amount of home purchases will be adversely affected. One of the greatest problems in this area is not the potential power of the government but the fact that there has tended to be little or no coördination of policies in this field with those applied in the general field of credit management. Thus, in the period immediately following the war, there was little attempt to tighten the terms of credit in order to lessen the attractiveness of home purchase. It is the contention of many that this has resulted in a greater-than-necessary inflation in the price of homes.

  Other effects are bound to result from such actions as the accelerated amortization provisions for expansion necessary for national defense, changes in depreciation allowed for tax purposes, and other changes in the interpretation of tax laws. These aspects of governmental policy do not generally come within the scope of fiscal policy but should be mentioned because they are closely related, and—as in the case of accelerated amortization—may have an influence as great or greater than some of the broader policies adopted.

All fiscal theory is somewhat in conflict with the principle of maintaining a close relation between the costs of government and the size of the tax burden. Although the case against a policy of an annually balanced budget is overwhelming, there is reason to be concerned about the growth of an attitude which completely ignores the fact that there should be any such close relationship. In this event, the problem of persuading the public that any expenditure is excessive may become more difficult than is desirable.

Equally difficult problems arise in the field of administration. The problem of devising ways and means of gaining the sort of flexibility required by the uncertainties described above is practically insoluble at the present time. Even in the field of debt management, where more extensive powers are delegated than in any other area of economic control, the possibility that banks and other industrial holders of short-term debt will let it run out without repurchasing makes it exceedingly difficult for the Federal Reserve to take vigorous action. Political pressures are also felt by the Federal Reserve, and these are often strongly against the exercise of the full power delegated to the Board. As pointed out earlier there is a serious problem of assuring the internal coördination of the policies of the separate divisions of the executive branch of the government. Certainly the sort of flexibility suggested by earlier analysis is not likely to be achieved for some time unless radical and novel new instruments of exercising fiscal influence upon the economy are devised.

A final word must be said about the balanced budget as an instrument of stabilization policy. This proposition, advanced by

Kaldor and others, suggests that it is possible either to stimulate
or to restrict the economy by large-scale variations in total expenditures matched by equal changes in revenues.[6] The basic theory
underlying this proposition can be approved without making the
assumption that the theory offers guidance to the policy maker.
Any such short-run variations in total budget expenditures and
receipts as required by this approach would seriously disturb
the private sector of the economy and would require an administrative and political flexibility completely impossible in the modern world. Even the changes in governmental staff would cause
difficulties. When the problem of estimating the size of the
variation required to get desired results is considered the problems
are further multiplied, as the degree of response of the economy
to such changes would be even less predictable than that to a
change in expenditures or revenues alone. This is true in part
because of the radical shifts in the role of government required
by such a program. It is obvious that no such approach will be
seriously considered at the present time, and it can thus be
dismissed from further consideration.

Monetary Theory

The revival of interest in monetary policy stems from the realization that monetary policy must be coördinated with fiscal policy.
This realization is based upon the experience since the end of
World War II both in the United States and Europe and has
been aided by the closer integration of monetary theory with
modern income analysis.

In view of the emphasis that has been placed upon the Keynesian revolution and problems of depression, it is not surprising
that the radical improvement in the field of monetary theory
has been slowly gaining the recognition it deserves. A decline in

[6] N. Kaldor, "The Quantitative Aspects of the Full Employment Problem in
Britain," in William H. Beveridge, *Full Employment in a Free Society*, New York,
1945, Appendix C.

emphasis upon qualitative credit control by banks and a new emphasis upon quantitative controls is one major advance. There has also been a growth in understanding of the effects of the monetary and banking system upon the economy as a whole. The nature of this advance is measured by the fact that as recently as the early 1920's the significance of open market operations of the Federal Reserve Banks was not understood. Even in 1931 the Federal Reserve authorities felt compelled to raise discount rates and tighten credit to protect the United States against the outflow of gold reserves. In 1937 the increase in reserve requirements, thought necessary to mop up excess reserves, was a reflection of a monetary policy insensitive to modern analysis.

Nothing has been of greater importance, however, than the successful revival of monetary policy in the period since 1951 when central bankers once again began to exercise their responsibilities in the United States economy. In spite of predictions of disaster, the transition from a fully supported bond market to one subject to the varying influences of the Federal Reserve, based upon the state of the economy, has been successfully accomplished. The Federal Reserve has gained prestige as a consequence. The mildness of the recession of 1953-1954 also aided in the revival of interest in the value of monetary policy. Although the restrictive credit policies of early 1953 were sharply criticized, the quick reversal of policy and the favorable reaction of the economy to the adjustment were proof that the central banking authorities had learned their lesson and would not hesitate to change policies when conditions changed. It also helped dispel some of the fear that monetary policy could never prove an effective stimulant to the economy.

Basic monetary theory has two strings to its bow. First, is the availability of credit and the supply of money; second, is the cost of credit or the interest rate. If the supply of money is reduced or even held constant in the face of rising output, either of two consequences will follow: A decline in the level of prices, or a decline in the volume of goods and services produced. In view of the rigidities in the institutional structure preventing the downward adjustment of the price level, the latter is the more likely outcome. This suggests the first lesson of monetary theory: the necessity of maintaining an adequate supply of money and credit at all times. This cannot be assured by use of monetary controls alone, and it may be necessary to combine fiscal with monetary policy to achieve the result desired. Further problems arise because of the tendency for the velocity of circulation of the existing monetary supply to vary directly with the business cycle. As levels of business decline, the velocity of circulation of the money supply will tend to fall. This suggests that monetary officials must therefore be prepared to vary the supply of money somewhat more than necessary to keep pace with the growth of output, first satisfying the desire of the public and the business community for large amounts of liquid assets and then retiring a part of the money supply as the desire for liquidity declines.

Variation in the cost of credit or the interest rate has been heavily discounted as an effective instrument of control by the disciples of Keynes and a newer group who seem to favor expansion at any cost. Two arguments have been advanced against the effectiveness of interest rate changes upon the volume of money and credit. First, interest is such a minor cost, except in the case of public utilities and other business with relatively high levels of fixed investment in capital equipment of long life expectancy, that any practical variation in interest costs will have insignificant effects. Second, they argue that response of savers to a decline in the rate of interest may be to increase their rate of saving and their desire for liquid assets. They believe that further complications arise because the speculative motive for holding cash is enhanced in a period of low interest rates and possibly declining prices. There is also little reason, say the Keynesians, for the return from investment to rise, because expectations are much

more volatile than the rate of interest and are the primary determinants of investment decisions.

The above argument was first developed in a period of profound depression and would probably still hold in such a period.
However, in any other period the pessimistic conclusions do not
necessarily follow. The cost of credit can make a difference to
marginal borrowers and may be becoming more important as
mortgage credit and consumer credit play a large role. Expectations are also affected by the actions of the central bank and
may be favorably or unfavorably influenced as a result of changes
in credit policy. But the most important point is not how much
credit policy may influence business to expand but how strategic
it may be in preventing an overissue of money and credit leading
to inflation and a speculative boom of serious proportions. Credit
controls are important, not only as they accomplish the direct
results desired, but as they encourage the maintenance of the
level of investment required for stable growth and permit the
maintenance of a stable international trade.

The potency of monetary policy as an instrument to prevent
inflationary developments must be emphasized. Monetary authorities have the power to control the total supply of money, assuming an appropriate fiscal policy. This can be done by use of
open-market operations, changes in the rediscount rate and
variations in reserve requirements. The consequences of a restrictive policy will be to raise the rate of interest. But the strength
of a restrictive monetary policy is not limited by the response
of borrowers to increases in the rate of interest. No matter how
high or low the rate of interest, banks cannot lend if their reserves
are already fully committed. As a consequence the effect of a
restrictive policy may often be to force the banks to ration credit
among their potential customers. Difficulties arise due to the
large volume of outstanding government debt and the effect of
restrictive policies upon current market values of long-term issues.
Problems also arise due to the large amount of short-term gov-

ernment debt which can be allowed to run off and satisfy the desires of the holders for cash. However, recent experience suggests that the limitations upon the power of central bank officials arising from such causes are exaggerated and that effective limits to credit expansion can be achieved without forcing either the short- or long-term rates to excessively high levels. In part, this is the result of the rather sluggish adjustment of interest rates and the tendency for rationing to be used as a substitute for rate increases.

The real problem of monetary theory is not the power of central bank officials to limit the money and credit supply but the question of the degree of restrictive action required in any given instance. This problem is similar to that faced in the field of fiscal policy but made even more troublesome by the fear of monetary officials that if the action taken proves too vigorous, it cannot be reversed in time to prevent serious consequences. This point may be debated at length but remains a troublesome one for anyone responsible for taking positive action in a period of uncertainty. Much greater confidence could be felt by monetary officials if they could be assured that the appropriate reversal of fiscal policy would be immediately forthcoming in the event that their action precipitated a decline. No such assurance can be given at the present time, and this justifies a certain degree of timidity on the part of monetary officials. Unfortunately, the longer they postpone action the more likely will be a violent reaction to a policy of restraint.

When it is also realized that monetary powers now delegated to a central bank can be taken away by a disgruntled legislature, the difficult position of central bank officials is appreciated. It is also true that the more successful the stabilization policies of government, the more likely it is that central bankers will be uncertain about the appropriate action at the moment. As was the case in fiscal policy, there is danger that in a full-employment economy there will be many occasions when institutional forces operating in the field of price, wage, and profit relationships will tend to be forcing up prices. In such a case a restrictive policy may well force a certain amount of unemployment. In this event, the long-run stability of the economy requires the solution of the underlying cause of the difficulty and thus the use of the sanction of unemployment, at least temporarily, to indicate the need for more basic adjustments. Any other course will place the monetary and fiscal officials in a position of underwriting and ultimately sanctioning the forces that are leading to inflation. Such a course is untenable—there is little reason to believe that under such a policy the difficulties will not continue to grow to the point where political forces are substituted for economic in the determination of the distribution of income.

The Conflict Between Price Stabilization and Full Employment

The compatibility of stabilization of prices and the maintenance of full employment is one of the thorny issues not yet covered. There are those who allege that no solution is possible and, giving their allegiance to stable prices, deny the advisability of government intervention to preserve full employment. Others, including myself, believe that the problem must be solved if anything like current economic and political freedom is to be maintained. Still another group denies that the issue is a critical one and refuses to become concerned.

Several approaches can be taken to this problem. One has received a great deal of support—an appeal to business, labor, and agriculture to exercise discipline and restraint so that stability of prices is maintained even in a sellers' market. How such restraint can be assured is a mystery. It is the function of every labor leader and corporation executive to maximize the economic benefits of those who hire him. In all cases there is the difficult problem of defining what is a moderate policy in a dynamic economy. Certainly the past successes of the agricultural bloc have not lessened the faith of agricultural leaders in the benefits to be derived from government intervention on their behalf. The critical issue arises when the individual, firm, or industry finds that forces beyond his control cause him to suffer losses or a decline in income level. But a stable price level requires that some prices and incomes fall while others rise as a result of changes in consumer demand, technology, and international trade. Such variations within the total economy are essential if the transfer of resources and labor is to take place without direct intervention of the government. Full employment has been identified with individual security and economic advancement for everyone. This, and the growth of large organizations, have created many institutional barriers to downward price and wage adjustments. But if only upward price inducements are relied upon to achieve the transfers required, the trend must be inflationary. If the government takes action to prevent a general rise of prices, the first result may be unemployment. Whether this would be sufficient to break down some of the barriers to wage and price adjustments is uncertain, but the public reaction which will follow is one that few governments will be able to resist. The growth of unemployment is also bound to be destructive to the maximization of the output of the economy and thus be against the interests of the country as a whole. What is at issue is the failure to maintain the sort of competitive conditions required in a free economy.

Several facts tend to modify this analysis and give support to the group that does not believe that the danger is as great as alleged. First is the growth of productivity, which permits a rise in real-wage rate, profits, and incomes without disturbance to the stability of prices. Second is the fact that collective bargaining in large industries usually results in labor contracts of considerable duration. Because of this, there have been occasions when wages have lagged behind the increase in demand, thus exercising a restraining force. Finally, there is reason to believe that the large corporation does not always try to maximize its short-run profits and frequently charges less than the market will permit. Corporations can justify such a policy in terms of the maintenance of good will and of gaining a larger share of the market. They may also have some concept of public responsibility which would require them to make no more profits than necessary to sustain a going concern. The problem is adequate appraisal of the importance of these factors in terms of the threat of inflation. There is no question that in a period of rising prices these factors may slow up the pace of the advance. They do nothing to give to the price structure the sort of flexibility required for the long-run maintenance of a healthy economy adjusting to changes in the market.

In addition, there is danger that labor, industry, and agriculture are all organized to bring pressure upon the government to offset a decline in income in any sector by inflationary fiscal and credit policies. For example, during the decline in auto sales in 1956, President Curtice of General Motors condemned the tightening of credit by the Federal Reserve System and blamed it for the declining sales of the auto industry.[7] This statement was made in the face of generally favorable economic conditions and slowly rising industrial prices. Agriculture and labor both realize that they can hope for rising incomes and a relatively larger share of total national income only in a sellers' market. From the beginning of time, agriculture sections have favored cheap money and rising prices. Labor has a greater stake in preserving price stability than ever before due to the growth in pension plans and other retirement benefits. But labor leaders know that wages are more important than pensions and that resistance to higher wages is substantially lessened in a period of boom. They, therefore, favor governmental policies designed to sustain a sellers' market indefinitely into the future.

Thus, it seems clear that the conflict between a full employment commitment and price stabilization is real and requires

[7] *New York Times,* January 18, 1956.

more attention than it has yet received. Public policy must reflect this fact. Greater tolerance of variations in the short-run position of the economy is required. Such variations might be accepted if the extent of unemployment and aggregate income variation were limited to some maximum figure established in advance. Such a compromise is certainly more likely to be achieved than one requiring a reversion to a hands-off policy on questions of employment stabilization and concentration upon the maintenance of price stability. Such a policy would probably breed so violent a reaction that all hope of achieving a moderate position might well be lost.

The facts suggest that the first point to be established is the limited capacity of either monetary or fiscal policy to assure the complete stability of the economy at all times. The second point is to provide assurance of government action to prevent either a cumulative inflation or deflation from getting underway. Only as such a program is defined with clarity is there hope of gaining for it public acceptance. The best means of assuring such results might be that of stabilizing personal income payments. Allowance for the growth of population and the increase in productivity could be made by permitting a steady rise in incomes so that normal expansion could take place without deflationary tendencies. Price increases would be checked by placing an upper limit upon the growth of personal incomes. A floor below which personal income would not be permitted to fall could prevent a cumulative decline in income and thus an unlimited decline in total demand and employment. It must be stressed that this is a policy that does not guarantee perfection. Shifts in investment demand, changes in liquidity preferences, and the attitudes of consumers would still cause considerable variation in both employment and prices. But these variations could be limited in amount and duration, and it is hoped that public acceptance would be maintained. The greatest danger is that the institutional barriers preventing the sort of internal adjustment of price and wage relationships required in a dynamic economy would operate to such a degree that unemployment would continue for an excessive period of time. In this event there is an unhappy choice to be made: to continue to bring pressure through the sanction of unemployment for the freeing of prices and wages or the acceptance of inflation to achieve full employment. The first years of such a policy would be the most difficult in view of the vested interests that have become established over the years. But if inflationary concessions should be made early in the game, hope of maintaining a balanced situation would be lost. The allowance of a certain amount of variation before any action is taken by the government would avoid the danger of whip-sawing the economy first in one direction and then another as a result of hurried governmental action. Built-in flexibility would operate, and normal provisions for unemployment insurance, public assistance, and so forth, would continue; but no direct fiscal action would be required until the limits of personal income variation had been exceeded. It is most important that there be wise use of monetary and credit policy in order to minimize the necessity for frequent fiscal action.

In the event that the limits were exceeded and direct fiscal action was required to bring the personal income payments trend back to normal, lower taxes and even consideration of negative taxes or cash grants to the public would be desirable. Such a policy would minimize the effect of governmental action upon the operation of the market and preserve, to the greatest extent possible, the sovereignty of consumers and producers in the field of resource allocation. Elsewhere I have suggested the further separation of such actions from the normal budget by use of a stabilization fund, and delegation of authority to draw from the fund or to add to it by the executive within clearly established limits.[8] This, coupled with the suggestion of cash grants on a

[8] Paul J. Strayer, "Stabilization of Personal Incomes—A Limited Fiscal Policy," *American Economic Review*, XL (December, 1950), 827-844.

per capita basis when support is in order, and a supplemental gross-income tax on income after exemptions when restraint is in order, is probably too radical a step to take at the present time. Certainly the response to these suggestions has been generally negative. In spite of my conviction of the merit of separating fiscal action for stabilization purposes from normal budget considerations, I am willing to concede that the public is not yet ready for such a procedure. As a result, there will be need to vary either basic rates of the income tax or exemption levels as a means of achieving the objective. There is a substantial advantage in using the basic rate as the primary instrument at the present time. Assuming the need for action in both directions, the possibility of raising rates that have been lowered is greater than lowering exemptions that have been raised. Administrative complications resulting from variation in the number of persons covered by the income tax should be avoided if possible. Finally, there is reason to believe that so long as the current excises are imposed, any permanent reduction in total tax requirements should be taken in the form of the elimination of excises rather than the reduction of the base of the individual income tax.

The most troublesome issue suggested by the approach outlined above is that of the degree of imbalance which will be permitted before positive fiscal action is required. A lower limit might be set by stating that any decline in personal incomes registered for a full quarter would call for positive action. In view of the growth trends arising out of both population increases and rising productivity, this would be a conservative limit. The upper limit is more difficult to establish. Assuming that normal growth requires an increase of approximately $15 billion annually, how much more than this can be tolerated without action?[9] Tolerance on the upper side should probably be somewhat less than on the lower. The best way of preventing inflation is to stop it before it gets started. If this is not done, some groups will obtain an

[9] U.S. Department of Commerce, *National Income*, 1954, p. 165.

early advantage, thus justifying subsequent concessions to others
in order to even up discrepancies which have arisen in wage
rates, profits, or sector incomes. In view of the close interrelationships that have grown up in the relations among wages, prices,
and profits, many of which are institutionalized in one way or
another, this policy suggestion is essential. There still remains
the problem of definition of such an upper limit. At the moment
I would suggest that $5 billion in excess of estimated normal
personal income is an outside figure and that even less might
prove to be desirable. If action were to be taken on the basis
of a record for a quarter, a rise of even less than $5 billion
might well call for action.

  If, in addition to a countercyclical variation in tax receipts,
some program could be arranged for varying the amounts made
available to the states for sustenance of their basic construction
and service programs, the objective outlined above might prove
to be more acceptable. The critical issue remains that of the
tolerance of the public for any variation on the downward side,
and its willingness to accept the necessity of tax increases in a
period of boom and general prosperity solely for the purpose of
checking inflation. The most difficult problem lies at the lower
limit of tolerance, where the shoe really pinches and the pressures
begin to be felt.

Conclusions

  A review of the foregoing will reveal that this is one of the
few discussions of stabilization policy currently available that
makes no mention of the multiplier and acceleration principles.
This is a conscious oversight and is justified by the desire to stress
the unknown factors which must be considered if an intelligent
public policy is to be followed. The multiplier tells us that money
injected into the income stream via investment spending becomes
income for someone, and this income in turn will be spent again.

The critical question is how much will be spent and how rapidly. The acceleration principle states that a given change in the level of consumer spending can lead, under certain circumstances, to greater percentage response in investment spending. The critical question in this case is how frequently this relationship may hold, as there are many instances when surplus capacity and expectational factors may make the principle inoperative. The multiplier ends up pointing out the well-established fact of the continuous nature of income flows. The accelerator suggests some of the complexities of a modern industrial system and some of the difficulties of sustaining a constant volume of investment for long periods of time. In neither case can specific quantitative relationships be predicted in advance. A prediction remains in the realm of an art rather than a science. In the case of the multiplier, the problem becomes even more complicated because the true multiplier will depend upon the marginal rate of taxation of the newly injected funds as well as the propensities of individuals to spend or save. As a consequence, these advances in theoretical understanding do not serve to answer the critical questions of how much restraint or stimulus is required or how long restraint or stimulus will be necessary.

Two conclusions follow from this analysis. First, a tolerance for variations in levels of income and employment (and even prices) will be required of the people of the United States if they are to preserve a free economy. No economist is capable of devising means of preventing all fluctuations. Second, not even the combined power of fiscal and monetary policies of government will assure a limit to the variability of the economy that will be tolerable for all. If excessive variations are to be prevented, it will be necessary to pay increasing attention to the structure of economic institutions and the complex relationships among prices, wages, and employment. It is in this area that the greatest fruits are to be gathered if preventive action is to be taken to avoid the necessity for frequent resort to corrective measures. Unfortunately, the capacity of economists to do this job is limited inasmuch as traditional market analysis has yet to be clothed with the dynamic element so necessary for guidance of policy issues.

One final word is required to emphasize the necessity of using fiscal, monetary, and credit policies in a complementary fashion. The frequent disputes among advocates of either one or the other of these instruments seem unrealistic and unwise.[10] As political realities are considered, this point becomes even more important, for it is in the monetary and credit area that the greatest flexibility is possible; and it is in the fiscal area that the greatest danger of abuse of governmental powers is possible. It is also true that it is easier to accomplish one's objective if there is more than a single means of bringing the power of government to bear on the situation. As, in the case of raising maximum revenues, there is advantage in having more than a single tax source, so there is advantage in using all available instruments for stabilization. While fiscal policy will be the primary means of stimulating the economy in periods of depression, and monetary policy may prove to be the primary instrument of restraining a boom, in both cases there is need for complementary action so that the strain on the primary instrument does not become too great.

We may conclude that, although we know less about the causes and cures for economic instability than we first believed after the awakening of the 1930's, there is reason to believe that the extremes of that period can and will be avoided. The job is one that government must assume and cannot avoid because of the leverage it now brings to bear on the economy and the popular pressures that have made it assume this responsibility. The question yet to be decided is whether governments will act responsibly and with wisdom and restraint, or whether they will

[10] Paul J. Strayer, "An Appraisal of Current Fiscal Theory," *American Economic Review, Proceedings,* XLII (1952), 138-146.

cause in turn the growth of new difficulties different, but no less serious, than those so much feared in the past. It is this question that will occupy the remainder of this book and should be ever on the minds of the people and their leaders.

CHAPTER X

Public Expenditure Policy

Some of the theoretical problems of effective control of public expenditures in the public interest have been suggested in previous chapters. It is the purpose of this chapter to review the major issues of policy in the United States. Economics can help develop the analysis and can greatly increase the range and scope of the discussion, but it cannot give scientific support for policy conclusions.

The increase in the size and significance of government expenditures has been documented in the earlier chapters of this study and elsewhere. Measured in absolute terms; or in relative terms; or as they affect employment, market prices, income distribution, capital formation, income, and employment; or in terms of any other possible classification the story is the same. The significance of government expenditures has greatly increased in the past 30 years. This seems to be apart of a long-run trend toward increased government expenditures that has not yet come to an end. It should also be noted that, in spite of the influence of war and defense expenditures, the growth of basic government services and welfare expenditures has also been more rapid than the growth in the private sector of the economy.[1]

---

[1] Solomon Fabricant, *Government in Economic Life*, Thirty-fifth Annual Report, National Bureau of Economic Research, Inc., May, 1955, p. 3.

We find that, as a result of these trends, the power of government to act for good or ill has been enhanced, and that the political process intrudes more and more into the sphere previously reserved for the market. The market for an increasing share of the total product of private industry is a government market.[2] Although there may be competitive bidding among suppliers, scarce resources are being used, and the purpose of their use is determined by political forces rather than private demand. In addition, the costs of doing business are modified by taxation and subsidies or free services provided by government. If the tax is on net income there is less reason to believe that it can have direct bearing upon the costs of business, but it will increase risk and adversely affect savings and investment incentives.[3] Income distribution will also be affected by both taxation and governmental expenditures. In addition to the effect on distribution of income among income classes, government will affect the distribution of income among occupational groups, industries, and geographic regions. Secondary repercussions upon saving, investment, and consumption patterns are also growing and will have their influence upon the level of total economic security.

In this era of big government it is important, therefore, to be sure that expenditures, taxes, and debt-management policies are designed not only to promote the maximization of welfare, however this may be defined, but also to maintain a stable and growing economy compatible with the preservation of a democratic political system. Of greatest importance is avoidance of discriminatory effects other than those clearly desired by the

[2] Government net purchases from business have increased from $362 million in 1929 to $24,621 million in 1955. During the war years and in the period of the Korean episode the rate was even higher. U.S. Department of Commerce, *National Income, 1954 Edition*, Table 9, pp. 172-173; *Survey of Current Business*, July, 1956, Table 9, p. 15.

[3] E. D. Domar and R. A. Musgrave, "Proportional Income Taxation and Risk-Taking," *Quarterly Journal of Economics*, LVIII (1944), 389-422. In this article the authors show that government shares in the losses of business as well as in the profits, thus lessening the adverse effects of taxation upon risk-taking. But they ignore the effects of taxation upon risk when there are never any profits to set losses against.

majority. This suggests that the larger the government the more thought and energy must be devoted to the consideration of the implications of alternative means of accomplishing certain desired objectives with the minimum interference with the rest of the economy. Of great importance is the preservation of a climate favorable to the sustaining of a rate of growth sufficient to maintain the defenses of the United States at a level made necessary by the Russian threat, and sufficient to answer the popular demands for an ever increasing standard of living.

Government Expenditures and Economic Welfare

No enterprise in the field of economics has proved to be more frustrating than the effort to find economic justification for the maximization of human satisfactions. Although the neoclassical writers believed that they had achieved this objective, it is now widely conceded that they built their structure upon assumptions that will not hold water. The impossibility of making interpersonal comparisons and the lack of any ordinal system for comparison among two states of welfare make anything but the more obvious propositions impossible to prove.

One of the greatest sources of difficulty is that in the field of government expenditure there is seldom a market price for the product of government and therefore it is impossible to apply economic analysis. It is easy to advise public officials that public expenditures should be carried to the point where the value of private goods given up is equal to the value resulting from the government program, but who can tell when this point has been reached? It is equally fruitless to advise that all government expenditures should be carried forward to the point where the satisfactions derived from government outlays are equal. In those cases where government charges for its services, it is more nearly practical to make some use of economic analysis, but even in this case there may often be reasons for abandonment of the

analysis for some other objective. The area that is closest to that
of private enterprise, namely the sale of public power or the
provision of other public services at a price, can follow principles
closely related to those found in the market place. It is frequently
suggested that a system of pricing which reflects the relative
advantage of use at different times will prove to be superior for
almost all public enterprises. The question arises as to the proper
allocation of uncovered costs if such a pricing system fails to
cover all costs. Still another set of problems arises if the government wishes to make the people more nearly aware of the costs
of publicly provided services. An excellent example is found in
the development of user charges for public highways. In this
case, it is believed that the public should be more conscious of
the costs they force on government due to the growth in numbers
of cars on the road and the great increase in the number of miles
driven.

The question therefore remains, if there is all this uncertainty
why have people made increasing demands upon governments?
The answer seems to be found not in economic analysis or even
the vague concept of welfare maximization but rather in the
changing character of economic, social, and political views. Certainly it is not surprising that a modern industrial society requires
more highly educated men and women than did a more primitive
agricultural society. It is not surprising that, in a society which
values material goods highly, the growth in the use of the automobile has caused the states considerable expense as the number
of cars and the miles they are driven have increased over the years.

Still another source of growing demands upon society and government arises out of the changing valuation placed upon health,
welfare, and security in a society that can afford for the first time
the luxury of systematically making some provision for these areas
of concern. This tendency has been aided by the changes in
family organization resulting from new values and the shift from
the farm to urban areas. Finally, there has been a growing realiza-

tion that in the modern wage economy there is little chance for the individual to fend for himself if the principal employers in his area are refusing to provide employment opportunities. What has been said suggests that it is much more useful to look at changes in the environment in which we live than to attempt to determine some criteria for maximization of welfare. When it is realized that changes in technology, changes in taste, and changes in the ways in which our society organizes people and business firms are occurring constantly, it is clear that no one system will satisfy all people for all time.

We must realize that certain public expenditures generate forces that will lead to later demands upon the government. For example, the rise in educational standards and the growth in communication facilities have both operated to raise the level of performance expected by the people from their governments. The bad health records revealed by physical examinations of draftees gave publicity to the need for public health expenditures, and probably hastened the day when more public funds are spent for health. Still other interrelationships may be found. The growth of farm surpluses coupled with the malnutrition of many poor children combined to create public acceptance of a free-lunch program. So it goes. There is no purely economic rationale for much of what is done, but much of it seems to make sense. Finally, we must stress again and again that the relationships are always changing, and policies which may have made sense some years ago may be obsolete today.

One of the clearest examples of changes in public-expenditure demands is found in the complex repercussions resulting from the changes in marriage age and size of family which have taken place in the brief period since the end of World War II. Where many school systems had excess elementary facilities at the start of the war, inadequate facilities are now the rule. Movement to the suburbs has also greatly accentuated the problems—often new populations of many thousands spring up overnight and demand

all public facilities at once, crowding what many older communities have done over many years into a few months. The
financing of these outlays is further complicated by the growing
tendency to separate industrial and residential communities. The
bedroom community that has been developed in a short space
of time must either rely upon some higher level of government
for assistance, or suffer the consequences of trying to finance all
its capital programs without the benefit of any industrial base.

Each day the public administrator and the legislative representative must answer the question: How much government is required and where has government grown too big? No economic
analysis will answer this question. Only the good judgment of
those concerned can provide an answer. More and more attention
must then be turned to the consideration of both the long-run
objectives of the society in which we live and the more immediate
demands of the moment. Certainly there is good reason to believe
that the postponement of governmental action to meet real demands of the public will only lead to later waste and inefficiency.
It may even lead to excessive action once the dam has broken.
On the other hand, there is need to consider the political and
institutional repercussions of alternative policies. This suggests
that there are real values in leaving to the individual or the family
the control over the bulk of the family budget. As much as economists might believe that their judgments are superior to those
of the majority, this feeling cannot be put into action without
their views being imposed against the will of the people. This
suggests that, if assistance is in order, there is virtue in giving
the spending unit the funds required and imposing the minimum
of restraint. Income supplements and transfer payments are then
generally to be favored over expansion of directly provided governmental services, assuming other things to be equal. It is obvious
that when a government can provide the service with greater
efficiency than the private market or, the national interest requires

that certain standards are to be maintained, then government must do the job.

A definite trend away from the use of means tests and other attempts to restrict public assistance to only an extremely small group is found in the extension of contributory pension plans for the aged, unemployment insurance, and the suggestion of negative taxes or direct consumer subsidies in the form of variable family allowances. These plans assume that it is desirable to make unqualified grants for a basic minimum standard of living and thus to encourage individuals who have the will and the capacity to provide additional amounts as they choose. Transfer expenditures can be used in this way to further the basic democratic objective of equal opportunity and individual security. What must be avoided is action favoring special groups who happen to have political advantage, and are willing to use it at the expense of the majority. Such seems to be the case where the aged and blind have obtained special tax status far in advance of that granted to other equally deserving groups. Similar dangers exist in the area of farm income stabilization plans. The other hazard to be avoided is that of the destruction of incentives. Although little is known about the point at which a minimum guarantee becomes too high, experience suggests that the danger, although exaggerated, is real. A good case in point was the frequent abuse of the unemployment provisions of the GI Bill of Rights which allowed veterans a weekly compensation of $20 for 52 weeks. Similar abuse of the educational provisions of the same bill is a matter of record. In neither case does the abuse necessarily condemn the act, but it suggests the dangers that could grow. Administrative reforms could have prevented many of these abuses, but the same forces that create the abuse tend also to perpetuate administrative laxity. Administrative policy no less than economic policy is ultimately subject to political control and motivated by political forces. This must again remind us that no policy recommendation can be made without consideration of all the possible avenues for abuse or difficulty. If this were done, there would be less surprise when programs turned out to be less than perfect. In another sense this suggests that there are more limitations upon the use of government power than are often found in the blue-prints made by model builders or those who are primarily motivated by an acute awareness of social problems.

One important factor has retarded the rate of increase in government expenditure in the United States and has probably left this country short of government services. This is the generally negative attitude toward government and fear of government that have continued over the years. Although we are willing to blame the government for adversity and are becoming more willing to charge it with increased responsibilities for our welfare, we place the government employee in a lower status than the private employee and are reluctant to grant sufficient sums for the government fully to discharge its obligations. Conservative interests and taxpayer organizations generally capitalize upon this attitude and do their best to nurture it. They point up every item of waste that can be found and imply that it is only in governmental operations that mistakes are made and that private industry is faultless. States rights advocates have found new recruits by pointing out that the wealthier industrial states contribute more to the federal budget than they get back in the form of federal grants or federal services. Similar views are advanced by advocates of municipal home rule. Thus, although these same states or local governments should profit from a federal or state grant program that would raise the level of health and education in the poorer states and localities where a significant part of the industrial work force is raised, they tend to hold back. It is my conviction that the public receives more for its tax dollar than any other dollar it spends. This in spite of the fact that there are many obvious means of improving the way in which the public economy is run and the projects that are undertaken.

The trend toward increasing government expenditures is the

result of many forces. The record shows that after every war there has been a permanent increase in the level of government spending. The experience of the great depression of the 1930's suggests that a period of economic instability has the same effects, particularly if there is widespread want and distress. The largest other force that seems to be responsible for the increase in government welfare expenditures is the whole complex of industrialization and urbanization. The experience in the United States has been that industrialization has been associated with changes in family organization; changes in social organization, which lessen the effectiveness of community volunteers and other neighborly means of assistance to those in distress; the growth of specialization and dependence upon cash income; and the growing vulnerability of whole cities and regions to a shift in industrial profits. These changes have worked to increase the dependence of the individual upon collective action. Add to this the growing complexity of the industrial economy, growing concentration of population, and the problems of communication and transportation, and it is easy to see why the total level of government expenditures has gone up both absolutely and relatively.

One of the most important lessons to be learned is that those who would like to avoid the complete politicalization of the economic process should do their best to prevent the damming up of unfulfilled wants so that there is once again need for governmental intervention on an emergency basis to clear the market and to guarantee the basic income required for decent living. If a major depression should get underway after a period when basic government services had been held back, there would be another period of frantic governmental expansion reminiscent of the early days of the New Deal, when improvisation and experimentation were the rule. We would be fortunate if in such a period we could avoid gross abuse of governmental powers. Imperfect as the New Deal was, it is still remarkable that there was so little graft and as much good will as tended to prevail.

Finally, it must be realized that there is danger that in the event of a real depression there could develop a sharp reaction against the basic economic and political values which are assumed to be worth preserving as the best means of continuing a strong democracy.

Although there are no scientific criteria that can determine the proper level of government expenditures, there is reason to believe that, in the sort of democracy that now prevails in the United States, it is well to yield gracefully to the popular demands that continue to grow as the result of well-established needs and aspirations. It is particularly important to create in the public mind the faith that government as now constituted can and will act in the public interest. The real policy issue comes down to a question of timing and the practical question of avoiding over-compensation so that there is created an inflationary bias. These questions will be discussed below and again in the chapter on tax policy, as they are at the heart of the policy issues that must be resolved. One thing is clear—we can no longer tolerate a major depression if we wish to preserve either the economic or political institutions we now favor.

The basic conservatism of American politics and the lack of even a single well-organized minority party favoring radical revision of the basic economic and political framework, can be attributed in large measure to the success with which the economy has continued to operate. Although the sociologists point out the many rigidities in the social structure, and the pessimistic point out the many workers in the lower income brackets who cannot provide adequately for their families, they overlook the important fact that children do break through class lines, and whole regions and occupational groups have enjoyed spectacular increases in their standard of living. The poorer sections of the South continue to export labor surplus to the industrial centers of the North and are also being rapidly transformed by the growing industrialization of the South. It is also important to note that the

poor have been gaining in real income more rapidly than the
rich. The fact is that the United States is unique among the
nations of the world in its ability to demonstrate continued increases in the real income of the people. We are an optimistic
country and so far our hopes have been justified. The interesting
thought recently advanced by Potter that the frontier thesis of
Turner can be extended to include the frontier of expanding
industrial opportunity does much to clarify the interaction of the
economic and political forces at work over the past century.[4]

With this background, it is becoming more and more evident
that the ability of the United States to continue past growth trends
will be determined by the wisdom and foresight used by the state
when it substitutes collective action for the market and uses its
powers to redistribute real income. The preservation of economic
stability with continued growth is an objective which must be
held high among those factors considered in establishing any
policy. It is to this aspect of expenditure policy that we must
therefore turn.

Economic Stabilization

In the literature of expenditure policy as it relates to economic
stabilization two main lines of thought loom largest. First is the
stabilizing influence of large budgets. Second is the commitment
of the federal government to increase or decrease its expenditures
in the event of a decline or rise in business. Included among the
commitments that would lead to countercyclical variation in federal expenditures are the farm support programs, unemployment
insurance, pension programs, and public assistance programs.
The advantage of the built-in-flexibility approach is that no new
legislation is required to initiate action, and the question of timing
is answered in advance and need not be raised once the commitment to support or spend under certain well-defined circumstances has been made.

[4] David M. Potter, *People of Plenty,* Chicago, 1954.

A third approach has been followed to some extent since the building of the pyramids. This is the conscious manipulation of public expenditures so that they act as a counterweight to variations in private expenditures. For the most part, emphasis has been placed upon the use of public works to fill in the gap when private investment declines. Although there has been a great deal of discussion of the desirability of preplanning of works programs so that they might be instituted almost as rapidly as the items in the built-in category mentioned above, this has not been done on any large scale; and in past depressions new legislation has been required to gain the objective desired. Somewhat in-between these two types of expenditure variations is the control by the executive branch of the rate of spending within existing programs so that the government's demand will vary countercyclically. Although discretion is limited by the total appropriation not yet spent, there is a considerable leeway within the budget as it now is made. This type of discretionary policy was followed to a limited extent at the early stages of the Korean crisis.

The limitations of the built-in-flexibility approach are such that it cannot be relied upon as the primary policy.[5] The fact that a substantial fall in income and employment and perhaps prices is required before the automatic increase in government outlays takes place is the most significant limitation. Although the sums involved are not to be ignored and, when combined with the countercyclical variation in revenue, may partly offset a variation in national income produced in the private sector, there is no assurance that built-in flexibility could ever either prevent a further decline, or bring about a turn for the better in the event of a major inflationary or depressionary movement.[6] If the cycle

[5] Committee for Economic Development, *Taxes and the Budget: A Program for Prosperity in a Free Economy,* New York, 1947. Even in this early formulation of the built-in flexibility approach the Committee for Economic Development conceded that public works might be necessary in the event of a major depression.

[6] David W. Lusher, "The Stabilizing Effectiveness of Budget Flexibility," and Joseph A. Pechman, "Yield of the Individual Income Tax During a Recession," both in *Policies to Combat Depression,* Princeton, 1956.

is mild and has within it some self-corrective forces, the automatic plan is ideal, but no one yet has the wisdom to predict in advance when this will be the case. The verdict must remain that built-in flexibility is good as far as it goes, but is insufficient to assure that government action will be strong enough to give the results desired.

The more positive public works advocates have concentrated upon needs in periods of depression. At one time they believed that stagnation was inevitable and that a permanent increase in public investment was required to maintain full employment.[7] Agreement upon the desirability of a public works program in the event of a major depression can be obtained from all political viewpoints. Much more difficult is the obverse policy of cutting back in the event of a boom or inflation. Still another problem is that of operating a countercyclical works program in the federal system of the United States. Most public facilities are built, maintained, and operated by states and local governments. For example, of the total new public construction activity in 1956 of $13.4 billion, $9.8 billion was entirely state and local, $0.9 billion was financed with the help of federal aid, and only $2.8 billion was direct federal construction.[8] But state and local governments in a period of depression face the same problems as private business in undertaking an investment program on their own. Credit may not be available; interest terms may be exorbitant; prudence may dictate a conservative policy until the full impact of the depression has registered; and, most of all, revenue declines may make it difficult for state or local government to meet even its existing commitments. Thus the normal reaction is for state and local governments to cut back rather than to increase their capital expenditures in depression. A large increase in federal expenditures may, therefore, only offset the decline in

[7] A. H. Hansen, "Economic Progress and Declining Population Growth," *American Economic Review*, XXIX (1939), 1-15. Also see his *Fiscal Policy and Business Cycles*, New York, 1941, especially pp. 38-46.
[8] *Economic Report of the President*, January, 1957, Table E-30, p. 156.

state and local expenditures. This was the case throughout most of the New Deal. The increase of federal aid may help prevent this perverse reaction, but unless the federal government is willing to make outright grants without any future obligations the state and local authorities may not wish to accept the federal assistance.[9]

If a direct federal program is developed on a large scale, there is the further difficulty that it will either encroach upon the area normally reserved for the states and local governments or upon the area of private investment. In the latter case there is again the danger that the increased federal outlay will not lead to an increase in total investment but only the substitution of government for private investment. In the former case the balance in the federal system tends to be upset with the loss of those political and administrative advantages that are associated with a decentralized form of government. In either case there is danger of creating an adverse psychological reaction as a result of drastic departures from established procedures.

In view of these difficulties, it has been suggested that a reservoir of fully approved public works should be maintained by the federal government at all times and that this reservoir should be carefully designed to avoid the dangers cited above. This would mean that items of lesser priority would make up the bulk of the list. But if this were the policy the program could be validly critized as inefficient and wasteful. Inefficiency might also arise if projects were kept on the shelf without revision, as they would rapidly become obsolete. The major gain to be realized by maintaining a shelf of preplanned works projects would be that of reducing the lag between the determination of the need and the actual outlay of money by the government. This lag, sizeable at best, is the reason why it is generally conceded that a public works program can be used only in the event of a major

[9] E. C. Brown, "Fiscal Policy in the 'Thirties': A Reappraisal," *American Economic Review*, XLVI (December, 1956), 857-879.

depression and is not well designed for use in minor fluctuations.[10] A more reasonable solution is that of greatly extending the amount of federal grants or subsidies to the states and local governments so that they could maintain their normal works programs without incurring additional financial obligations. In this case the number of federal "make work" projects could be reduced, and the violence done to the federal system would be substantially less. The difficulty of working out the terms and conditions that would apply is still substantial, but in this approach there is much that is desirable.[11]

Although discussions of public works programs as a stabilizer pay lip service to the idea that they can be varied at the top of a boom as well as at the bottom, little thought has been given to this aspect of the problem. At the outset there is a superficial appeal in the idea that only the timing of works expenditures is involved and the questions of the proper size and scope of governmental activity need not be raised since the increase at the bottom of a depression can be offset at the top of a boom. It is often suggested that over the cycle the total spent will remain the same as if more traditional budget procedures were followed. This is not likely to be the case.

First, there is no certainty that the cycles in the future will be symmetrical or that, in any cycle, the appropriate policy will call for a reduction in public works at the top of the boom equal to that which was added at the bottom. Second, there is good reason for the public to want to increase public works in prosperity. In a period of prosperity there may be an upward shift in the demand schedule for public improvements as the capacity for their financing increases, as the public chooses to use a part of the rise in real income for collective wants, and as the rise in real income leads to an increased use of many public facilities. Auto and

---

[10] National Resources Planning Board, *The Economic Effects of the Federal Public Works Expenditures, 1933-1938,* Washington, 1940.

[11] James A. Maxwell, *Federal Grants and the Business Cycle,* New York, 1952.

truck mileage increases, recreation facilities are more frequently used as families have more free income, school enrollments increase as the period of education is extended, water and power demands increase, postal traffic grows.

Recent experience also suggests that there is a tendency for the rate of population growth to rise in periods of prosperity and fall in depression. The significance of this lies in the magnitude of the shift in birth rates and marriage age and the consequent effects upon needed facilities such as schools, hospitals, and housing. In face of such developments, it does not make sense to tell the voter that he should postpone his demand for some public improvement until the uncertain day of the next depression. If the need exists now it must be met if it does not deny the satisfaction of some more important need. Overexpansion can be avoided with profit. Speculation, of the type indulged in by some communities that built municipal improvements with an eye to promotion of land sales or at the instigation of the real estate promoters, should be avoided. At best, however, the results that could be expected are far short of the sort of model that has been projected. All that a reasonable man should expect is that the rate of public investment not rise excessively in periods of prosperity, but rise it probably will. If, at least, the existing rate were maintained, or perhaps slightly increased in a depression, an important contribution would be made. If more is attempted, there are likely to be serious repercussions.

The greatest danger of public works programs is that they created vested interests which successfully prevent a cutback when it is desired; or, their abandonment may involve such waste that prudence suggests their continuance, even if general economic conditions are no longer favorable. We could imagine the final result of an unsophisticated approach to public works leading to either greater instability or the rapid and permanent socialization of total investment.

Still another argument in favor of a public-expenditure approach to economic stabilization deserves analysis from the point of view of its long-run effects upon the structure of the economy and the political framework. This is the idea that by the selective use of public expenditures it will be possible to offset the effects of shifts in demand or other changes that leave a region or town in distress while other areas are less severely hit. Carried further, it offers relief to whole industries that are more than normally sensitive to the variations of a cyclical nature.

This reasoning tends to break down when subject to critical appraisal. In the first place, the type of project that can be appropriately undertaken in a public program probably involves substantially different inputs of labor and materials than are involved in the decline of private business.[12] In the second place, there is good reason to fear a commitment to put a floor under every region or industry that tends to suffer more than the average. It is business losses and relative income differentials that are the motivating forces required to bring about a shift of factors of production in a market economy. Technological changes, style, and other changes all require that labor, capital, and management move smoothly and rapidly from one employment to another. This cannot be accomplished if government programs guarantee a favorable income to all regardless of the industry or region in which they live. A program of selective aid might lead to either a tendency for stagnation, or at least to the slowing up of economic development as the mobility of labor and capital is reduced. The temporary postponement of the immediate crisis may also cause inflation. In the latter case, we could easily follow the pattern which tends to develop in the early stages of a war or defense buildup where the entire burden of bringing about the necessary shifts of factors is achieved by increasing profit margins and wage rates so that the only possibility is an upward movement of the average.

[12] E. J. Howenstine, Jr., "An Inventory of Public Construction Needs," *American Economic Review*, XXXVIII (1948), 353-366.

A final argument advanced to justify the increase in government-directed projects in a depression is that the real cost of government projects employing idle factors is zero or, in a slightly modified version, that there is bound to be an upward shift in the marginal value of government projects.[13] Both these statements are true if one's assumptions are narrow. But they are of very limited value as guides for policy, because they ignore the fact that there are alternate means of using the powers of government to bring about the reëmployment of idle factors which do not involve their direct employment by the government. The most obvious is tax reduction or, if necessary, negative taxes or a system of family allowances. We find, therefore, that the proposition about the costlessness of government employment is not true. If alternate means of bringing about full employment are considered, it then becomes necessary to consider the opportunity costs of such employment before the final decision can be made. This should also make clear that when the structure of the economic system is considered those who are interested in maintaining a market-controlled economy will favor the use of the indirect rather than the direct method of reëmploying idle workers.

Looking at the political and administrative aspects of public works variation over the cycle raises additional objections. If no planning has been done in advance, either hasty improvisation is likely to occur which will lead to waste; or, if the cautious, conservative policy followed by Secretary Ickes is repeated, little spending will in fact result. The diffusion of responsibility that is characteristic of the American political system makes it exceedingly difficult to prevent waste. At the federal level there is a different danger than at the state or local level. The danger arises not so much from corruption in the usual sense, but rather from waste on a grand scale by the diversion of money to sub-

[13] Paul Samuelson, "Principles and Rules in Modern Fiscal Policy: A Neo-Classical Reformulation," *Money, Trade, and Economic Growth*, New York, 1951.

marginal projects. Although there is no reason to favor the type
of corruption practiced by the local courthouse gang, there is at
least a closer relationship between their projects and the popular
demands of the public than may be found in some major federal
program that is so big it is impossible for anyone but the expert
to understand what is involved. There is the further danger that
federal officials dispensing billions of dollars exercise a more
subversive influence upon business than any local official dispensing only thousands or millions.[14]

This analysis of the danger involved in large scale government
projects is not made because of any belief that the government
official or politician is less honest than the businessman, because
the evidence seems to point the other way. The corrupter is
the businessman; the corrupted is the government servant who on
occasion proves to be vulnerable to congressional pressures resulting from interest in the local community. For every corrupt
public official there are probably many times over that number
who have been approached by members of the business community seeking favors and have been turned down in spite of attractive propositions. There is a high degree of morality among
public servants that should not be ignored because of the frailty
of a few. The bright light of publicity and congressional inquiry
makes every public transaction vulnerable, while few private contracts are subject to public scrutiny.

Paying my respects, therefore, to public officials generally and
their excellent record over the years, I still fear the merging of
public and private business on any larger scale than is necessary.
I share with R. M. MacIver his belief that there are great advantages in the separation of the management of the economic and
political aspects of our life as far as possible. I fear the concentration of power as a corrosive influence upon the public at large
as well as upon those given the responsibility of discharging

---

[14] H. C. Simons, *Economic Policy for a Free Society,* Chicago, 1948, pp. 13-14.

their duties as dispensers of the fruits of our productive powers.[15] Competition is not always a satisfactory means of determining who should get the maximum reward and in many cases it is ineffective, but collusion is worse and is likely to grow if power is even more highly concentrated as the result of rapid extension of governmental activity.

We must conclude that the view which seems most reasonable is one that attempts to devise the ways and means of stabilizing the public sector over the cycle and at the same time leaves that administration of public activity in the hands of the governmental jurisdiction that is normally responsible for it. In view of the sharp limitation upon the powers of states and local governments in the event of a major depression, this can be done only if there is worked out some system of federal subsidies or grants that will help out the states and local governments when they need it. The chances of doing this now are rather slim. Equalization of income among the states becomes a smaller stumbling block when all states need aid. Opposition to the undertaking of a new federal responsibility is less when the question is not that of the responsibility but rather the means of discharging it.

These conclusions leave the primary responsibility for stabilization to other devices; the conclusions also assume that these devices will be used effectively. Among the devices suggested is that of variation of transfer expenditures with an eye to the stabilization of personal incomes. Although this is in the expenditure side of the budget, discussion of this proposal will be deferred to the chapter on revenue policy, since the analysis is closely related to tax policy, and in many cases there is reason to think of variations in transfer expenditures as similar in almost all respects to variation in tax levies.

A brief mention of still another possibility is required to complete this analysis of the stabilization aspects of expenditure policy. This is the much discussed balanced-budget route to full

[15] R. M. MacIver, *Democracy and the Economic Challenge,* New York, 1952.

employment given early expression in Kaldor's appendix to Beveridge's postwar study of *Full Employment in a Free Society.*[16] Briefly, it is held that if total expenditures and taxes are increased together in a period of unemployment, the net effect will be to stimulate employment and income by activating what would otherwise have been idle purchasing power. In a period of boom a sharp cut in both expenditures and revenues would supposedly produce the opposite effect.

A critical analysis of this route to stability raises doubts about its effectiveness. The limits of variation of the total budget are rather sharp, unless one believes that radical shifts can be made in the whole structure of the political and economic organization of society over the course of the business cycle. This is obviously impossible, and therefore there cannot be the unlimited variation in the total budget required by the theory. In the second place, the analysis supporting the original proposals assumed that the variation in public budgets would have only slight or negligible effects upon the behavior of investors and consumers in the private sector. This is highly unlikely, as the experience of recent years suggests the sensitivity of both groups to changes in government budget and emphasizes the effect of government plans upon expectations. We may conclude that, although interesting, this theoretical exposition of the possibilities for using the balanced-budget approach to economic stabilization policy offers little of practical value. However, it has served to call attention to the fact that the larger budgets of the current period may act as stabilizing forces if they are maintained over the cycle. It also follows that there is some danger that a sharp reduction in total governmental expenditures could be a source of difficulty if it occurred under unfavorable conditions. To this extent there is some merit in the oft-repeated statement that the United States economy is dependent upon large-scale military outlays to sustain

[16] See also T. Haavelmo, "Multiplier Effects of a Balanced Budget," *Econometrica,* XIII (1945), 311-318.

the prosperity of recent years. Although such a thought is repugnant to anyone who realizes the tremendous possibilities for economic progress if only a part of the resources now used for military purposes were released for civilian enjoyment, it has the merit of pointing out the difficulties in a period of readjustment from high defense expenditures. It also realistically reflects the fact that, should it be possible to cut military outlays, there is little chance that other government programs would take their place for some time, and, in the transition, a depressing influence might be felt.

Political and Administrative Aspects

Control of the expenditure process is divided between the legislature and the executive. The formulation of programs usually starts in a department or agency, is reviewed by the executive office, and then is transmitted as the executive budget to the legislature. In the case of new programs, the initiative may be taken by the legislative branch as it proposes a bill to establish a new agency or to give to some existing agency new responsibilities. In all cases, the legislature will review all spending proposals and usually hold public hearings. After review, appropriations are voted and money is then available for spending by the operating agencies of government under the general supervision of the chief executive. This budget process is lengthy and detailed; and, although many improvements have been made, it is more rather than less like the system which prevailed before recent economic developments focused so much attention upon the strategic role of the budget. This fact severely limits the possibility of achieving the goals of maximization of welfare and maintenance of economic stability. Unless the executive and legislative branches work together, there is bound to be difficulty in gaining effective control of expenditures in the public interest. At the federal level the process can be described in great detail, and considerable progress has been made in recent years to rationalize it so that the type of information necessary for analysis is generally available. At the state and local level there is considerable diversity in the practices over the country, and the compilation of basic data for analysis is both difficult and time consuming.

The most obvious limitation placed upon effective expenditure control by political and administrative realities is that the procedures now followed make it exceedingly difficult for the broader economic interests to be kept in the forefront, or for the total program to be considered as a whole.[17] At the executive level, each department, bureau, and agency tries to get a preferred position for itself in the total budget. It is often successful if it can gain strong congressional support or has a broadly based popular appeal. No executive can completely control his departments' requests under such conditions. At the legislative level, the piecemeal consideration of the major appropriations by small committees or subcommittees gives great strength to vested interests and prevents the consideration of competing demands simultaneously. A further limitation is found in the traditional emphasis upon administrative detail and an item-by-item review of proposed expenditures, rather than on program and policy in broad terms. Although this tendency is being modified at the federal level, and much greater emphasis is now placed upon program budgeting, this is in addition to, not in place of, detailed budget analysis. At the state and local level there is even greater need for improvement.

Resolution of these difficulties is further complicated by the almost complete separation of the expenditure and revenue sides of the budget in both the executive and legislative branches.

---

[17] For an excellent discussion of the budget process and some of the recent attempts to reform budget procedures, such as the Legislative Budget experience of 1946-1948, the Omnibus Appropriations Bill for fiscal 1951, and proposals for a Joint Committee on the Budget, see Jesse Burkhead, *Government Budgeting,* New York, 1956, especially chap. 12.

Although sensitivity to the revenue requirements of government projects is universal, the separate consideration of revenue policy sometimes leads to unfortunate results. One of the worst is for tax authorities to advocate tax cuts before expenditure requirements have been determined and with little or no regard to generally prevailing economic conditions. A conspicuous example of this is found in the tax cut of 1948 when inflation was still the major problem. Although this action later proved to be fortunate in view of the recession of 1949, it was done for the wrong reasons, and on the basis of political rather than economic considerations. The earlier cut of 1947 and the President's veto of it is evidence of new strength on the executive level but does not guarantee such action in the future.

Most proposals to improve the budget process increasingly tend to favor the strength of the executive branch and the delegation of greater administrative discretion to the operating departments. The need for better coördination of different aspects of the programs of government is stressed, and great emphasis has been placed upon stabilization policy issues in recent years. Two suggestions have received the greatest attention. First, the development of the program budget to assure consideration of the main functions of government rather than the bits-and-pieces approach which tends to occur if appropriations are granted by agencies and subdivisions of agencies for personnel, supplies, rent, administration, and so forth.[18] The program budget also permits review of the total program at a single time, even if many agencies are involved ultimately in its administration. The second suggestion is that of increasing the strength of the executive as leader of his party by developing a greater sense of party responsibility.[19]

[18] Arthur Smithies, *The Budgetary Process in the United States,* New York, 1955; Committee for Economic Development, *Control of Federal Government Expenditures,* New York, 1955.
[19] American Political Science Association, "A Report of the Committee on Political Parties," *Toward a More Responsible Two-Party System,* vol. XLIV (September, 1950).

If the executive and legislative majority were of the same party the executive budget would receive the support of Congress or state legislatures as a matter of course. Internal debates over the program would be thrashed out in advance in party meetings or assemblies. It is claimed that in addition to the advantage in terms of better program and economic orientation the increase in party responsibility would make the voter more nearly aware of the big issues and the government more sensitive to them. As the government operates today, the extreme diffusion of power makes it difficult to center responsibility upon either the executive, the legislature, or the party for mistakes of commission or omission. The problem of party responsibility if the executive and legislative branches are in opposition has not really been faced except by those who make the unrealistic assumption that we will modify our constitution to establish a parliamentary form of government.

Although both of these approaches have much to commend them, and are, in fact, ideas that have already influenced the operation of the federal government, they include in them much wishful thinking. As advanced by their more enthusiastic supporters, the possibility of gaining the objective in pure form and the advantages that will accrue as a result are exaggerated. In spite of the standard cliché about the incomprehensibility of the federal budget and the stress upon its size, it has for many years contained the basic information necessary to give the public all it can comprehend about the major programs of the federal government. In fact, the *Budget in Brief,* a pamphlet of budget highlights, contains most of the information required by the voter. Some further improvements are desirable to aid analysis by experts and for the purpose of control—especially presentation of more information about the future implications of federal programs once they have been undertaken. This information might help prevent a commitment to spend billions under an initial appropriation of millions. Greater discretionary authority for the exercise of good management is also desirable so that the executive will not find the road to more efficient discharge of his function blocked by budgetary restrictions. Thinking in terms of program rather than bits and pieces will help, but it is not likely that the government administrator will ever achieve the discretionary authority of many business managers. The legitimate interest of the public and its representatives in the maintenance of uniformly high standards throughout the government, and the necessity of full accountability to the public for all money appropriated, makes it difficult to pattern government operations in the same manner as business.

The major difficulty that cannot be corrected by changes in procedure or form is one which arises due to the size of the budget of the federal government. Many of its functions involve dimensions and ideas completely foreign to the layman and to most legislators. Even at the state and local level the popular appraisal of governmental policy encounters similar barriers, although public awareness of inadequate services or excessive expenditures may develop somewhat quicker. This point is most vividly illustrated in the case of the military budget. The sums involved defy comprehension; while secrecy prevents both meaningful breakdowns of this total and the reporting of expert, up-to-date assessments of the dangers which make necessary the expenditure of such sums in the first place. Rivalry among the three branches of the service further confuses the issue as each branch appeals to the public to give it support at the cost of the others. New complications arise when persons in high places assert that the country cannot afford to spend as much as it is currently spending without endangering the basic industrial fabric on which the whole military supply system rests, while others assert with equal vigor that we cannot afford the risks to our security that follow from spending so little. Although democratic theory places great stress upon public debate and discussion and the faith that a balanced judgment will result from the exercise of the popular will, in this area, the cards are stacked against such an outcome because there can be no complete discussion of all the relevant elements. We must conclude that in such cases the public must rely upon the good judgment of elected and appointed officials and in the improvement of internal controls and analysis. Protection against gross abuses is also afforded by the necessity of gaining agreement among all parties concerned —the professional military, their civilian departmental superiors, the executive office, the military affairs committees of Congress, the whole Congress, and finally the public.

The idea of party responsibility, like that of many economic policy recommendations, is based upon a neat model of the way in which the system should work if there were no variables operating in unpredictable fashion or according to forces that are in conflict with the primary goal of the sponsor. Rational economic policy would certainly be aided if all the extraneous considerations that arise in consumers' and investors' minds were absent. But the political system of the United States is even less orderly than the economic. The base of the political parties is at the state and local level, and the elected representative is spokesman for his local interests fully as much as he is for the national. It must also be remembered that the political structure of the United States gives the chief executive major responsibilities as a national leader and symbol. Under a system of party responsibility, he would be only a spokesman for his party and the servant of his party leaders. We may conclude that such a system would be well nigh impossible to impose within anything like the framework of our political system and that, if it were achieved by some miraculous change in the political system, the results might be less favorable than expected. What is most to be feared is that the process of gaining agreement on party policy would require such compromises that the resulting public policy recommendations would be lacking in force, and the strong political leader or statesman would tend to be supressed. One of the strengths of the system that now prevails is that in periods of crisis the executive has been able to speak in the public interest and push both the public and his party into taking a position well in advance of that which they would adopt lacking such leadership. We must also remember that the representative or senator from a safe constituency can often afford to ignore short-run party issues and focus almost all of his attention upon the major national issues. Certainly the congressmen from the one-party South have made important contributions to national policy because they know that they can act without worrying about the reaction of the national party organization. It is also well to remember that politics is much the same whatever the system. The much-admired British parliamentary system did not prevent a Munich, nor has it been able to resolve all the complex postwar problems leading to inflation and to a foreign trade deficit.[20]

It is true that the United States has a long way to go in developing a sense of governmental responsibility and popular understanding as to what are issues of national import. This could be advanced if political leaders and parties became more forthright in their stand on national issues, but this will come only as the public demands it. In other words, what should come first is a more positive public attitude toward government; then increased party responsibility would follow. Responsibility in this sense would then become equivalent to responsiveness to major issues of policy.

The problem of local and sectional interests and their frequent conflict with the national interest cannot be resolved by a simple gadget. What is involved is the use of political power by those who have it. As long as the power exists, it will be used. The only practical means of containing and preventing the abuse of

[20] For a good critique of party responsibility see: Austin Ranney, "Toward a More Responsible Two-Party System," *American Political Science Review*, XLV (June, 1951), 488-499; Julius Turner, "Responsible Parties: A Dissent from the Floor," *American Political Science Review*, XLV (March, 1951), 143-152; David Butler, "American Myths About British Parties," *Virginia Quarterly Review*, XXXI (1955), 46-56.

political power is to generate an offsetting power or public reaction based upon realization that the advantage of the few is at the expense of the many. An example of this is found in the growth of industry leadership in favor of lower tariffs as more leaders become aware of the importance of exports and the connection between free imports and export demand. One of the dangers of party responsibility is that it might be possible for the logrolling that has been so common in congressional circles to be even more successful if the process were within the party caucus and thus completely hidden from view.

Perhaps the greatest barrier to the development of a more responsible public policy is the difficulty of expressing the major issues of economic policy in terms that can be readily understood by the public or even the responsible political officials. Experience since the passage of the Employment Act of 1946 suggests that the President shares this disability and cannot be moved much more rapidly than the public. Although there has been general acceptance of the responsibility of the government for economic stabilization, the consideration of ways and means of discharging this responsibility is still at an elementary level. This is true in spite of the availability of professional advice at both executive and congressional levels. For example, the importance of the possible increase in cost of servicing the public debt loomed much larger in the recent debate over Treasury policy than it should, largely because it was a cost easily understood by the average man. Similarly, attention is focused upon minor items of expenditure when the issue of governmental waste and efficiency is raised because it is a way of gaining public attention. An example of this approach can be found in any taxpayer association pamphlet and is vividly illustrated in the congressional inquiry that made much ado about oyster forks for the Navy. Even the expert must deal in particulars of minor import if he is to be heard. We thus face a major dilemma of the role and place of the expert in an economy that has become so complex as to defy comprehension by any single man. If he is given too much power it will tend to destroy the responsiveness of the government to public demands and create the danger of manipulation of the public by the expert. On the other hand, if he is ignored there is danger that governments will be forced to act ignorantly.

The sort of problem that has yet to be resolved is that typified by the question of the annually balanced budget. The public tends to favor this rule, for it cannot comprehend the difference between the principles that apply in cases of personal finance and public finance. Thus, we may find the government cutting back its support of the market and raising taxes in an effort to balance the budget at a time when this will adversely affect income and employment. On the other hand, tax cuts and expenditure increases which are possible in periods of prosperity may aggravate the problem of inflation, or cause greater difficulties in the future. The danger of this sort of action is now considerably less than was the case at the outset of the Great Depression of the 1930's; but the persistence of this sort of thinking leads to uneasiness in periods when there are good reasons for an unbalanced budget. It is also destructive to confidence and business spending.[21]

Another major problem is that of making the best use of the potential leaders our political system produces. This is a particularly aggravating problem in Congress where the seniority rule gives positions of great power and influence to men who are not necessarily the best qualified for the job. Not the least of the difficulties that result are those associated with the conservative bias of the older person. Before a Congressman gains seniority on an important committee he is apt to be well past his prime, and once given his position he may continue until death or physical infirmity forces him to retire from Congress. Great damage can and will continue to be done to the democratic

[21] The case for the balanced budget is well made in Jesse Burkhead, *op. cit.,* chap. 17.

process as long as this system prevails. As is the case in so many areas, however, it is hard to find an acceptable subtitute for the seniority rule. This is a particularly difficult problem in the House of Representatives, where the large number of members makes selective appointments even more difficult than in the Senate.

The main conclusion arising out of this analysis of the political and administrative aspects of the problem reinforces the earlier generalization that the machinery of government is not well designed to take on any more responsibilities than it now has. This conclusion is based on both theoretical and practical analysis. The impossibility of predicting economic developments in advance, or even the exact reaction of the economy to specific measures of known dimensions and subject to control by government, indicates that current economic theory is not yet developed to the point where it can be used to tell those responsible for policy exactly what their choices should be. Even less well developed than economics theory is the analysis of the political and administrative implications of alternative courses of action. It is fear of radically changing fundamental political structure and social relationships that leads many individuals to view with a jaundiced eye proposals for more positive governmental policy. Finally, it must be recognized that there are many instances when the policy that seems to be most desirable for purely economic reasons may be in sharp conflict with that which is necessary for political reasons. Thus, in the postwar inflation, the political case for large amounts of foreign aid and generous assistance for veterans of the armed forces overbalanced the case that could be made for a reduction in government expenditures as a means of reducing the inflationary pressures in the market.

Experience with the administration of a rational economic policy and the control of expenditures with an eye to the objectives established above is confined in large measure to the period since the inception of the New Deal. Although in earlier periods there was some recognition of the necessity of a positive gov-

ernment policy, it was largely confined to the area of money
and credit and, even in this case, based upon rules of thumb
not too different from the budgetary rule of the annually balanced
budget. The early experience with monetary and credit management and the more recent experience with more ambitious and
comprehensive economic programs does not instill confidence.
The Federal Reserve Board, given an unusual degree of independence, staffed by experts, and with sources of intelligence
of unusual breadth through the system of nation-wide member
banks, has been found wanting by most students who have tested
Reserve policies in retrospect. From the inception of the New
Deal there has been a tendency for fads and fashion to guide
policy as much as firm analysis or real understanding. In critical
periods when major shifts in the economic climate were developing, public policy has been inadequate. In 1937, both fiscal
and monetary policies were too restrictive and helped precipitate
the sharp and severe depression of 1937-1938. In 1945-1946,
predictions of a postwar recession and widespread unemployment
led to the maintenance of easy money and to a policy of tax
reduction that helped perpetuate the inflation of the immediate
postwar period. In 1950, the President was still asking for authority to control inflation when the recession of 1949-1950 was
well underway. In mid-1951, the government was asking for
increased direct controls to deal with a predicted renewal of inflationary pressures in the fall; but, in spite of the failure to gain
this power, these pressures never developed. In late 1953 and
early 1954, the government proved to be correct in deciding that
there was no need for an all-out attack on the current recession,
but the Democratic minority was most critical in its condemnation
of this policy and favored, on the basis of economic analysis, a
major revision of fiscal and monetary policy to combat a coming
depression.

   We must conclude that there is no reason to believe that the
sort of budgetary policy suggested in the early version of the

Full Employment Bill or in later proposals of a similar type can be adopted without creating the danger of government inter-vention of the wrong sort and the hastening of the process of more and more governmental direction of the economy as first one experiment and then another is tried. As long as it is im-possible to predict the course of private spending a year or more in advance, there can be no justification for variation in expendi-tures in anticipation of such fluctuations. What can be done is to wait until known deficiencies develop and then act to offset them. In this case there are bound to be lags, as the political process cannot be made to respond quickly to every minor shift in eco-nomic conditions. Finally, there is reason to believe that if maximum efficiency is desired and the maintenance of something like the market economy now prevailing is favored, expenditure variation is not as effective as revenue variation—with the excep-tion of countercyclical variation in transfer expenditures.

Granting this analysis, there remains the major issue of finding ways and means of stabilizing the expenditures of states and local governments over the cycle. This can be done only if the states find some means of offsetting the loss of revenue in depressions. The possibility of building reserve funds in prosperity to be used in depression has been suggested many times.[22] The main diffi-culty is that this assumes the maintenance of high tax rates in prosperity and a willingness to hold large surpluses. This is not easy to do in view of the uncertainty of the timing or magnitude of the depression that is the reason for the building of the surplus, and in view of the general resistance to the maintenance of high tax rates. Further complications arise in the handling of the surplus funds if they are built up. If the state tries to invest them in the market it may find that it is forced to realize upon them at a substantial discount. If such sales became general among

[22] Louis Shere and Carl Shoup, "Use of Reserve Funds to Stabilize Revenue Available for Expenditures," State of New York, *Report of the New York State Commission for the Revision of the Tax Laws*, Albany, 1932, Memorandum Number Eleven.

the states they would aggravate the deflation in security prices, and thus affect the general liquidity of the entire economy.

It is clear, therefore, that federal power must be used if a successful countercyclical state plan is to be developed. It is unrealistic to believe that in times of prosperity it would be either desirable or possible for the states to build up credits with the federal government sufficient to assure the maintenance of full programs in depression. There is also no reason to believe that the building of a surplus in prosperity would be desirable stabilization policy. If surplus funds were used for retirement of public debt or retired from circulation, the maintenance of continued prosperity might be threatened. If the funds turned in to the federal government were spent and only token recognition of the obligation to the states were made, the result would be to increase the size of the federal budget expenditures financed by the generally inferior state tax systems. Few would consciously favor such a plan.

On the other hand, a plan of granting credits in depression with a commitment to repay in prosperity would cause most of the same difficulties to arise. The inevitable conclusion is that the best plan would be to make outright unconditional grants in depression on the basis of need so that the true expansive influence of federal financial power could be used and so that the states would benefit without loss of subsequent power. In this sort of plan the main problem would be to establish standards for variable grants and a sufficiently firm commitment to permit the reduction of grants when the need no longer existed.

Conclusions

Recent trends have increased the importance of government expenditures to the point where the economic health of the country may be said to be affected as much by the volume and direction of these expenditures as by any other single force.

In terms of control, it is clear that government policy is still in the primitive stage. Theoretical guides are lacking, and conflicts in objectives complicate the problem. One of the major dangers is that the progress recently made in fitting government into a model of the economic system via the income approach and by the use of national income accounting will mislead the policy-maker and give him a false sense of understanding and power. This is particularly true of those who take the suggestions of model makers literally and ignore the uncertainties of both economic and political dynamics. The most guilty are those who are willing to give almost absolute priority to the achievement of full employment. At some point the issue of employment stabilization and political and economic freedom comes into conflict. It is the consciousness of this issue that is so important to the policy-maker if he is to avoid taking action that leads to collectivization of the economy and the destruction of the basic political framework that we now profess to hold in such high esteem. On the other hand, the negative position that has characterized the opposition to any positive government intervention, except for the benefit of special interest groups, will certainly cause a reaction which would lead us in the same direction. A balance and a tolerance of both some political and some economic imperfections is required. This plea is basically for mature judgment and realization that the complexities of life do not permit the achievement of the planner's utopia. The chance of maintaining such a moderate policy in the field of expenditure is largely dependent upon the avoidance of external disturbances of a major sort, such as war and the good luck to be able to get by the next few years without a major depression. There is no magic formula that will assure this favorable environment, but the power of reason can point out the dangers inherent in alternative policies, and we can hope for the best.

ıı

Tax Policy I

ıı

Tax policy, like expenditure policy, requires analysis of both the specific effects of individual taxes and of the aggregative effects of the tax system as a whole. Like expenditure policy, tax policy views depend upon the individual's philosophy and value system. Even when a citizen realizes the necessity for high taxes he can be persuaded that his own taxes are too high and that someone else should bear a larger part of the total burden. Like high expenditures, high taxes have become a major force determining the general economic climate, and they are even more important in their specific effects upon the way in which business is organized and income realized. It is also true that under current conditions and because of the limitations of our theoretical knowledge, decisions about tax policy are based primarily upon ethical or moral judgments. The parallel can be continued even further into the realm of the strategic role of tax policy in determining the future of the federal system of government and the future of a market-dominated economic structure.

The pervasive influence of taxation need not be labored in a period when from 20 to 30 percent of the total income produced in the United States is taken by government to finance government purchases, government employment on its own projects, and transfer expenditures. But the average or aggregate percentage does not fully tell the story. When business corporations pay 52 percent of their net income in taxes; when individual income tax rates range from 20 percent to 91 percent; when excise taxes range up to 50 percent or higher ad valorem; and when extreme differentials are created by special features of the law such as capital gains, percentage depletion, family partnerships, additional allowances for the aged, and failure to include certain types of income such as pension contributions by employers and sums invested in deferred compensation plans, the possible ramifications of tax policy are revealed. Additional effects will result from the redistributive aspects of the tax system, both among individuals and regions.

Finally, it must be pointed out that the realistic formulation of tax policy requires administrative and political realities to be weighed fully as much as economic considerations. A theoretically perfect tax poorly administered can have more adverse effects that a cruder tax well administered. Political limits to taxable capacity are variable depending upon the structure of the tax system. As a rule the political tolerance of heavy taxes is greater if a variety of levies are used. This is due to the greater tax consciousness generated by high rates and the fact that with high rates the imperfections and side effects that result from tax law or administration become more significant.

Tax Theory

The theory of taxation still lacks both precision and unity. The most formal aspect of tax theory is the incidence of taxation, but incidence is usually but a special case in the general theory of price determination. As a result much of the theory of incidence is of limited use in the measurement of the true burden of taxation. Economic analysis is of value but it cannot serve as a complete policy guide, and as price theory becomes more realistic incidence becomes less certain. Special care must be taken to avoid false inferences about the significance of tax shifting frequently implied by textbook writers. For example, when it is said that a tax is shifted forward to the purchaser this does not mean that the burden in terms of income or profits is fully avoided by the seller. In spite of the fact that the final consumer will have to pay more, even the monopolist of purely competitive value theory cannot avoid loss of profits as the result of an increase in an excise tax. Recent investigations in the field of corporate price policy suggest that even the old assumption that an income tax can never be shifted is subject to question because the assumptions of profit maximization in the short run do not always hold. The theory of tax capitalization and the theory of the relation of indirect taxes and the price level remain in a primitive stage. As an attempt is made to apply more recent theories of monopolistic and imperfect competition to tax incidence, the degree of uncertainty tends to increase. We are forced to the conclusion that incidence theory is still inadequate and reveals the limitations of much of price theory as applied to specific cases.

Even more limited in value is the traditional theory of tax burden distribution. The inadequacy of the criteria of ability-to-pay, faculty, and benefit as guides to policy are obvious. They have no exact meaning and provide no rational basis for action beyond the deep-seated social or moral convictions of those who would use them. Attempts to go further than this have bogged down in spurious reasoning growing out of the alleged diminishing utility of successive additions to income. It is now generally conceded that the impossibility of making interpersonal comparisons makes invalid use of this theory for analysis and that even if the case is granted intuitively it does not prove the case for progression. This is true because to resolve the critical issue of progression, regression, or proportion in the tax burden distribution, knowledge of the rate at which the utility of income declines is required.[1] Proper judgment of these issues also requires that the reasonableness of the income differentials resulting from the operation of the market system be assessed. If large incomes result from the imperfect operation of the system, a much higher rate of progression or a system of selective taxation to tax the unearned increments can be justified. However, to make such an assessment requires perfection of tools of analysis not now available. Under such circumstances, no tax burden distribution will be satisfactory. Political and social judgments even more than economic analysis will determine policy.

To avoid, for a moment, the negative approach, it is well to point out that there can now be said to be limited acceptance of certain basic postulates of taxation. These are that persons in equal circumstances should be treated equally, that tax revenues should vary countercyclically, that taxes should be imposed upon those with low incomes at a lower rate than those with high, that taxes should be lighter on a large family than a small one, and finally that taxes are to be justified not only as a means of balancing the budget but also as a means of reducing private consumption and investment expenditures. Taxes must be restrictive in order to release productive factors for government use. Greater popular appreciation of the last point would do much to remove the negative attitude toward taxation, although it can never prevent the general reaction that rationalizes opposition to each tax by claiming that it is unjust, or opposition based upon a hope to have one's cake and eat it too. More limited acceptance is given to the ideas that direct taxes are to be preferred to indirect taxes, that the individual income tax is the best tax, and that taxation should be used consciously to bring about more equal distribution of income and wealth.

The most controversial area of policy is that concerned with

[1] For an excellent review of the literature see Walter J. Blum and Harry Kalven, Jr., "The Uneasy Case for Progressive Taxation," *The University of Chicago Law Review*, XIX (1952), 417-520.

the use of taxation for other than the raising of revenues required to balance the budget. It is frequently claimed that taxes should be imposed "for revenue only." The use of taxation for either the purpose of social control or economic stabilization is opposed by an articulate minority. In a milder form this same view is found in the writing of those who advocate the principle of neutrality in taxation or those who favor a "leave them as you find them" position. Although this noninterventionist approach seems to imply a position of neutrality with regard to most of the pressing issues of policy, it requires, no less than an interventionist approach, a commitment of the sponsor. His commitment must be to the *status quo,* whereas the commitment of the interventionist is to an ideal not yet realized. There is nothing sacred, however, in the *status quo* and in many instances it can be argued that the most enlightened policy, as well as the most realistic policy, may require substantial modification of the results of the market system. Use of taxation as the instrument with which to achieve a given purpose should be based upon a judgment that it is the best means of accomplishing the objective in mind. If this is the case, it is certainly as good a use of taxation as any other. One reason for favoring the use of taxation as an instrument of social control is that, in some instances, it may involve less undesirable political and arbitrary administrative side effects than more direct means of accomplishing the same objective. For example, it has often been pointed out that the tariff is a relatively innocuous means of affecting the flow of international trade as compared to the use of import quotas, exchange controls, and other similar devices. The great advantage of the use of the tariff, or a tax, is that it still leaves the individual producer and consumer free to compete without appeal to political or administrative authority for approval. Although some tariffs are nearly prohibitive in nature, this freedom is still of value in international trade and avoids the necessity of building a large bureaucracy to administer more detailed regulations.

Tax Limits

As the result of the severity of taxation much attention has been recently given to the question of the limits of taxable capacity. Some contend that tax limits can be expressed in terms of a percentage of the national income or in terms of tax rates.[2] These claims have not proved to be of value.[3] A much more reasonable conclusion is that the limit that will first apply is determined by variable political forces. These include such factors as past experience, quality of administration, and balance in the tax system, including such items as the severity of specific rates, the purpose for which revenues are required, and extent to which the economic system has in it elements which prevent taxes from becoming effective. Escalator clauses in wage contracts which reflect increases in the consumer price index resulting from increases in excise or sales taxes are an important example of an institutional force limiting the effectiveness of taxation. Either political or institutional forces can operate in such a way that either the public will refuse to accept higher tax rates or tax increases will be ineffective due to offsetting wage and price increases. The fear that taxes might reach a level causing a decline in total output so large that the tax rate increase is offset by a reduction in the tax base is exaggerated in the United States. So long as Congress controls the imposition of taxes, other limits are much more likely. The popular myth that tax reduction might so increase the tax base that total revenue would remain the same or even increase is equally unlikely. Although it is easy to demonstrate that revenue yields would increase in

[2] Colin Clark, "Public Finance and Changes in the Value of Money," *Economic Journal,* LV (1945), 371-389.
[3] J. A. Pechman and T. Mayer, "Mr. Colin Clark on the Limits of Taxation," *Review of Economics and Statistics,* XXXIV (1952), 232-242.

specific instances when the demand for the taxed product is
highly responsive to changes in price, there is no reason to believe
that the total national product is so responsive to changes in
tax rates. In periods of full employment this outcome is particularly unlikely, as in the short run the only means of increasing
output would be to add to the labor force or to get the existing
labor force to work longer hours. With more free income the
average worker is just as likely to do the opposite: work fewer
hours and encourage members of his family to leave the labor
market. We must conclude that, although any specific tax can
be pushed to its limits so that less revenue is obtained by raising
rates, the controlling limits for the economy as a whole are
the political tolerance of taxes and the possibility of manipulation
of wage and price relations to avoid the full impact of taxation.
These limits are real and must be respected in the formulation
of policy, but the general fear that the capacity of the United
States to meet its financial obligations is now severely tested in
some fundamental economic sense is not realistic.

A related issue is the effect of taxation upon the rate of saving
and investment. It is frequently asserted that current rates of
taxation are drying up the sources of capital and making it unattractive to invest such capital as there is available. The record
investment boom of recent years is evidence that in the short
run, at least, these fears are exaggerated. To some extent the
issue is falsely drawn, inasmuch as the favorable treatment of
capital gains, percentage depletion allowances, and other tax
differentials have greatly lessened the severity of taxation of
investment income. However, the basic issue is the extent to
which taxation will cause a decline in the rate of growth which
would take place if some other pattern of taxation were used. It
is probable that high rates will reduce savings. The corporate
income tax is a particularly important tax from this viewpoint,
as it is the corporation that controls the largest part of the
savings and investment decisions in the economy of the United

States. The maintenance of a 52 percent corporation net-income tax rate will have a cumulative effect upon the ability of corporations to expand out of retained earnings.

Some economists favor the maintenance of high taxes as a means of reducing the volume of savings. This group believes that unless taxes mop up excess savings they will become greater than the volume of investment for which there is an outlet and thus cause a depression. This view follows closely the early versions of the Keynesian theory, although similar views have been advanced by the underconsumptionists for a much longer period. Although savings can be reduced by taxation, it does not follow that this is a wise policy even when investment spending lags. This is the case because the same tax that reduces saving may adversely affect the rate of investment by reducing the net return available after tax. The independence of the investment variable in the Keynesian system has thus misled many policy-makers. Another view that has greater force is that the maintenance of a high rate of investment is not wise and that a somewhat higher rate of current consumption and lower rate of investment would be desirable in a country as prosperous as the United States.[4] Two arguments can be raised against this position. First, industrial expansion must continue at past rates or even higher rates if the national security of the United States is to be protected against the threat of the Russians, who are using the power of the state to maintain a high rate of industrial expansion. Second, the importance of a high rate of growth and a steady improvement in standards of living as a force preventing political discontent makes it a political necessity to continue to expand at a rate comparable to that achieved in the past. There is reason to believe that it is much more difficult to maintain a free economy in a stagnant or slowly expanding economy than in one that is

[4] Paul A. Samuelson asserts that tax policy and fiscal policy can be adjusted to favor any desired rate of growth. "The New Look in Tax and Fiscal Policy," Joint Committee on the Economic Report, *Federal Tax Policy for Economic Growth and Stability*, Washington, 1955.

enjoying a reasonably high rate of growth. Although a growing economy may be more vulnerable to cyclical fluctuations, an economy in equilibrium is one that offers less opportunity for the individual and might well become rigid and inflexible with a marked stratification of the social structure. Under such circumstances most frustrations with one's lot would find expression only through political channels instead of being diverted into a struggle for economic advancement. Although it is possible to favor the exchange of economic growth potential for greater stability and security, it is doubtful if many would favor the exchange of freedom for stability and negligible growth.

The case against high rates of taxation as a barrier to both the low-income indivdual and the small business developing to compete with the wealthy individual or giant corporation has been made by both Wright and Butters and Lintner.[5] High rates of taxation cumulatively limit the possibilities of an individual acquiring a large fortune, or the expansion of a small business firm from retained earnings or individual contributions of wealthy investors. As a result, those who built up a fortune or business in a period of low taxation will find it easier to protect their relative position so long as high rates prevail.

As was pointed out above, the existing tax system is not as severe as is generally believed. The Harvard studies of the effects of taxation upon business and incentives suggest that the possibilities of tax avoidance have permitted the continuance of high rates of savings and investment and have even led some investors to undertake risks who might have followed a more conservative policy had not the possibilities of large capital gains subject to low tax rates been made available.[6]

---

[5] David McCord Wright, "Income Redistribution Reconsidered," *Income, Employment and Public Policy,* New York, 1948; J. Keith Butters and John Lintner, *Effect of Federal Taxes on Growing Enterprises,* Boston, 1945.

[6] For a summary of these studies see J. Keith Butters, "Taxation, Incentives, and Financial Capacity," *American Economic Review, Proceedings,* XLIV (1954), 504-519.

The Ideal Tax System

Even greater difficulty is encountered in the formulation of a theory of the ideal, model, or just tax system for the long run. Tax policy cannot be evaluated, however, unless some criteria exist. Equity is generally conceded to be one of the most important considerations, but who is to define it? The public interest is to be promoted, but how can the public interest be defined so as to present a meaningful guide to the policy maker? The democratic process assumes that the process of public debate and controversy will result in a resolution of the major differences and a compromise satisfactory to all but the extremes on either side. However, the actual functioning of the legislative process and the extent of public knowledge about major issues of taxation is such that current tax policy reflects much more nearly powerful pressure groups and the thinking of a relatively few strategically placed individuals than the public at large. Blough has suggested that the Treasury should be recognized as the one powerful agency in the taxing process to have kept the public interest foremost; but, since the change in administration in 1953, the Treasury has chosen to withdraw from public debate and certainly conceives of the public interest in a very different way than was the case in the day of Blough's service as head of the Tax Research Division.[7]

The major recodification of all federal tax legislation in the Revenue Act of 1954 first appeared in print in the form of a bill drafted by the Ways and Means Committee. This bill incorporated all of the compromises between the Committee, the Treasury, the Joint Committee on Internal Revenue, and the powerful lobbies. This major job of revising the federal law was done without any serious public debate except over some relatively minor provisions. The failure of the administration or the Treasury to present their ideal tax proposals to the public has

[7] Roy Blough, *The Federal Taxing Process,* New York, 1952, p. 122.

reduced the chance of making major reforms in the federal tax system in the near future. The fact that the bill as passed extends even further some of the special provisions of the law favoring limited numbers of taxpayers, implies endorsement by the administration of a policy of achieving equity by extending to all the special privileges of a few. This is a dangerous policy as it may lead to a breakdown of public confidence in government and the destruction of the tax base.

The standard textbook treatment of the issue of long-range tax policy usually bypasses the difficult issue of translating the glittering generalities of equity, administrative convenience, certainty, and ability, which go back to the days of Adam Smith, into specific guides for policy. Each of us can give these principles content, but few will agree on a total program or the relative priority assigned to items on which there can be general agreement. One of the most widely accepted principles is that taxes should not be arbitrary or capricious in their effect upon individuals or groups, but those who favor the use of tax power to provide an incentive for certain types of activity have always been willing consciously to use taxes in a selective manner to achieve their end. The principle of convenience and certainty is often in conflict with the laudable desire to make full allowance for special cases or circumstances so that a more refined adjustment of tax to ability can be achieved. Even the principle that those in equal circumstances should be treated equally defies exact expression due to the difficulty of defining equal circumstances. It is not difficult for interest groups to find ways of claiming special treatment in the name of the national interest, but it is difficult to prove the adverse effects of exceptions without resort to a level of generalization and abstraction that removes the argument from the popular level. A conspicuous example of this type of problem is found in the case of the special treatment now given to all extractive industries via the percentage depletion allowance and capital gains. Starting with the statement that it is in the national interest to have large proven reserves of strategic minerals and metals and the fact that a large amount of money may be spent in exploration without any return, the oil, sulphur, and other extractive industries have achieved a tax position more favorable than that of any other industry and have been able to extend this position over the years, in spite of opposition by tax experts and others in a position to judge the reasonableness of the special provisions granted. Everyone can understand the national interest in maintenance of large oil reserves, but few can comprehend the complex technical issues of percentage depletion, capital gains, and allowance for current exploration costs. Even a widespread knowledge of the general availability of large reserves of coal, sand, gravel, and mollusk and oyster shells has not prevented these industries from gaining a part of the special provisions allowed oil, uranium, sulphur, and other more strategic materials.[8] It should be noted, however, that all departures from tax justice are not in favor of certain pressure groups. The limitation of capital losses, the failure to devise an acceptable averaging scheme for individual income taxpayers, and the failure to make adjustment for the declines in the value of money all work to the disadvantage of certain taxpayers.

We must conclude that at the present time there are no rules or guides that can serve as a rigid framework for the analysis of tax policy. Each critic must devise his own, and in the process as much thought must be given to political matters as to purely economic. This will mean that the debate over tax policy will range over the whole area of economics and politics; and the results will reflect popular prejudices, errors, and misconceptions about these matters as much as the ultimate truth. This state of affairs is not to the liking of those who want everything wrapped in tidy bundles and put in its proper place for all time. Tolerance

[8] Joint Committee on the Economic Report, *Federal Tax Policy for Economic Growth and Stability,* Washington, 1955. See papers in Section IX and the exchange of letters between Rex G. Baker, general counsel, Humble Oil and Refining Co., and Erwin N. Griswold, Dean, Harvard Law School, in the Appendix.

of change, inconsistencies, and outright error is required. But
this is the way of a democracy and much to be preferred to the
rigid and equally imperfect results which would be produced by a
dictatorial government.

Current Issues and Possibilities of Reform

Three major areas of tax policy can be distinguished for purposes of discussion. These are: (1) the problem of equity in
tax burden distrubtion, including both the question of the fairness of individual taxes and the question of the proper distribution of the total tax burden by income class; (2) the relation of
tax policy to the stabilization of income, employment, and prices;
(3) the relation of tax policy to economic incentives and economic growth. Problems of state and local taxes will be covered
in Chapter XIII. No effective reform of the tax system can be
achieved unless in the pursuit of each objective the possibility of
successfully achieving all other objectives is kept in mind. Thus,
although each area will be discussed separately, frequent references will be made to the interrelationships among all of them.

Equity

The subjective nature of the concept of equity and tax burden
distribution is at the heart of the policy problem. Objectives
determine conclusions, but objectives are notoriously diverse and
are too often expressed in such a vague fashion that it is exceedingly difficult to build a logical system upon them. Additional
difficulty results from the internal inconsistencies of much popular
thinking about tax policy and the general tendency to focus upon
the particulars of policy as they affect the individual, firm, or
industry, rather than the economy or society as a whole. This conflict between the individual and general interest is inevitable. The
impact of a tax upon the individual is clear and immediate. The

payment of any tax is painful. In a competitive, democratic society it is acceptable to use legal means to reduce this burden. Taxes are tolerated as necessary evils and, except in rare cases of taxes clearly imposed for regulatory purposes or for punitive purposes, taxes are never enthusiastically approved.

In attempting an analysis of this issue it is also necessary to realize that tax incidence theory is incapable of giving precise answers to the question of the real burden imposed by any tax. Thus, there can be a legitimate controversy over the effects that will result from either the existing or some proposed tax system. We must conclude that the pursuit of the ideal will always be frustrated by both lack of knowledge and the conflict in views over the ideal, which will continue as long as freedom of expression and the popular franchise is maintained. If this is the case there is reason to emphasize the process by which policy is made rather than to concentrate entirely upon the result.

Equity in tax policy requires that all the electorate have as full knowledge as possible of the current law or suggested changes in it. Today, many tax laws are misleading, and the public is more often ignorant of even the more obvious facts than not. For example, the average man is misled by the frequent identification of marginal with average or effective tax rates. The community-property provisions of the individual income tax grant a much larger tax relief to the married man with a high income than has been realized by the public at large. Capital gains, preferential rates for certain industries, pension provisions, and other technical provisions of the income tax law further confuse the issue so that the fact that most individuals are not subject to the full impact of the progressive rate schedules is concealed from the public. Indirect taxation, such as sales and excise taxes, may be objected to on similar grounds. The consumer may not realize that the purchase price of the commodity he is buying includes a tax or if he does, the small sum paid relatively frequently minimizes the true nature of the burden imposed. As a result, not only is violence done to some one group's concept of equity but the resulting distribution of the tax burden is in opposition to the basic tenets of democratic theory. This sort of problem will often generate its own corrective influences, but greater awareness of its existence would do much to keep it from growing, as it may have a tendency to do in a period of high revenue requirements.

The "$64" question facing the tax-policy-maker remains that of the proper distribution of the tax burden among all members of the community. An equalitarian bias prevalent in most democracies has found expression in the widespread use of progressive income and death duties. Although it is impossible to give a scientific justification for either greater or less progression, several facts can throw light upon the issue now before the policy-maker and the public at large. First, it is only in a progressive tax system that many of the most troublesome issues of tax law and administration arise.[9] For example, the inequity resulting from fluctuating incomes is much less if rates are proportionate than if they are progressive. Capital gains taxation would not present so many difficulties under a proportionate system, and the tendency for many deferred-income payment plans to develop would be reduced if all income were taxed at the same rate. The limitation of allowance of capital losses reflects both social and economic biases for which no justification can be found.

Second, the revolution in income taxation and the generally high levels of taxation now required have made obsolete the popular view that the wealthy can finance the greatest part of the cost of government. The verdict that the Lord must love the poor because He made so many of them must now read the Lord loves the poor as He has given them most of the tax base of the nation. With over 80 percent of the total taxable income in the first bracket of the individual income tax, there is no chance that a substantial relief in the burden of the poor or the middle class can be obtained by any conceivable increase in the top bracket

[9] Walter J. Blum and Harry Kalven, Jr., *op. cit.*

rates. This fact does not prevent the continued use of the individual tax as an instrument of income equalization but suggests that,
in addition to limiting the size of the largest incomes after tax,
any subsidy of the lowest income groups will require a substantial contribution from those who are only slightly better off. An
example of this fact is found in the social security program which
achieves important income equalization results by imposing proportionate tax rates.

Third, the current practice of imposing high rates under a
steeply progressive schedule and then making such rates ineffective by extending the loopholes in the law, creates overwhelming
incentives to find means of realizing income in a form subject
to the preferential rates. The effect of the tax law is therefore to
redirect capital and to force management and individuals to make
decisions solely for tax purposes. If the public desires this result,
there is no means of proving the public wrong; but the danger
is that the public does not realize the imperfections of the current
law and is ignorant of its effect. Not the least of the effects which
result are those which distort the distribution of tax burdens
among equals. This then resolves into an argument about the relative weight to be given the use of tax incentives in order to achieve
some public purpose on the one hand, and the principle of equity
that holds that persons and businesses in equal circumstances
should be subject to equal burdens, on the other. It is my contention that the latter case has lost the political and administrative
battle and that a better balance would be achieved if there were
fewer special cases and more nearly equal treatment of all. A
particularly disturbing reaction is that of certain interest groups
which have been successful in extending a special tax incentive
well beyond the purpose for which it was designed, in a callous
and calculated use of pressure to achieve a preferred status. Inasmuch as the stakes are higher with high revenue requirements, it
is this point that demands increasing attention. This issue has
been discussed at length in articles and is viewed with alarm by

many experts in the field, but the trend toward more and more special rates or favored sources of income and wealth continues.[10]

An important source of differential taxation arises from the taxation of capital gains. The differential between the high marginal rates on ordinary income and that of 25 percent on capital gains realized after six months holding is so large that numerous devices have been developed to permit the realization of what would otherwise be ordinary income in the form of capital gains. It has also encouraged sales of property or closely held firms to larger corporations in order to take advantage of the preferential rate. Additional discrimination is the result of the failure of the law to bring accrued gains to account on the death of the taxpayer. Thus, he and his heirs may forever escape an income tax upon gains which have accrued during a lifetime but are not realized before death. In this case there is an advantage in holding assets longer than would normally be the case. The granting of capital gains treatment to other income, including income from the sale of cattle held for breeding purposes and coal royalties is evidence of the tendency to extend preferential treatment of certain sources of income as the result of political pressure-group activity. Although the limitation of capital losses offsets some of the potential tax relief available, this is of minor importance in a period of expansion and in the case where capital gains treatment has been extended to areas which would normally be thought of as current income.

The case for special treatment of capital gains is often based upon the claim that they are not income. In this view national income accountants concur. But as Seltzer has pointed out, there is a much less clear line between what is called capital gains and

[10] Joseph A. Pechman, "Erosion of the Individual Income Tax," *National Tax Journal*, X (1957), 1-25; C. Lowell Harriss, "Erosion of the Federal Estate and Gift Tax Bases," *Proceedings of the Forty-eighth National Tax Conference of the National Tax Association*, 1955, pp. 350-358; Paul J. Strayer, "The Individual Income Tax and Income Distribution," *American Economic Review*, XLV (1955), 430-440; Joint Committee on the Economic Report, *Federal Tax Policy for Economic Growth and Stability*, Washington, 1955, pp. 251-311.

what is called income than is generally realized.[11] Capital gains
result from changes in the value of money—so does ordinary
income. Conventional accounting practices generally fail to reflect
the fact that the cost of goods sold and depreciation are artificially
low in a period of rising prices. Capital gains result from sudden
and unexpected shifts in demand or technology—so does ordinary
income, as the reëvaluation of assets permits profits to be realized
over time as the result of higher prices. Most important, however,
is the fact that many gains merely reflect the fact that ordinary
income has not been distributed but retained in a business and
used to increase the capital or book value of the company. It is
this possibility that makes it so attractive today for a corporation
to retain a large percentage of its earnings rather than to distribute
them and have them taxed as dividends. Other considerations may
also lead to a high rate of corporate saving; but the capital gains
law will often tip the scales in its favor, or at least lead to a
higher rate of retention than would otherwise be the case. The
most persuasive case against capital gains is found when they reflect a fall in interest rates on fixed income securities. Although
dealers or speculators in bonds may gain, the investor who sells
one security and buys another wonders why he should be taxed.
His case is certainly different from that of the investor who enjoys
an increase in capital value due to an increase in earning capacity.

Another major source of discrimination in the present law is
found in the provisions for exemptions and deductions from
taxable income and their administration. The most flagrant abuses
are in connection with the allowance for expenses. Although there
is no way of measuring the extent of the excessive deductions
taken as business expenses, it is the belief of almost all observers
that the expense account and the provision by companies of free
services such as automobiles, club memberships, and entertainment
allowances are abused. In this case the problem is one of admin-

[11] Lawrence H. Seltzer, *The Nature and Tax Treatment of Capital Gains and
Losses,* New York, 1951.

istration and enforcement. The law should be tightened to make it more difficult to claim excessive amounts. Perhaps the most effective means would be to make an example of the most flagrant violators and then to rely upon the corporations to police themselves. This assumes that Congress would favor such a step and grant the Internal Revenue Service sufficient funds to employ the investigators required to enforce a strict interpretation of the law. In this connection it is important to realize that inadequate staffs for the administration and enforcement of tax laws are at the bottom of many of our current problems. This is a clear case of a "penny wise, pound foolish" policy and suggests a radical revision in current thinking is required. The Treasury has shown many times that additional personnel cannot only improve the enforcement of the law but also bring in many times the cost of their salaries in additional revenue. The tendency of the politician to want to avoid punitive action may help explain this failure in personnel policy, but it is growing more serious as additional burdens have been thrust upon the Treasury in recent years. Laxity in enforcement cannot be allowed to continue without damage to the whole tax system.

One of the most troublesome areas of tax policy is that of the proper coördination of the corporation income tax and the individual income tax. Starting with the premise that the corporation is a legal fiction and that the stockholders' interest in the profits of the corporation may be thought of as similar to that of a partner's, the conclusion is reached that taxation of both corporate income and dividend income is discriminatory and unfair. This conclusion has led to many proposals to eliminate this abuse. Plans have ranged from the suggestion of treating corporate profits on a partnership basis, requiring stockholders to pay on accrued but unrealized earnings, to the recently adopted dividend credit.

Most of these analyses assume that the corporation income tax is not shifted forward to the consumer, and fail to differentiate between the large public corporation, where management decisions are divorced from ownership, and the private corporation, which is more like a partnership.[12] The question of incidence is important, as some of those who argue most vigorously for elimination of double taxation of corporate income also claim that the tax is shifted. One can not have it both ways. If the tax is shifted there is no discrimination against stockholders but rather against the purchaser. In spite of the recent articles suggesting the possibility of shifting of the corporation income tax, it is probably true that the bulk of the tax is not shifted. This assumption is followed in this analysis.

In the case of the public corporation, the purchaser of shares will discount the tax and pay a lower price for shares as a result. Any relief will thus give to him a windfall of substantial proportions once the tax has been in effect for a long enough time for the market to reflect the new situation. Goode has argued this case most persuasively, and also points out that the distribution of stock ownership is such that the burden of corporate income taxes is distributed progressively by income class. The problem of finding an alternative source of revenue is also neglected by most advocates of reform. Estimated to produce $21.6 billion in the fiscal year 1958, or 27 percent of all federal revenues, replacement would be difficult unless there is a substantial reduction in total revenue requirements. Even in this event, the desire of the individual taxpayer to share directly in any tax reduction suggests that the corporation income tax is here to stay.

Still another complication is found in the possibility of tax avoidance by retention of earnings. Some solution to the problem of undistributed profits is required. The partnership method might work in the case of the small, closely held corporation. In this case each shareholder would be taxed on his total earnings whether distributed or not. In the case of the public corporation whose stock is widely distributed and whose stockholders have

12 Richard Goode, *The Corporation Income Tax,* New York, 1951.

little or no determination in the dividend policies of the company such a method would not work. The most practical suggestion seems to be the use of a withholding tax on undistributed profits and the granting of a tax credit or allowance for sums withheld when individual income tax liabilities are figured on dividends. The change in the 1954 code permitting the deduction of $50 of dividend income and an allowance of 4 percent of dividend income against total income tax liabilities, gives the same benefit to the wealthy taxpayer and to the poor, assuming the poor have enough income to get the full benefit of the credit. At the one extreme the widow with dividend income but no tax liability gets no relief, while the top bracket taxpayer, who is least severely discriminated against as a result of double taxation, gets the full relief from his tax liability.[13] Although no great damage is done by the 4 percent credit, the extension of this method of granting relief would result in the application of a lower tax rate to "unearned income" or investment income received by top bracket taxpayers than to "earned" or salaried income. Historically, just the reverse has been the declared policy of most governments, justified on the ground that property income gives the recipient greater security, power and, in general, a greater capacity to pay taxes.

Modification of current tax provisions is also suggested in order to discourage the alleged advantage of bond financing and financing from retained earnings. On the former point, there is evidence that tax provisions are often of less importance than the level of stock prices, questions of management control, and so forth.[14] On the latter point, there is no question but that taxation has been of real significance. In periods of great prosperity the decision to retain a large part of earnings for expansion seems inevitable, so long as high rates of personal-income taxation continue. As

[13] Daniel M. Holland, "The Differential Tax Burden on Stockholders," *American Economic Review*, XLV (1955), 415-429.

[14] Dan Troop Smith, *Effects of Taxation on Corporate Financial Policy*, Boston, 1952.

a result of the advantage given to bond financing in certain cases, it is true that some companies may become more vulnerable in the event of business fluctuations. It also remains true, however, that the entire economy has become so interrelated that no general liquidation can be afforded in any event. Finally there is need to remember that in the case of the large public corporation the danger of failure or default on bonded indebtedness is remote. The variety of products, the strong financial position of these companies, and the ready access they have to the capital markets of the country suggests that it is most unlikely that they should be faced with a financial crisis. Because the small company is the one most likely to find it necessary to retain earnings for expansion and for tax minimization purposes, it seldom finds it possible to issue bonds rather than stocks.

Another major issue is that of the proper level of the personal exemptions and deductions under the individual income tax. The broadening of the base of the individual income tax to include most low-income families and individuals has been the most significant development in the field of taxation in recent years. The lowering of exemption levels in the 1940's, the effects of inflation, and the rise in real incomes in the postwar period have steadily increased both the number of taxpayers and the size of the tax base. These changes have been made possible by the development of collection at the source on a pay-as-you-go basis. As a result, the equally radical increase in revenue requirements has been met, for the most part, without resort to indirect taxation or taxes on spending which are less capable of being adjusted to the individual circumstances of the taxpayer.

These developments have led some critics to object to the burden on the low-income taxpayer and the failure of the individual income tax to provide for the complete exemption of a minimum of subsistence. It is, therefore, desirable to review these changes critically and to consider the need for an adjustment of exemption levels. In this review both the question of the relation of exemptions to the equitable distribution of the tax burden and the economic effects of low exemptions will be considered.

From the beginning of the income tax in 1913 until World War II, the exemption levels were so high that only the relatively wealthy, top income brackets were brought within their scope. As recently as 1934 only 4 million returns were made, in contrast to the roughly 50 million in recent years. In the prewar years it could be said that exemptions provided for more than a minimum of subsistence. But it would be misleading to suggest that those in the lower income brackets were free from necessity of contributing toward the cost of government. In the years of high exemptions much greater relative reliance was placed upon indirect taxes with the result that, although hidden, the burden upon the low-income groups was substantial and generally believed to be regressive over a wide range. The progressive income tax became, therefore, a progressive superstructure added to a regressive base. Although valuable in so far as it applied, it was not of great significance in determination of the real burden of the mass of the taxpayers with modest incomes. A review of the history of income taxation in this country and in England from its first use in 1799 leads to the conclusion that, in spite of the claims of many writers in the field of taxation, the exemption of a minimum of subsistence from all taxation has never been seriously attempted. Actual policy has been determined by revenue requirements, administrative capacity, and political considerations.[15] For example, in World War II the choice faced by the administration and Congresss was between more or less dependence upon inflationary financing of the war and additional taxes of wide applicability. Granted the decision to attempt to increase the tax yield, the choice of means was between the extension of the individual income tax to bring the mass of the public within its scope and the use of indirect levies of equal severity but less capable of being used in a manner designed to adjust the tax liability to the individ-

[15] Paul J. Strayer, *The Taxation of Small Incomes,* New York, 1939.

ual circumstances of the taxpayer. It is to the credit of the administration and Congress that they chose to emphasize the use of the income tax rather than the cruder instrument of sales taxation of some kind.

Perhaps the most significant economic result of the greater role of the individual income tax has been the increased sensitivity of the federal tax system to fluctuations in the level of income and employment over the business cycle. Once considered to be an objection to the use of income taxes by those who favored the annual balance of the federal budget, this feature of the federal revenue system is now widely accepted by those who wish to increase the extent of automatic or built-in flexibility of revenues to temper the severity of the business cycle. The growth in acceptance of this viewpoint is evidenced by its endorsement by many congressional leaders and even business groups. It must be remembered, however, that while the sensitivity of the total revenue system of the federal government has been increased by broadening the base of the income tax, the relative sensitivity of the individual income tax alone has not necessarily been increased. A major advance in the same direction has been reduction in the lag between receipt of income and payment of tax liabilities made possible by collection at the source and the requirement that taxpayers not subject to source deductions estimate their tax liabilities in advance and pay on this estimated tax during the year of income receipt. From most points of view this is a great improvement over the old system of permitting the taxpayer to settle his tax in the year following receipt of income. The necessity of requiring large tax payments in a year of sharply declining income or of small tax payments in a year of rapidly rising income is avoided. Even more important is the knowledge that a change in tax rates or exemption levels can be made effective at once and be reflected in the take-home pay of the mass of wage earners.

Two features of the income tax add greatly to its sensitivity in response to changes in levels of national income. These are the exemptions which, if left at constant levels, affect countercyclically the amount of the total income subject to tax and second, the progressive rate structure which will increase the average tax rates as incomes rise and reduce the average tax rate when incomes fall. As a result, a given percentage change in gross-income payments will result in a larger percentage change in tax receipts. This will offset, in part, the forces leading to either a rise or fall in income levels. Coupled with a similar tendency for expenditures to vary countercyclically, the result is to temper somewhat the tendency for the economy to become vulnerable to cumulative periods of deflation or inflation. Although the advantages of this built-in flexibility can be exaggerated, it is not to be ignored as a step in the right direction.

One other change in the income tax that has occurred in recent years deserves special mention. This is the fact that the inclusion of the low-income recipient within the scope of the tax, and the increase in the level of the initial rates applicable to the first bracket of taxable income, have changed the possibility of using the tax as a means of income redistribution. The income redistribution potential of the tax has been further modified by the increase in the means offered under the law for the legal minimization of the nominally confiscatory rates applicable to large incomes. Although it is theoretically possible to achieve a great variety of results under a tax of the general dimensions currently imposed in the United States, the resistance to high rates and the necessity of heavy taxation of the lower brackets where the bulk of all income is concentrated, makes the practical possibility of greater redistribution of income by taxation a remote possibility.

The most disturbing fact is that at the same time there is evidence that significant differentials in tax burden are developing not on the basis of total income but on the basis of source of income. This trend leads to the conclusion that more attention should be paid to questions of equity and avoidance of distortions in the impact of the tax rather than nominally punitive rate schedules which are ineffective. Exemption policy must seek to achieve equity for all. Recent extensions of extra exemptions and deductions for the aged and for certain retirement income suggests that discrimination can become as great at high- as at low-income levels. Looked at from another point of view, the heavier the tax load the more important the pattern of expenditures. With an ultimate ceiling of 100 percent at the top, the larger the revenue requirements the higher the basic rate and the lower the exemption level will tend to be. Both the higher basic rate and the lower exemption level have the effect of lessening the spread between the relative burden at bottom and top.

A critical appraisal of current practices requires a balanced judgment based not only upon the effects of exemptions and deductions upon economic stability and growth but also on the effects of current law upon revenue, equity, administrative practicality, and other widely held objectives of a more subjective nature, such as the level of exemptions and deductions required to maintain family strength and stability.

CHAPTER XII

Tax Policy II

The main features of the current law can be outlined briefly. Each taxpayer is allowed to deduct from his net income $600 for himself, $600 for his wife if he files a joint return, and $600 for each dependent. Additional sums of $600 are deductible for those over 65 years of age and for the blind. The deduction for dependents is limited to children under 19 years of age and to close relatives for whom the taxpayer contributes over half of the support. In the 1954 code an exception to the general rule that no deduction would be allowed, if the dependent made $600 or more, was made in the case of students, so long as the taxpayer continued to contribute over half of their support.

A second group of deductions is found in the area of business expenses, depreciation, and business losses. These items are deductible from gross income to arrive at adjusted gross income and conform rather closely to the prevailing accounting concepts of deductions necessary to arrive at net income.

A third group are deductions from adjusted gross income required to arrive at taxable income. These include expenses not connected with a trade or business, expenses incurred in connection with employment for which the taxpayer is not reimbursed, and the special deductions allowed for charity, unusually heavy medical expenses, and so forth. This group includes such important items as deductions for nonbusiness taxes paid by the taxpayer to state and local governments; interest, including mortgage interest; and casualty losses and thefts. Some aspects of this area must be included in this analysis. To provide a means of avoiding the complications which would arise if all taxpayers were required to itemize each deduction in this category, the law permits the use of a standard deduction of 10 percent of adjusted gross income in lieu of an itemized statement for this whole group of items. This is limited to $1000 for each taxpayer. If the standard deduction is used, no other deduction will be permitted. The Statistics of Income for 1954 indicate that, of approximately 43 million taxable returns, only some 15 million were returned with itemized deductions.[1] Although this is a larger percentage of itemized returns than that found in previous years, it is an indication of the relative generosity of the sums allowed under the standard deduction.

A final point must be discussed in this outline of the main features of the law. This is the extension of the community property treatment to the income of married couples and its recent extension, to a limited extent, to heads of families. Although the justification for this provision is entirely different from that of the deductions and exemptions, it has the significant effect of sharply reducing the effect of the progressive rate schedules upon some married couples and leaving the single individual to bear the full brunt of progression. Thus, when the comparative burden of individuals and married couples is analyzed, the effect of income splitting is of even greater importance than the effect of additional exemptions when the husband is the primary wage earner and his taxable income is large. It is impossible to discuss the merits of the personal exemptions without reference to this fact.

The major criticisms of the current provisions of the law permitting the above outlined exemptions and deductions can be divided into two categories. First, those that criticize the law on

---

[1] U.S. Treasury Department, Internal Revenue Service, *Statistics of Income, 1954; Individual Income Tax Returns for 1954,* Washington, 1957.

the grounds of equity or on the basis of the social repercussions of current practices. Second, criticism which is based on the belief that the economic effects of current practices are adverse. On the first ground two major objections are raised: (1) That the exemptions are too low and place an undue burden upon the low-income groups, and (2) that both the exemptions and deductions are arbitrary and discriminate without reason or justification among taxpayers. On the first count, frequent reference is made to the failure of the tax law to reflect the change in cost of living since low exemption levels have been in effect. The one increase from $500 to $600 made at the end of the war obviously fails fully to reflect the rise in prices since that time. Another and perhaps more insidious aspect of this reaction has been the tendency for labor to claim that take-home pay after deduction for income and social security taxes should be the measure of their wage scale rather than income before taxes. This is insidious because it would, if followed as a policy, negate the effect of a tax increase designated to stop an inflationary development of serious proportions. The fact that similar claims to profits after taxes have been made by business in periods of inflation suggests that this may well become a problem of major proportions in the future. The more reasonable argument that the level of exemptions should be raised to improve the distribution of income after taxes must be considered both from the social and economic viewpoint. In the face of large current revenue requirements a reduction of the existing, heavy excise taxes, such as those on transportation, cosmetics, tobacco, admissions, and liquor, before increasing the level of exemptions seems to be the more desirable course. The argument that this would further emphasize reliance upon a single source of revenue is deemed important by some, but in circumstances that would permit a real reduction in revenues there is much to be said for giving the priority to the elimination of selective excises not only upon the ground of equity but also to relieve the industries affected of the arbitrary effects of the current law.

A final reason to make some effort to raise the level of individual exemptions is found in the borderline area which stresses the discriminatory nature of current exemption provisions. Greatest objection is raised about the burden borne by the single individual with low income as compared to the married couple. With the standard deduction, a single individual will pay a 20 percent tax on income above $666.66, while the married couple will not start paying tax until their income is $1333.33. The 20 percent tax on the difference is $133.33, no small sum for the single man to pay on a minimal income. The need for the community-property provision of the 1948 act which removed the discrimination between residents of community-property states and noncommunity-property states is clear and no particular objection is raised to the method used to remove the discrimination. There is, however, no justification for the discriminatory burden upon the single. A solution may be found in a more realistic relation of the exemption levels of the single person to the married and in the adjustment of the tax brackets or rates of either the single or the married to bring the two into line. At the present time, the effect of income splitting is to give the married a set of rate brackets just twice as wide as those of the single person. Thus the married couple must have $4000 of taxable income before the second-bracket rate applies, whereas the single person will pay the second-bracket rate on taxable income above $2000. When the rates become even more progressive in the upper brackets, this difference becomes substantial and can be expressed in vivid terms by thinking of the benefit the wife brings to her husband as a dowry that becomes increasingly valuable as the income of the husband rises through the brackets until he has reached the top, then diminishes in value as the husband's income rises further and further above the point where progression in rate brackets stops.[2]

[2] Ludwig S. Helborn has estimated that under the terms of the 1951 law a wife with no income had a cash value of as much as $11,457,000 if her husband earned $309,000, and was subject to maximum tax rates on this sum. Ludwig S. Helborn, "Uncle Sam's Dowry," *National Tax Association Proceedings,* 1951, pp. 310-314.

Objection to the income-splitting features of the law are centered upon the benefit given to the wealthy individual who marries the woman with no income of her own and finds that in addition to the benefits they jointly share from her unpaid contribution to the running of the household his tax liability is greatly reduced by the community-property provisions of the law. At the other extreme, the current law allows only a slight adjustment in the tax status of a married couple when each continues to earn the same income after marriage that they individually earned before marriage. It is difficult to see how the taxpaying capacity of two individuals earning $5000 a year before marriage is increased as the result of their marital status. Between these two extremes are found a multitude of possible cases. As a rough adjustment to correct some of the discrimination against the single, it is suggested that the brackets used in case of married couples be made somewhat narrower than is now the case. The increased revenue should be applied to the reduction in rates across the board.

A final source of discrimination among those to whom the exemption level is important and who are at the margin in terms of living standards is the relative ease with which the income tax can be assessed against the wage earner subject to deduction at the source and the difficulty of getting comparable coverage of the self-employed with similar incomes. This latter group includes farmers, small shopkeepers, many in service trades and professions. Although this discrimination arises because of administrative limitations, it cannot be ignored in the appraisal of the individual income tax.

One may conclude that the problems of the relative burden assessed against the single and married and the problem of evasion and avoidance are valid objections to current practices. However, so long as the federal revenue system relies as much at it does at the present time upon indirect levies of an even more arbitrary impact which discriminate against individuals, firms, and industries, there is a strong presumption in favor of the maintenance of current levels of exemption with only minor adjustments and concentration upon the reduction of the more objectionable levies as declining revenue requirements permit.

The second objection to current levels of exemption and tax deduction mentioned above is that the economic effects of taxation of the lower income brackets will be adverse to the maintenance of both economic stability and continued growth. The group that holds this view stresses the necessity of maintaining high levels of consumption demand, and fear the development of another period of stagnation due to the imbalance between savings and investment intentions in an economy characterized by widespread inequality of income distribution. This same group will often hold that redistribution of the tax burden in favor of the lower-income groups and against the upper- would give the government the resources with which to support a program of public investment that would be more productive of the national interest than the private investment that it might replace. This view was presented with some vigor in the recession of 1953 and earlier in the slump of 1949.

A careful appraisal of this view and its emphasis upon the desirability of strengthening consumer demand must lead to a critical analysis of the prediction that there will be a stagnation of investment opportunities and a tendency for redundant savings. Also required is an estimate of the effect of a redistribution of the burden of taxation from bottom to top upon the investment outlook or, if the burden is to be relieved at the bottom without increases at the top, the effectiveness of such action as opposed to an equal reduction of top-bracket rates. Finally, there is need to calculate the threat of inflation which would follow a policy of general tax relief.

The basic principle that the maintenance of aggregate demand is essential, if both stability in the short run and long-term growth are to be assured, is not subject to dispute. The importance of consumer demand as a determinant of investment prospects is also granted. But there are many other forces affecting the decision of the investor. One of the most important is the effect of taxation upon the return realized after taxes and thus upon the judgment of the investor about the future. The latter aspect of the problem may be even more significant than the former due to the emphasis often found among the investor groups upon such considerations. A favorable tax climate may stimulate the investor as much or more than an increase in yields on outstanding investments. It follows, therefore, that, even if the stagnation thesis is accepted, a policy designed to stimulate consumer demand alone would be less successful than one granting some tax relief to both consumer and investor groups. Such a policy could be helpful. It would raise the expectations of the investor group, since both consumer demand and return of capital would be improved. Any other policy would be viewed with suspicion by the investor who is probably as interested in the attitude of the government as he is in the specific measure it adopts.

At the present time, the lowering of the tax burden upon the lowest-income group can be considered only as revenue requirements permit or as other sources of revenue are found. As indicated above, priority should be given to the reduction or removal of excise levies, as they are discriminatory both among individuals and among industries. In view of their magnitude, there is little chance that any substantial reduction in income tax can be permitted unless there is a radical change in the level of public expenditures.

If there is a depression and there is need for counteraction on the fiscal front, then it would be wise to grant some relief to both low- and high-income-tax brackets. But, in view of the possible need for later action to offset a boom or inflationary tendencies, the relief to the lower brackets should take the form of a reduced rate rather than an increase in exemption levels. This is recommended because there is reason to believe that, once the level of exemptions is raised, there will be little chance of reversing the action short of a major catastrophe, such as war. We may conclude, therefore, that, in the event that revenue requirements are permanently reduced, priority should be given to the reduction of excise levies while countercyclical variations in levels of taxation can be best accomplished by variation in rate structure rather than exemption level. Finally, there is little evidence that the stagnation thesis is a basis for a selective policy of tax reduction. In the first place, there is grave doubt about its validity in the current economic situation. In the second place, if such a difficulty should arise, there is a strong case for action that would stimulate both consumption and investment spending.

Although often discussed, the distribution of the tax burden on the basis of benefit or user charges deserves separate consideration. Prime examples of this sort of tax are the gasoline tax and certain license fees or charges. The gasoline tax varies with miles driven and with the weight and speed of the vehicle using the road. Thus, it is closely related to the wear and tear on the highways by the user. The problem of the maintenance of an adequate highway system for the growing volume of both commercial and pleasure traffic suggests that the traditional emphasis upon the maintenance of highways financed out of general funds needs to be reconsidered. In view of the tremendous cost that is involved, and the problem of meeting these expenses in competition with other equally pressing demands, the use of the market mechanism to relate use to cost of service seems to be in order. So long as this connection is not made, there is probably no limit to the possible growth in car ownership and peak demands placed upon our highways. By establishing a price for highway accommodations, the consumer will be left free to choose how much he wishes to pay for. Unless this is done, the individual will continue to think of highways as a free commodity and never fully realize that there are large real costs involved.[3] Highway finance should become

[3] Committee for Economic Development, *Modernizing the Nation's Highways*, New York, 1956.

more like public utility finance. The growth of toll roads is evidence that something like this is occurring under the pressure of current demands, but this is still a small program and cannot be carried much further if current difficulties in financing toll highways continue.

Distribution by Income Class

The central issue of tax-burden distribution by income class has been left for the end of this section because it is both the most controversial issue in the field of equity and the one least likely to be resolved on the basis of economic analysis. It is also my belief that many of the problems of aggregate-tax-burden distribution cannot be discussed intelligently unless one is first aware of the uneven incidence of tax burdens within a given income class. Factual studies of the actual distribution of the present tax system are difficult to make. The inadequacies of the theory of incidence require those who attempt such an estimate to use assumptions of questionable validity, and the imperfections in data about income distribution before taxes and about the consumption pattern further complicate the problem. Much of our income statistics are derived from individual income-tax returns, and in spite of attempts to adjust these data to reflect the difference between taxable income and true income there is a wide margin of error left.[4] Sources of difficulty include: the problem of the influence of the tax system upon the way in which, and the time at which, income is realized; the expenses to be deducted from gross income to arrive at net income; and the question of proper treatment of income in kind, such as that derived from ownership of a home. A realistic study of the real burden should also include information about the past history of those who fall into each income group at any particular point in time. Thus,

[4] David M. Holland and C. Harry Kahn, "Comparison of Personal and Taxable Income," Joint Committee on the Economic Report, *Federal Tax Policy for Economic Growth and Stability*, Washington, 1955.

many of those who are in the lowest income brackets or even those who have negative incomes are not destitute but are able to draw on capital, and over the years average a reasonably decent living or even maintain a very high standard of living. The use of the conventional accounting year as the period for income determination and tax computations is the source of many of these difficulties; awareness of this fact does not, however, provide a solution.

The best estimate available indicates that the burden of all federal, state, and local taxes is at best proportionate in relation to income until a fairly high level of income is reached at the $5000 level.[5] Above this point it is generally conceded to be somewhat progressive, although not nearly so much so as a superficial reference to the marginal rate schedules of the individual income tax would suggest. The latter point is the consequence of the possibility of the higher-income group taking advantage of the various devices for minimizing the burden of taxation mentioned above such as, expense accounts, pension plans, stock options, percentage depletion, capital gains, and the privilege of investing in tax-exempt state and local securities. As nearly as can be determined, few taxpayers actually pay as much as 50 percent of their true income in taxes, although many will be subject to marginal rates above 50 percent on that part of their income subject to the full impact of the law.[6] The generally severe burdens imposed upon the lower-income groups are the result of the heavy weight of the indirect excises, sales taxes, and property taxes, many of which result in a regressive distribution of the tax burden by income class. The exemptions and progressive rates of the individual income tax prove to be important, therefore, not only to produce a generally progressive distribution of the tax

[5] Richard A. Musgrave, "Incidence of the Tax Structure and Its Effects on Consumption," Joint Committee on the Economic Report, *Federal Tax Policy for Economic Growth and Stability,* Washington, 1955, pp. 96-106.

[6] J. Keith Butters, Lawrence E. Thompson, and Lynn L. Bollinger, *Effects of Taxation on Investment by Individuals,* Boston, 1953, pp. 85-88.

burden but also to offset the tendency for the burden of the great majority of taxpayers to be regressive. The concentration of the bulk of the total individual income in the middle and lower income brackets plus the width of the first bracket of the federal tax of $2000 ($4000 for married couples), plus the standard deduction, makes exemptions the important means of imposing progression for the great majority, not progressive rates. This is true because the initial rate of 20 percent is applied to a larger and larger part of the total income the more income exceeds exemptions and deductions, or to a lower and lower percentage of the total income the closer that income is to the exemption level.

Opinions about this distribution vary from those who claim that it is too progressive and favor a drastic reduction of income and death-tax rates to those who emphasize the regressive taxes paid by the lower-income groups and favor their reduction and more severe taxation of the wealthy. It is of interest to note that few commentators are satisfied with the current distribution. Almost all discussions fail to point out, however, that the burden of taxation at both top and bottom is offset, in part at least, as the result of the benefits received by all citizens. The protest made in the name of the poor, who are obviously not in a position to pay much to government without substantial sacrifice, ignores the benefits this same group may receive. Recent studies indicate that some of the regressiveness of tax burden distribution is offset by the distribution of the benefits of government both directly, as the result of transfer payments, and indirectly in the form of goods and services or subsidies.

More to the point, however, is the fact that under current law there is little chance of further taxation of the rich replacing any substantial part of the revenue lost as the result of relief to the poor. The Tax Foundation estimates that a flat rate of 20 percent applied to all taxable income would produce 85 percent of the total collected in 1955. A 50 percent maximum would yield 98 percent and a 70 percent maximum would yield 99.5 percent of all the revenue obtained in 1955.[7] It is clear that rates of 91 percent are unrealistic and unwise. At this point there may be no purpose in seeking additional income; but even if this is not true, there is obvious reason to seek means of avoiding such levies. Until the law is cleaned up to prevent the use of various means of tax avoidance, it is idle to talk in terms of rates even so high as those that now nominally prevail.

The reverse of the above propositions is also true. There can be no realistic exemption of the bottom groups as a whole. The increase in exemption under the individual income tax from $600 to $700 would reduce the tax yields by about $2.5 billion.[8] The repeal of all federal excises would cost about $10 billion. Particularly difficult is the problem of states and local governments which rely for the most part on taxes such as the general sales tax, the property tax, and excises. So long as there is reason to believe in the maintenance of strong states and local governments, they must be, in so far as possible, financially independent. They cannot give up the best sources of revenue now available and accepted by their residents. In many cases it can also be said that the harm done by regressive state and local taxes is much less than the harm and social cost that would result from the failure of the state or locality to provide adequate services at the local or state level. This is a judgment that cannot be proved but one on which there can be general agreement among those who believe that the real benefit of many collectively provided services is much greater than that resulting from even the last expenditures of the poor.

In conclusion, I believe that there is much greater need for tax reform that prevents or minimizes the differential impact of taxation on individuals wth equal incomes than there is of a wholesale attempt to make it more progressive. Current tax distribution

[7] Tax Foundation, Inc., *Are High Surtax Rates Worthwhile?* New York, 1957.
[8] Joint Committee on the Economic Report, *The Federal Revenue System: Facts and Problems,* Washington, 1956, p. 13.

and the distribution of benefits favoring the lowest-income groups and adding to their security, is now tolerable. If there is to be a drive to improve the lot of the poor, the increase in welfare programs and transfer payments would be a better way of achieving this end than a wholesale reduction in taxes. The equalization of individual tax burdens will cost a considerable amount of revenue, inasmuch as certain taxes of a selective nature will have to be given up. A part of this can be recouped by removal of the loopholes in existing levies, but this option is open primarily to the federal government. As a means of achieving this result the top-bracket rates under the individual income tax could be substantially lowered in exchange for tightening the treatment of family partnerships, capital gains, depletion, tax exempt securities, and expense accounts, and other loopholes. As a result, the true impact of the tax might well be more progressive rather than less.

The question of the connection between payment of taxes and the obligations of citizenship must also be considered. Although much nonsense has been written about the connection between tax consciousness and good citizenship, the complete exemption of low-income groups from any contribution to the costs of government further increases the possibility that the political struggle between the "haves" and "have nots" might grow to the point where it would seriously weaken our economy and social structure. The impossibilty of maintaining anything like current budgets with the complete exemption of any significant group suggests that any such attempt would be to stimulate a serious inflation. This is also a destructive force and gives further reason to doubt the desirability of complete exemption for even a small group at the very bottom.

Finally, there is danger that excessive equalization of income would lessen the possibilty of social mobility rather than increase it. If positions of power and prestige were solely determined by one's position in the hierarchy of management, the professions, government, or by some social arbiter, the possibility of a change in status due to some good fortune would be sub-stantially lessened, and the loss of position due to misfortune would also be less frequent, leaving most persons in the unen-viable position of knowing much more certainly than can now be the case what their status will be forever into the future. This might also prove to be the straw that would significantly affect incentives to maximize output and thus lessen the rate of future growth, if it did not cause an absolute decline. This argument had been fully developed by Frank Graham and suggested that the only place where fully progressive rate schedules can be safely applied is in the estate and inheritance field. Although this position is *not* one shared by the author, it is a reasonable one and consistent as worked out by Graham with his basic commitment to equality of opportunity and the preservation of the maximum incentives for a free market system. Favoring very heavy inheritance taxes after the bare minimum has been allowed for protection of dependents, he would restrict the income tax to a proportionate rate, assuming that the degree of market competition had been significantly increased. At the time he wrote, Graham was not adverse to some progression so long as the competitive forces of the market were so restricted and the results of the market place were so much distorted.[9]

One of the strange developments of the past period is that while the individual income tax and the corporation income tax have been so greatly increased in severity, little has been done to strengthen the effectiveness of the estate and gift tax since the period of the 1930's. In spite of a wealth of material proving the ineffectiveness of the present system of death taxes and gift taxes, there seems to be little appeal to the thought of greatly increasing their severity. The trend seems to have been in the opposite direction. As recently as the 1954 code revision, a new loophole was opened by the provision that irrevocable life insurance policies could be bought by the donor and excluded

[9] Frank D. Graham, *Social Goals and Economic Institutions,* Princeton, 1942.

from his estate so long as he no longer had any option over the disposition of the assets. Why this is the case is hard to explain, except in terms of the hope of all of us that we may become the beneficiaries of some bequest. In view of the relatively mild effects of death duties on incentives and the obvious relationship to equality of opportunity, it is still hard to see why this source has been so neglected. Still another source of avoidance has been favored by the large estates. This is the charitable foundation which permits the bulk of the estate to escape taxation but allows control of the stock of the financial institution to be maintained by the true heirs. Among those who have gained advantage from this source are the Ford, Mellon, and Sloan Foundations. If one of the purposes of estate taxation is to force the distribution of economic power, this device should be banned.

This entire section on the distribution of the tax burden must end on a pessimistic note. Although there is growing awareness of the imperfections of the current tax-burden distribution, the tendency seems to have been to extend rather than restrict the opportunities for avoidance and evasion. In the process, there has developed a tendency for the burden on property income to become lower than the burden on salary or wage income, and also a tendency for the extension and multiplication of differentials in the tax burdens borne by persons in otherwise equal circumstances. While some poor unfortunates may bear the full brunt of the highly progressive rates effective today, others may escape almost entirely. As a result there is too much attention directed to the question of tax-burden minimization. Investment and other economic decisions may be made with an eye to tax savings rather than to the best opportunity for a favorable return. This leads to the distortion of investment and may adversely affect the long-term rate of growth of the country. There is, further, the danger that compliance will suffer in the future as more and more persons become familiar with the differential impact of the tax system. If all persons think of taxation as a racket, their compliance will

capacity. On the other hand, there is danger that changes in revenue laws will cause either an unforeseen and unnoticed response tending to necessitate later corrective action or may be discounted so that the desired stimulus or restraint is not effective. For example, the recent change in income-tax policy permitting more rapid depreciation for tax purposes and the temporary allowance for accelerated depreciation for investment required for national defense purposes may have substantially increased the amount of present investment. Although there may be little reason to believe that the income effects of more rapid depreciation are significant, the increased availability of funds for investment resulting from more rapid depreciation may be of importance. There is danger that this stimulus will cause a bunching of investment detrimental to the sustaining of an even rate over the long pull. This is not a prediction, for many forces could intervene to prevent such a development—a renewal of war tension, more rapid development of new technology, and so forth. But the danger is real and suggests that for most purposes there is virtue in maintaining the tax structure with the minimum of changes. The discounting of revenue changes so that they have minimal effects can be illustrated by assuming changes in the rate of corporation taxation on a countercyclical basis. If expected, this would have less effect than might appear in simplified models. The corporation would realize that new investment might well produce income in a period of high taxation rather than low. Certainly the stimulation to corporate expansion would be substantially less than that which would result from a belief that the corporate tax rate were to be permanently lowered. Still another example of a change that might have undesirable effects would be the result of a policy which suddenly granted to all stockholders a full credit for corporation income taxes paid at the source. This would produce a windfall to all stockholders, as current prices reflect dividend policies and book values resulting from the current law. The danger of a sudden change would be that it would encourage a new wave of speculation in the stock market. Even if the lost revenue were replaced, the repercussions of such a radical change in past policy might well be disturbing to the stability of the economy.[13]

We may conclude that there is often a conflict between flexibility and stability in tax practices. Even uncertainty as to the future severity of tax laws can produce disturbing repercussions. This suggests that there should be a special effort made to minimize the structural changes in tax law when the primary reason for change is to stimulate or restrain the economy as a whole. This in turn suggests that the area where changes can be made is rather sharply restricted. Minimal side effects would seem to follow from variation in the basic rate of the income tax, as it would produce large effects on disposable income with a minimum change in rate structure and minimum disturbance of normal business practices. Still another possibility would be the use of negative taxes or cash grants to inject money into the system, leaving ordinary taxes without change. In the event of inflation, broad-based levies must be used if the restrictive force is not to become complicated by side effects of unknown magnitude.

All these generalizations neglect the problem of gaining acceptance from Congress for the changes that are required. Ideally, Congress should delegate to the executive the power to vary basic tax rates in the same way and according to the same standards that apply to the Federal Reserve Board control of interest rates and the general availability of credit. The chances of such a delegation of power by Congress are remote in view of political tradition and the sensitivity of individual congressmen and senators to taxpayer response to changes in his tax bill. The built-in flexibility found in the current law can only modify, not offset the severity of fluctuations. In a period of crisis, Congress may respond rapidly as it did in 1950 and 1951, but even in this

[13] Carl Shoup, "Taxation and Fiscal Policy," in Max F. Milliken, ed., *Income Stabilization for a Developing Democracy*, New Haven, 1953.

case the general fear of World War III and early planning for a much larger build-up of military strength than later proved to be required made the action of Congress less remarkable than has been alleged. When the President and the Treasury ask for $10 billion and make a strong case for such an amount, and the Congress passes an increase calculated to produce $5 or $6 billion, the record cannot be cited as an example of radical change in congressional willingness to use its tax powers to the full extent required for stabilization policy.

Perhaps the greatest achievement of the recent congresses has been their generally tough attitude toward tax reduction. Although this may be based largely upon a misguided faith in the sanctity of the annually balanced budget, it lessens somewhat the danger of tax reduction leading to a generally inflationary bias. This point must be qualified by reference to the cut of 1948, which was resisted by the administration. The greatest danger is that in response to administration pleas for tax rate changes, the lag in the legislative process will cause variations to be too little and too late. If this happens, there is even danger that there can be times when the cut or increase does not become effective until the trend it was designed to offset has reversed itself and thus will become not a stabilizing but a "destabilizing" measure. It must be concluded that there is no magic formula that will guarantee the sort of response on the revenue side that is called for in most models. Some tolerance of fluctuations must be permitted so that the direction of the action required of Congress will be made clear and the need felt acutely enough so that action will be taken. If in the future some delegation of power to the executive is made, permitting variation in tax rates, less time will elapse between the start of an adverse trend and the response to it; but even in this case there is some merit in not acting too soon for fear of whipsawing the economy first in one direction and then another.

The final point which must be made is that there are occasions when fiscal policy is ineffective if the objective is to maintain both full employment and price stabilty. There are even some occasions when the total index of prices may be inadequate to serve as a policy guide if internal relationships such as occurred in 1955 and early 1956 point to a rise in industrial prices offset by a fall in agricultural prices. When these occasions arise, there is no case for tax variation but reason to worry about the internal price, wage, and profit relationships. There is danger that any rise in unemployment will set in motion responses that will cause inflation. It is in this situation that the most severe test of stabilization policy will be found. The one hope is that there may be such generally deflationary forces at work in the long run that the danger of inflation will not be felt. Little comfort can be taken from this possibility, however, as there are so many institutional pressures leading toward rising prices.

This discussion of the use of taxation as an instrument of stabilization must end on the same note as that covering the possibility of variable expenditures. In a period of marked inflation or depression, there is little question but that taxation is one of the powerful tools with which to promote stability. There is no reason to believe, however, that there is either the knowledge or the disposition on the part of the public and Congress to use taxation in a manner that would assure perfect results. This is to be regretted, in that there are so many advantages to the variation of revenues rather than the variation of expenditures. The market can still maintain its full vigor when revenues fluctuate, in sharp contrast to the effect of variable expenditures. The point made in the earlier chapter on stabilization remains true. The first line of defense against economic fluctuations must be monetary and credit policy, not fiscal policy.

Effects of Taxation on Incentives and Growth

In order to know the effects of taxation upon incentives and growth prospects, it is first necessary to know what are the factors

controlling incentive and economic expansion. In spite of the renewed interest of economists the world over in these matters,
knowledge and facts are lacking. Taxes affect incentives in two
contradictory ways. One is to reduce the reward for effort expended so that a comparison between more work and more leisure
should result in some diminution in the amount of work done.
The other is the income effect, which stimulates some persons to
attempt to offset the loss caused by taxation with the expenditure
of greater effort. The net result of these two influences cannot
be measured. It is likely to be small in either direction because of
the multiplicity of forces that provide incentive to the individual
and the relatively few individuals who have the option of working
more or less hard in a modern society. The studies of incentive
effects made so far in the United States suggests this hypothesis
to be correct, at least as far as corporation executives are concerned.[14] Some greater concern has been felt in England about the
adverse effects of taxation upon the worker. But the British problem is complicated by the scarcity of goods, the traditional class-
mindedness of the British worker, and the pressures upon the
worker in the period of the war and reconstruction. Finally, there
can be no total balance sheet struck unless the possiblity of increasing incentives by the expenditure of additional revenues is
considered. Certainly this is the result to be expected as a result
of expenditures raising the level of education and health of the
average citizen. Even expenditures for highways may have this
effect.

The one area where incentives are most adversely affected by
high rates is investment. The progressive income tax is bound
to change the odds for new enterprises and may adversely affect
even well-established ones. The latter case is less likely, as there
is more chance of carrying losses forward or back and having the

---

[14] Thomas H. Sanders, *Effects of Taxation on Executives*, Boston, 1951; Challis
A. Hall, Jr., *Effects of Taxation on Executive Compensation and Retirement Plans*.
Boston, 1951.

government share in them as well as profits. The more the law permits such carry-over and carry-back of losses, the less likely are the adverse repercussions of a progressive tax upon investment of well-established companies. There is also the possibility that rational calculation does not always motivate the investor and, like the long-shot gambler, he may take chances when the net returns are reduced by taxation that he would not have taken before. This effect might be thought of as similar to the income effect mentioned earlier in connection with indivdual incentives. The only study yet made on this point again suggests that something of this process has taken place among a significant number of taxpayers.[15] This point must be qualified, inasmuch as these individuals have been stimulated by the favorable rate on capital gains and a period of unusual prosperity. Finally, it is again necessary to qualify, with recognition of the possibility that the decline in incentive of private investors may be offset by the increase in government investment which would not have been possible unless the tax had been imposed in the first place. A good example is the investment of the government in the development of atomic energy, where the risks and the sums involved were so large that only the government could have undertaken them.

This brief review of the effects of taxation upon incentives makes it clear that present knowledge is insufficient to give precise answers. It is also true that the sweeping generalizations frequently made by business leaders and others about the destruction of incentives are merely assertions and are not based upon facts. The remarkable rise in output and productivity which has taken place in the period of high taxes is further proof of exaggeration by those who are most fearful.

The problem of growth is even less well understood than that of incentives. The reasons for marked variation in rates of economic expansion in different parts of the world are generally believed to be political and sociological as well as economic. One

15 J. Keith Butters, Lawrence E. Thompson, and Lynn L. Bollinger, *op. cit.*

fact can be firmly pinned down—growth requires saving and investment. The effects of taxation upon the capacity of the private sector of the economy to save are certain, at least in direction. The magnitude of the effect is, however, not certain. Some recent investigations suggest that the adverse effect may be less than usually believed, due to the fact that consumption patterns may be more affected by one's relative place in the hierarchy of incomes rather than by absolute income.[16] It is also true that the growth of corporate saving makes the corporation income tax more important than the individual income tax as a determinant of the net savings in any period. Finally, there is the important development of mortgage and consumer credit as a force leading even those subject to a high rate of taxation to save. All these points apply to a rich economy with a large amount of surplus income. In a more backward economy, the problem may be different, particularly if the growth of communications and education leads to the growth of desire for new products more rapidly than the economy can produce them. In this situation a high rate of taxation as a means of financing government saving and investment may be necessary. There remains the alternative of maintaining wide differentials in income distribution to encourage saving without government intervention. But in the modern world this is politically difficult to justify, and there is danger that the savings of the rich will find outlets in foreign investments without being offset by a flow of investment funds from abroad.

One of the most dangerous results of taxation may be the tendency for the investment that takes place to be distorted by taxation or as a result of government investment programs controlled for political purposes. In the United States there is now evidence that the decisions of investors are influenced unduly by tax considerations. The differential impact of current tax laws justifies this concern. In some of the underdeveloped countries

[16] James S. Duesenberry, *Income, Saving and the Theory of Consumer Behavior,* Cambridge, 1949.

of the world there is evidence that government investment programs are greatly influenced by feelings of national pride, desire for self-sufficiency, and the whims of the leading politicians. In any event, there can be distortion leading to a lower rate of real growth than that which would be found if the free market were to be the sole basis for the decision as to the best investment opportunities. To the extent the national interest requires the intervention of the state to correct for the bias of the market place, qualification of this point is required. Certainly this is true in such areas as public investment in schools and other public facilities necessary for the provision of basic governmental services. However, the problem of measurement of good or bad effects is insuperable. Until we perfect our ability to predict the future with perfect accuracy, there will never be a sure method of calculating the positive or negative effects of a given course of action. In view of this fact the sustaining of a high rate of investment is about all that can be used for comparative purposes. With a high rate it must be assumed that growth will be more rapid than with a low rate, although situations could be imagined where skillful investment of a small sum might produce greater results than inept investment of a larger sum. The difficulty is that no one can be sure about such comparisons except in the most obvious cases.

The most difficult question in the United States remains that of the level of taxation required to finance necessary public investment projects. There is no more controversial area of public policy. It is made so, not only by the highly emotional feelings of advocates on both sides, but also by the fact that the stakes for both public and private investment interests are so large. What is done in the public area will affect private investment and vice versa. In addition, the extension of the area of public investment, requiring the maintenance of high levels of taxation, particularly corporate and personal income taxation, may well limit the possibility of further growth of new and smaller corporations dependent on either retained earnings or individual investors for their financing. If this is the case, the structure of industry will become more rigid and the competitive position of the small company will deteriorate. Large companies can retain enough earnings and have such large depreciation accounts that they need never lack capital with which to keep abreast of new developments. More complex technology requires larger sums for product development. If additional sources of capital are required, the large company has a tremendous advantage in floating new issues of either stock or bonds. The small corporation has neither the internal funds nor access to the capital market.[17] In a period of high taxation, the small business has additional risks that cannot always be offset by income-averaging or by deduction from other sources of income. Attempts to resolve this dilemma by use of tax differentials favoring the small firm may reduce the adverse effects slightly, but unless a penalty is placed on size as such the small differential granted will still leave the giants in a much more favorable position.

Finally, there must be recognition of the fact that the tax law as it now stands encourages the large and small corporation to retain earnings as a means of financing expansion, rather than going to the market. To the extent that the market would better judge the comparative need of industry for new capital, this tendency may reduce somewhat the possibility of maximum growth.

We may conclude that the evidence to date does not suggest any serious deterioration in either incentives or growth potential in the United States. In view of the importance of many public investment programs, there is danger of inadequate rather than excessive spending of this type. As many others have pointed out, the country can grow as rapidly or as slowly as the people desire. If international problems could be solved so that national defense were not a matter of major concern, something could be said for

---

[17] J. K. Butters and John Lintner, *Effect of Federal Taxes on Growing Enterprises*, Boston, 1945.

a slower rate of growth. The most important reason for doubting the advantage of such a policy is that the body politic has become accustomed to a steady rise in productivity and expansion of real income as a solvent for all sorts of political and social pressures. If we should choose to have a less dynamic economy, serious political and social problems would be likely to arise. The most important area requiring attention at the present time is that of the differentials that have developed in the tax law encouraging certain types of investment at the expense of others. These have developed in part because of the excessively high marginal rates under the individual income tax and might be reduced if there could be agreement to cut the top brackets in exchange for the closing of loopholes. If this were done, then it would be possible to evaluate more objectively the merits of tax incentives for certain industries.

Conclusions

This discussion of tax policy should not end without an attempt at an overall appraisal of the revenue system of the United States today. This will be attempted in broad terms, and then a final word will be devoted to the subject of immediate reforms and the outlook for the future.

On the positive side, the tax system of the United States is equal to, if not superior to, the tax system of any other country in the world. No nation raises as large a part of its total revenues from income taxes as the United States. The United States tax burden is almost as large a percentage of national income as that of any nation in times of peace. Although no other nation has a federal system quite like that of the United States, it is of interest to note that none of the other federal systems has been able to give the same degree of financial independence to the subsidiary levels of government. Our tax system also compares favorably with others in terms of progressivity, although comparisons are made difficult by the prevalence of loopholes permitting tax avoidance in other nations as well as our own. The British probably carry progression further than anyone else, but this judgment must be qualified by recognition of the numerous avenues of escape from the full impact of the British law and the widespread discrepancies between one's impression of the distribution of income derived from inspection of tax returns and that derived from a visit to London and observation of the continuance of conspicuous consumption on a large scale. At the compliance level, there is some reason to believe that the British have a better record than the United States, but there are many nations with much poorer records. In terms of equity, judged by the ordinary standards of equal treatment of equals and the avoidance of discriminatory levies penalizing a few, the United States system is probably equal to that of any nation in the world. Our great wealth has permitted avoidance of many of the taxes on selected articles of consumption that have been required to raise revenues in most of the world. Finally, no other nation has found it possible to collect revenues sufficient to support a high level of governmental services, a military force necessary to meet the Russian threat, and generous assistance to the other nations of the free world. This is a great accomplishment, made possible by the tremendous wealth of the United States and a good revenue system.

On the negative side, there are several disturbing trends. First, is the tendency for the income tax to suffer as more and more technical amendments and provisions either exclude income from the base or grant preferential rates. This tendency not only limits the taxable capacity of the nation but also results in differential burden distribution which, in addition to being unfair, is disturbing to the best allocation of resources and thus economic expansion. The reaction to this trend is growing and could lead to serious repercussion. One dangerous tendency is the extension of more and more tax relief to special groups so that the tax base is reduced to the point where it is impossible to collect adequate revenues. Another is a growth of taxpayer reaction leading to additional compliance problems and widespread evasion of the law. Finally, there is danger that a small base and the consequent necessity of maintaining, or even raising rates, will seriously affect incentives and further distort the allocation of resources.

The second problem of importance is that of the revenue-raising capacity of the state and local governments. Needing to make up for expenditures deferred as a result of years of depression and war, states and localities find the going rough when sudden changes in the location of population and the baby boom of the postwar years add even more burdens. In addition, there have been complications arising out of the fact that old political boundaries make it difficult to achieve financial and administrative efficiency. The resistance to high taxes arising as a result of the sudden increase in federal requirements has made the problem of the states more difficult. Much could be done at the state and local level if political leadership were strong, but there remains the problem of pushing ahead with speed and the necessity of anticipating the possibility of an end to the boom of recent years. For both reasons, it is necessary to contemplate the necessity of making use of the greater revenue-raising capacity of the federal government in order to assure a healthy state and local financial structure and adequate state and local service levels. But this would create additional pressures at the federal level and might cause the aggravation of the earlier mentioned federal problems.

Finally, there is an intermediate position that must be taken with regard to the use of taxation as an instrument of economic stabilization. Granting the progress of recent years, there remain many gaps in our understanding of business cycles, particularly our ability to predict economic events in advance. Add to this the limited capacity of government to act quickly, to vary revenues, and its unwillingness to delegate authority over revenue matters, and one is forced to realize that the possibility of the frequent adjustments in taxes called for by model builders is remote. The response of taxpayers to any given change is also in the realm of the unknown, and further limits the possibility of achieving perfection in this field. The size of the tax bill, the development of current collection, and the improvements in theory all suggest that major swings can be offset by fiscal action; but the limitations suggested above indicate that minor swings cannot be prevented. The much discussed built-in flexibility of the revenue system acts in a favorable manner, but only as a moderator of the severity of fluctuations, not as a counterbalancing force. Depressions of the severity of the 1930's can be prevented, but the new era when the boom will continue indefinitely without end has not yet arrived. Some bad years are bound to come from time to time.

In view of these findings, public opinion should be rallied to support the revision of current tax laws in order to improve their coverage and to eliminate the special concessions granted in all but the most compelling cases. Even more important would be the elimination of the differential rates of taxation that have crept into the system and the avoidance of the political reaction that is bound to follow a greater public realization of the extent and magnitude of these differentials.

The second area in which major reforms are required is that of state and local finance. Although much can be done within the boundaries of the states, some greater use of federal revenue powers is required. The critical issue in this case is the terms on which federal grants will be made for such purposes as education, highways, health, and welfare. The needs are so great, however, that a breakthrough is required soon. National interest in education, highways, and health is such that no responsible nation can afford to stand by while the states let standards fall in any one of these important areas.

Finally, more work needs to be done in the development both of basic theory and of political and administrative techniques of countercyclical finance. If improvements in theory only tell us what not to do, progress will have been made. It is, however, in the area of political and administrative action that the greatest progress can be made in a short period of time. Extremely high taxes make the possibility of adverse effects just as great as favorable effects. Political pressures arise from the interests of well-organized minorities and often tend to obscure the national interest. Ways of maintaining the national interest and the problems of the economy as a whole in the forefront of the public's mind will continue to tax the ingenuity of all concerned for years to come. If perverse action can be avoided in the years ahead, substantial improvement over any policy that has yet been followed will have been achieved. No nation is in a better position to make this advance than the United States, but the answer depends as much on the leadership of politicians as it does on the perfection of the theories of economists.

The demand for tax reduction at any price sweeps the country from time to time. Republicans and Democrats try to win the voters' approval by claiming that only their party will reduce taxes. Unfortunately there is grave danger that instead of a reduction in total burdens, the average taxpayer will end up paying more not less taxes. This will happen in part through the growth of state and local expenditures but may also occur as a result of the extension of more federal assistance to needy areas or through the inevitable growth in the existing programs of the federal government. Led to believe that tax reduction is possible, the public may become aroused when it finds that instead of relief it is forced to pay more in all. It is in this case of real disappointment that there comes the real danger of irresponsible behavior and a real inflationary bias. If this event coincides with the growth in public awareness of the differential impact of the existing tax burden, then we may really fear for our stability.

We may conclude that in spite of an increased understanding of fiscal policy there are deep-seated reasons for resistance to its application by either Congress or the executive, and there must be a greater popular resistance to the evils of inflation before a more positive policy will be followed. This may be coming, as the result of the growth in the numbers of aged dependent upon pensions and social security. But even among this group there is always the danger that they will use their power to force an increase in the size of pensions rather than action to check inflation.

When it is realized that there is a good prospect that taxes will increase to cover increases in costs of government resulting from other than cyclical forces, the difficulties of gaining further increases to check inflationary tendencies are made more obvious. Add to this the growing realization of the uneven impact of federal, state, and local tax burdens, and the magnitude of the problem becomes even greater.

||||||||||||||||||||||||||||||||||||||||||||||||||||||||||||||||||||||||||||||||||||||||||||||||||||||||||||||||||||||||||||||||||||||||||||||||||

CHAPTER XIII

State and Local Tax Problems

||||||||||||||||||||||||||||||||||||||||||||||||||||||||||||||||||||||||||||||||||||||||||||||||||||||||||||||||||||||||||||||||||||||||||||||||||

Changes which have taken place in recent years have led to a crisis in the field of state and local finance. It must be remembered that states and local governments provide those services that are basic to the preservation of healthy communities. Even in the welfare field, where so much attention has been directed to the growth of federal programs, states and local governments still have the primary responsibility. Education, health and hospitals, relief, fire protection, police, and basic recreational facilities are the primary responsibility of states and local governments. Planning for the orderly development of our communities must be done at the state and local level. The great bulk of the basic highway facilities of the nation are built by states and local governments rather than the federal government. One way of illustrating the relative importance of state and local governments is to point out the fact that governmental employment is largely state and local, not federal. Of the total of over 7 million currently working for government, almost 5 million are state and local employees while only 2.1 million are federal employees if the armed services are excluded. This is a surprising figure to many who are impressed by the size of the federal budget. It reflects the dominance of the federal budget by such items as the purchase of the product of private companies and federal transfer payments. This is in contrast to the service function of state and local government.

Several reasons can be cited for the growth of difficulties in the finance of states and local governments. First has been the increase in total tax burdens. State governments as second claimants, and local governments as third claimants upon the taxpayer, find it increasingly difficult to raise revenues in spite of the growth in real incomes even after all taxes have been paid. Voters who have to pay so much to the federal government seek relief where they can find it. The job of state and local government will always be more difficult if the federal budget is $70 billion annually than if it is in the realm of $30 billion. A second and perhaps even more important reason for the plight of states and localities in this period of prosperity is the combination of the baby boom and the growing mobility of the population. This has required many new schools and new service facilities and personnel for the new suburban developments growing in what were once rural areas, and has often led to the separation of the industrial tax base from the area of most rapid population expansion. A third reason for difficulty has been the inflation of recent years. This has generally reduced the real value of the local property-tax base at a time when this can least be afforded. This has occurred because assessed values lag behind market values and because there is traditional resistance to a rise in the tax rate upon real estate in spite of the decline in assessments in relation to real values.[1] Inequities in assessment and poor administration of the local property tax have also hurt. Still another reason for the growing crisis in state and local finance is the increasingly conscious competition among the states and local governments for new industry, leading to offers of tax remission to new industry and corresponding reluctance on the part of states and local governments with established industries to increase taxes. Finally, one must cite

[1] Mabel Newcomer, "The Decline of the General Property Tax," *National Tax Journal*, VI (1953), 38-51; Clara Penniman, "The Role of Property Tax in Wisconsin Since 1929," *National Tax Journal*, LX (1956), 331-338.

an unfavorable political climate as a cause of difficulties in state and local finance. The factors that make for a good or bad political environment are almost impossible to isolate, but the contrast in the financial position of different states and localities which may result from such factors is notable. For example, contrast the current revenue system of the state of New Jersey with that of New York. Though both are wealthy industrial areas they are in complete contrast. New York has one of the best state revenue systems of the country and New Jersey one of the worst. A large part of the difference can be expressed in terms of political leadership, but what created the successful political leaders in the one case and prevented their rise to power in the other defies explanation.

The serious nature of the problem is well documented in areas such as public education, but the growth of public concern about it continues to lag. When the total problem is considered, it is staggering in its dimensions. Not only do we have to face the problem of raising our annual expenditures for public education by $5 or more billion annually,[2] but similar sums will soon be required for highways, health, and care of the aged and otherwise incapacitated. If there is to be a proper job of planning for better living and use of the greater leisure time which is expected to be available to all gainfully employed, still more outlays must be made to improve housing and provide for parks and other recreational facilities, public museums, concert halls, and adult education programs. The critical question is not whether such programs will be undertaken in the end, but how much deterioration in current standards will occur before governments respond to the felt needs of the community. It is also true that the longer expenditures are postponed the less well the job can be done and the more costly it will be to do anything. In many areas today the combination of the baby boom, resistance to taxes, population

[2] J. Frederic Dewhurst, *America's Needs and Resources, A New Survey,* New York, 1955.

shifts, and bad planning have already led to a deterioration in the level of service, particularly in the level of educational opportunity offered to the youth of the nation. This is not only of serious consequence to the youth affected but also to the country, as today's youth are the future professional, management, and labor resources upon which the capacity for further growth depends.

The failure of state and local government to perform adequately their service functions, and the national interest in this fact, have led many to the conclusion that there is now no alternative but the use of some federal financial assistance to avoid further deterioration in the fields of education and highways. This conclusion is distressing to two groups, those who wish to keep down the costs of government at any price and those who are genuinely fearful of the consequences of federal grants upon the vitality and continued independence of the states. To the first group the answer is clear. The cost of failure to spend for education and welfare will be greater in the end than the taxes required to maintain an adequate program. To the second group the answer must be that unless there is some radical change in state and local government capacity and willingness to finance needed services, there is no alternative. Some still hope for a sufficient decline in the requirements of the federal government to free the states from the pressures they now face, but this is largely dependent upon international conditions over which we have little control, and in view of political pressures in the states could not be guaranteed to work.

In addition to the expected growth in federal grants to the states, the trend toward the assumption by the states of a larger share of the financial responsibility for locally administered services will probably continue in the future. Not only is there a growing resistance to the dependence of local government upon the property tax but the jurisdiction of the typical local government unit is proving to be less and less related to the area most efficient either for administrative or for revenue purposes. Thus, the state will tend to use its greater financial powers not only to provide the necessary revenues but also to induce the local governments to merge or in other ways develop a means of coöperative provision of services on an efficient basis. In the postwar period, Pennsylvania's attempt to give local governments greater freedom in choice of revenue measures has not proved to be a practical solution of their problem.[3]

The big issue is not whether there will eventually be greater use of federal and state grants-in-aid but on what terms they will be made.[4] One of the primary sources of resistance to the growth of grants comes from the wealthier areas, who see in an extension of grants-in-aid more diversion of revenues collected within their jurisdiction and spent in some other. Such feelings have required a compromise in most grant programs so that even the wealthiest area is guaranteed a return of a large part of what was collected. This compromise tends to limit the possibility of equalization of service levels. Although there are arguments defending such a position, the weight of facts leads me to conclude that grants should be made to the greatest extent politically practicable to the area of greatest need so that the promise of truly equal opportunity for all can be achieved. Granting this objective, there remain difficult problems of measurement of capacity and need. No solution that fails to take into account the time dimension

[3] Carl Chronister, "Pennsylvania's Experience with Property Tax Alternatives," *1955 Proceedings,* National Tax Association, Sacramento, 1956, pp. 260-278.

[4] The first statement on this issue was made by George D. Strayer and Robert Murray Haig, *The Financing of Education in the State of New York,* New York, 1924. They said: "The state should insure equal educational facilities to every child within its borders at a uniform effort throughout the state in terms of the burden of taxation; the tax burden of education should throughout the state be uniform in relation to taxpaying ability, and the provision for schools should be uniform in relation to the educable population desiring education. Most of the supporters of this proposition, however, would not preclude any particular community from offering at its own expense a particularly rich and costly educational program. They would insist that there be an adequate minimum offered everywhere, the expense of which should be considered a prior claim on the states economic resources." p. 173.

will prove to be satisfactory, as many of the most serious problems today are found in areas of unquestioned wealth and long-range capacity to pay which are suffering from a violent shift in population. They therefore need to expand capital plant for all governmental services in a very short period of time. California is an excellent example of such an area. Among the richest of the 48 states, it is suffering the consequences of a population boom and the popular demand for the maintenance of high quality state services. School buildings, highways, and water are all in short supply, and must be expanded immediately if service levels are not to fall drasticaly. The state has now one of the highest tax burdens of any of the states, but more revenue is needed to provide for the expanded population.

Debt limits, and difficulty in gaining favorable terms for large bond issues of an untested community in the process of building all its basic facilities in a short period of time, are bound to be a cause of difficulty, even if the ultimate capacity of the community fully justifies the issue of all the debt required. Still another reason for the extension of special consideration to these rapidly growing communities is the effect of a sudden expansion upon the tax rate. Unless there is an unusually favorable influx of high-value industrial property along with residential development, the effect of such an expansion will be to force up the tax rate so sharply that resistance will develop. As a result, there is likely to be waste resulting from an attempt to provide the bare minimum in basic facilities, and neglect in meeting long-range requirements for education, water, sewer, and other needs. If these could be financed at low cost at the outset, there could be considerable saving. The savings made possible by providing basic facilities before land improvements increase the costs of installation can be considerable. All these points reinforce the earlier statement that the rapidity of growth may be as important a measure of capacity as wealth, income, or other commonly used measures. A solution to this problem requires either emergency grants or special loans by state or federal government. Assuming the development of a general grant-in-aid program of a permanent nature, the most reasonable solution would be the use of state and/or federal credit to make possible the finance of these extraordinary capital outlays at low rates and without regard to normal debt limtations. In most cases, use of state credit should permit a solution; but if the state is itself in difficulties, access to federal credit may be required.

The possibility that grants-in-aid can be used as a part of a stabilization program is still another point in their favor. Variable grants cannot be used so that total expenditures of states and local governments will offset changes in private expenditures, but much might be accomplished if state and local expenditures could be sustained at peak levels in the event of a depression. The limited capacity of states and local governments to finance needed improvements in periods of depression suggests that federal grants could be of immense value in sustaining high levels of state and local expenditures in the event of trouble. Although this would not of itself offset a decline in the area of private spending, it could prevent the aggravation of the difficulty by sustaining governmental expenditures and providing for the more orderly development of those facilities required by community growth and those services essential to good community life.

If it is also true that many of the states and localities will have additional burdens thrust upon them as a result of unemployment and the growth of need for public assistance of various sorts, the need for federal aid is made clear. The problem is that today there is provision for the use of federal grants only in the case of a limited number of programs of restricted coverage and no plans for the extension of additional grants-in-aid to the states in the event of a crisis. Planning for such grants should be done before the need arises. If this is not done, there is danger that the federal government will end up spending no less money; but, as the result of the emergency and the lack of previous planning, will do the job itself, bypassing the states. A repetition of the Works Progress Administration and the Public Works Administration programs of the Great Depression would go far to weaken the remaining vitality of the federal system, as we have known it in the past.

One final point must be made with regard to the operation of a federal grant program: The social issues raised by federal intervention in the affairs of the states are varied and complex. The primary reason that general grants have not yet been made in support of education is not budgetary but rather, the questions of segregation and the use of federal funds by parochial schools. On the first issue the solid South is fearful of federal grants as a device which would eventually raise the issue of desegregation even if the original appropriation did not so specify. On the latter issue there are two strong groups fighting on either side. Although the argument against the use of governmental funds without government control seems to be clear cut in terms of political tradition and theory, and the principle of separation of church and state is well established in the United States, a well-organized minority has been successful in keeping the issue alive. Here again the political factor seems to be the controlling element in the situation. The need for aid seems clear. The measurement of the extent of need is difficult but possible. It is the terms of the grant that are the question.

Some who would go so far as to argue against grants on general principles believe the extension of federal grants requires federal intervention of a kind that would seriously weaken the basic structure of our federal system. This argument is not supported by the facts in areas where grants have been made. In these cases there is a tendency for the federal government to be rather lax in the enforcement of standards found in the law. Although federal standards may do much to raise the level of performance in certain instances, the locus of political power in the hands of the state political organizations guarantees the continuance of a high degree of state autonomy.[5] Still another fact argues against the most extreme states-rights point of view. This is the changing interest of the country at large in the welfare of all sections of the country. International affairs, internal migration, and higher concepts of the basic minimum which should be the birthright of every citizen make the old states-rights position obsolete. What is really at issue is the capacity of the United States to solve its governmental problems in an orderly fashion. If we fail in this, the eventual political repercussions will become much more serious than anything feared by the advocates of an extreme states-rights position.

Another trend requires attention in this discussion of the financial problems of state and local government. This is the growth in the use of state and local "authorities" or independent corporations as a means of financing and administering certain local services, notably highways, public buildings, and schools. Used with notable success in the Port of New York to solve the problem of administering the traffic and port problems involving two states and by the federal government to provide for such emergency programs as the Reconstruction Finance Corporation and certain farm lending agencies, the use of authorities for general financing and administering of state and local projects has been a recent development. Two types of authority must be distinguished. In one, the full faith and credit of the state or local government is pledged. In the other, the bonds of the issuing authority must stand on their own in the market and are backed only by the revenue potential of the independent agency. The differential in interest rate which follows as a result of this difference may be considerable depending upon the age, function, and general financial condition of the issuing authority. At one extreme is found the Port of New York Authority with a large surplus and assured revenues from the tunnels and bridges under

[5] Leonard D. White, *The States and the Nation*, Baton Rouge, 1953, pp. 35-36.

its jurisdiction. At the other are some of the newer turnpike authorities with unproved traffic volume and no surplus or other source of revenue.

A variety of reasons have accounted for the rapid growth of authorities in the post-World War II period. Among the reasons have been the desire to hold down the size of the state or local budget; the desire, or necessity, because of debt limitations, to incur debt outside of the formal framework of the government; and the belief held by many that there are administrative advantages to be obtained by the creation of a separate agency loosely controlled by normal governmental machinery. Even the federal government has increased the role of authorities—notably in the highway program. Its hand has been forced by the rigid debt limit imposed by Congress and its desire to reduce the size of the budget.

Several questions arise as a result of a careful appraisal of the record. First, there is the question of the status of such agencies even when they are not backed by the full faith and credit of the government. Although there is little question that difficulties might arise causing some to fail, there is a nice question as to whether the governmental unit which has authorized the authority is responsible in the event of failure or of a reorganization which scales down the authorities' debt. When the full faith and credit of the authorizing government has been pledged, the issue is clear, but when this is not the case there remains the question of the ultimate responsibility of the government. It is easy to believe that pressure would develop from a variety of sources to force the government to assume responsibility, even in cases where this is not legally required. In this event, and in every case where the full faith and credit has been pledged, the governments involved are placed in a position of assuming a financial commitment with little control over the management of the agency which they have to support. This appears to be a serious objection to the use of authorities unless all other means have been tried.

In general, the recent enthusiasm for the authority as a means of solving the financial problems of state and local governments must be looked at with a jaundiced eye. The old principle of budget unity is violated, civil service standards are bypassed, and spoils politics can be encouraged by the authority device when the power of appointment is left in the hands of political officers. Independence in administrative control can mean not only freedom to follow businesslike methods but also freedom to ignore the wishes of the people and follow unbusinesslike methods.[6] A final objection is that authorities are often in a position to tax the public by imposing tolls and other charges without their decision being subjected to public debate. These points all suggest that authorities can be tolerated only in instances when there is no other means of finding a practical solution to the problem of gaining jurisdiction over an area beyond the boundaries of any single governmental unit. In all other cases they violate basic principles of government finance and should be rejected.

This discussion of state and local revenue problems cannot be left without some reference to ways and means of strengthening the state and local tax structure. The most obvious place where reform can be made is in the administration of the property tax. Long the most important and often the sole source of local revenue, the property tax has been poorly assessed and has generally declined in severity as assessments have lagged behind the rise in real values in the post-World War II period. The volumes that have been written on this problem and the failure of most states and localities to do anything about it indicates the difficulties in the way of reform. But anyone who is serious about the strengthening of state and local government must face the fact that it is in this area that much can be done to improve local finance. The most obvious reform would be to gain general ac-

[6] Joseph E. McLean, "Use and Abuse of Authorities," *National Municipal Review*, XLII (1953), 438-444.

ceptance for full-market-value assessments.[7] This would have the advantage of both lowering the nominally high tax rates and keeping pressure upon state and local officials to reassess property frequently and thus remove many of the worst inequities that have been the source of legitimate complaint against this tax. The other major reform should be the elimination of exemptions for new industry. The growing tendency for many of the states and local governments to offer many years of tax exemption to new industry may create serious problems in the years to come. Various studies of the effects of tax exemption as it relates to industrial location indicate that it is of little importance, in spite of the fact that many firms will use it as a bargaining point when dealing with local officials.[8] It can even be pointed out that the quality of the schools, roads, and other basic services in a community may be of greater long-run importance than the tax rate in attracting new firms. The moral of this is that state and local governments have only themselves to blame if they get into a position where one can be played against the other by prospective investors. Still another facet of this problem is appearing in the areas where state and local governments are not only offering tax exemption but also offering to construct plants and lease them to new industry on favorable terms. In this plan, long-term debt will be increased at the cost of borrowing capacity for new public projects, and many communities will find that in the end the problem of financing needed governmental services will be more rather than less difficult. The appeal of industrial development as a means of raising financial capacity may have merit, but the price paid by many communities may be too great. Even if industrial development brings higher income, it may not solve the financial problems of the community. High income may also bring demands for higher levels of government services.

[7] The recent decision of the courts in New Jersey to require full-value assessment should provide an interesting test case.

[8] John A. Larsen, *Taxes and Plant Location in Michigan,* CED Executive Study Group, School of Business Administration, University of Michigan, 1957.

At the state level, the problems of finance are so diverse that it is difficult to generalize about reforms which would guarantee adequate revenue. One generalization that can be safely ventured, however, is that all states need some broad-based tax, and preferably more than one, if they are both to meet the state revenue requirements and be in a position to make the grants-in-aid required by local governments. This means that adequate state revenues require some form of sales or income tax, if not both. Another possibility is the gross receipts tax, with exemptions, which combines some of the features of the sales and income taxes. It is surprising that there are still some states that have not been able to pass either type of tax and are dependent upon auto use taxes, including the gasoline tax, and selective excise taxes. As was mentioned above, some states seem to tax sin or the means of getting there, as they concentrate upon excises on liquor, tobacco, horse racing, and the automobile. Such a narrow tax base would prove to be particularly vulnerable in the event of a depression and cannot adequately finance the full burdens of state government even in the best periods. The choice among the various broad-based levies must be made realistically in view of the character of the state economic system; the political history of tax legislation; the current distribution of political power; and finally, the desire of the public and its leaders for progressive versus proportionate or regressive tax-burden distribution. In view of the generally proportionate distribution of the existing tax burden and the difficulty of local administration of progressive tax levies, I have a bias in favor of the use of the state individual and corporation income tax. In addition to the advantages usually associated with the income tax both in terms of the adjustment of taxes to individual circumstances and its countercyclical effects, the current allowance for state income taxes paid, in computation of federal income-tax burdens, permits the states to gain a large part of their income tax revenue at the expense of the federal government. If the effective federal rate is 50 percent, deductibility will halve the effective burden of state income taxation. This point must be noted in partial answer to the earlier point of the relatively weak position of state governments in competition for the taxpayer's dollar. Still another possibility is further coördination in the administration of state and federal income taxes. Coöperation in auditing of income tax returns and access by state tax officials to federal returns already has improved the ability of states effectively to enforce an income tax.[9] Further gains might be achieved by experiments with the use of state tax supplements on federal returns and even more coöperation in the administration of federal and state levies. Certainly, if states generally try to impose a broad-based income tax such as that now administered by the federal government, their problem could be solved only if some such devices are used. At the higher income levels, problems are created by the limited jurisdiction of state tax officials on income derived from sources outside of the state. Although this problem is a formidable one, and the problem of discriminatory double taxation has yet to be solved in spite of innumerable conferences and studies of the problem, greater progress might be made under the stimulus of federal leadership. The greatest difficulty is the reluctance of the states to give up peculiarities in their individual laws so that the two concepts of taxable income could be merged and efficiently administered by a single jurisdiction. A false sense of pride, local pressure groups, and plain cussedness all work against achievement of the desired end. One is forced again to state that many of the problems about which the states complain the most are of their own making and cannot be resolved without reform within their own jurisdictions.

The state retail-sales tax has proved to be the most lucrative source of state revenues. Of relatively recent origin, it was first widely used in the depression of the 1930's and has proved to be

[9] For a discussion of these and other possibilities see U.S. Treasury Department, *Federal-State-Local Tax Coordination*, Washington, 1952; Tax Institute, *Federal-State-Local Tax Correlation*, Princeton, 1957.

a good revenue producer in a period of rising incomes and sales. Contrary to the assumption of many, it is not an easy tax to administer and enforce. Particularly in areas near the border of a state that has no tax, the diversion of sales to the tax-free states presents real difficulties. Other problems of a continuing nature arise from the large number of retail establishments responsible for collection of the tax and the difficulty of defining retail sales. The typical low-rate tax now used in the states also creates the problem of differential rates on low-cost items due to the administrative difficulty of using less than a penny as the minimum tax collected. The typical solution is to draft a schedule of tax liabilities for such items as breaking to the nearest penny. States that attempted to use mill tokens have found the cost and irritation to the taxpayer not worth the greater equity in most cases. Still another limitation of the sales tax is the small base that results if food, clothing, services, and housing are excluded, and the very regressive distribution of the burden, if they are left in the tax base. The possibility of including such items as housing and services is remote, so the practical issue becomes that of inclusion or exclusion of food and clothing.[10]

One must conclude that there is no magic formula guaranteed to improve state revenue sources. The best feature of the sales tax is its acceptability as a source of state revenue in these days of high federal income taxes. But even those states with a sales tax are finding it difficult to raise sufficient revenue. If the choice is between inadequate state revenues and a sales tax, the answer is clear. In view of the advantages that can be derived by better education and welfare and service programs, there is a net gain to be had from even a regressive distribution of tax burdens. Preference for income taxes should not be carried to a point of stubborn resistance to the political facts of life.

[10] Exclusion of food and tobacco would remove $81.4 billion from the base, and clothing, accessories, and jewelry another $25.6 billion at the national level. U.S. Department of Commerce, *Survey of Current Business,* July, 1956, p. 21

The new value-added tax in Michigan [11] and the gross-receipts tax in Indiana [12] are relatively recent attempts to find acceptable solutions to the problems of adequate state revenue sources. The gross-receipts tax has the advantage of producing a relatively large amount of revenue from a low rate. Both have the disadvantage of being deceptive in their burden. The gross-receipts tax is particularly bad as it taxes relatively more severely the low-markup high-volume business as opposed to the high-markup low-volume business. In both cases, the continuance of tax liabilities on firms that may be losing money is a marked disadvantage from a countercyclical point of view, although of some advantage to hard-pressed treasury officials of state governments who cannot ignore the problem of revenue sources in a depression as can the federal treasury. Experience with the value-added tax is meager; and it is too early to tell what the verdict will be as to its potential, but the problem of depreciation allowances seems to be the most troublesome aspect of the tax to date. The real problem, however, is that the size of the revenue is limited by the fact that it is difficult to make this base any larger than that of the sales tax. Its use in Michigan is likely to be an exception due to the large volume of exports of manufactured goods from that state.

The inequities of the gross-receipts tax as it differentiates among firms according to the degree of integration and value added make it the least desirable of all the broad-based taxes. Attempts to avoid some of the worst sources of discrimination by differential rates and exemptions are bound to be arbitrary and inadequate. Although Indiana seems to have had reasonable success with the tax, it is not to be recommended.

---

[11] W. Lock, D. J. Ray, and H. D. Hamilton, "The Michigan Value-Added Tax," *National Tax Journal,* VIII (1955), 357-371. See also "Taxation of Business in Michigan," *1955 Proceedings,* National Tax Association, Sacramento, 1956, pp. 6-38.

[12] State of Indiana, Commission on State Tax and Financing Policy, *Final Recommendations, 1954,* Indianapolis, 1954, pp. 67-86.

Conclusions

This review of state and local revenue problems suggests that it is in this area that many of the most difficult problems of government finance are going to arise over the years. In spite of all that can be done at the state and local level, there is need for federal aid to meet the growing crisis in state and local finance. National interests are looming larger, and local interests are becoming less susceptible of purely local solution. Political boundaries have made obsolete many of the state and local units both as administrative and financial areas. Nonetheless, there is reason to preserve the advantage of decentralized government and local autonomy. How to accomplish this, in view of the multitude of problems that the states and their subdivisions must face is the issue. Some form of grant-in-aid seems to be the only answer. It is the responsibility of the states, which have the ultimate political power, to see that the grants are not destructive of their vital interests.

If some such program is adopted in the near future, much of the current discussion of reduction in federal taxation will prove to be illusive. If the states try to go it alone, the rise in state taxation will offset any reductions made possible at the federal level. The conclusion that follows is inevitable—the prospects of tax relief are remote and further tax increases are more likely. The one tempering influence is that of rising productivity. This suggests that even if taxes rise or continue at present levels, that part of income left after taxes can also rise if the growth of the economy continues at the rate we have known in the past. This further reënforces the need for a positive stabilization policy so that the gains of increased output can be sustained over the next few years.

Some of the more drastic solutions to the problems of state and local government should be mentioned, if only to indicate their inadequacy. One solution that has superficial appeal is a complete reorganization of state boundaries in order to create efficient administrative and economic units. This possibility, appealing in the abstract, has little or no chance of achievement. At the local level a similar proposal to merge and reorganize local jurisdictions has been made and again has much to support it. But in both cases the powers of established interests, the interests of office holders, the differentials in tax burdens, and the pure cussedness of individuals make the prospect of any extensive move in this direction remote. Another problem arises out of the differences in boundaries that might be suggested depending upon the interest that was being served.

The one area where success has been achieved is in the consolidated school district. In this case two factors work favorably. One is the fact that it is possible to develop a consolidated school without necessarily reorganizing the local governmental unit. Second, the schools have been out of the main stream of politics in many parts of the United States as is evidenced by the maintenance of fiscal autonomy for school budgets and the professionalization of the leadership of the schools. Thus, even when it is necessary to form a new school district to gain the consolidated school, the interests of the parents do not clash in the same manner as would be the case if the police departments of two adjacent areas were involved and the decision as to the selection of the new chief arose. Finally, there is the obvious advantage of the larger school district from a financial point of view. A varied program cannot be offered with any efficiency at the high-school level with less than 800 to 1000 students. The trend toward the differentiation of educational programs to suit all the children has been carried so far that there is now widespread acceptance of of this principle. The old-fashioned single program has ended with the one room school house. In this day of teacher shortages, there is also the obvious advantage of making the most of scarce resources—possible only if the school is of adequate size.

Still the greatest stumbling block is the basis for the apportionment of federal or state grants to state and local districts. This basis must include the capacity of the state or local district, the effort they have expended to meet their obligations, the state of economic conditions, and some consideration of a basic minimum below which no communty should fall. In the case of state grants to local communities, local assessed values are generally used to determine capacity, but there are many problems that arise from the unevenness of assessments and the necessity of equalization of assessed values. Typically, some differential is also included to account for special factors such as transportation, special classes for problem children, and so forth. In addition, few state-aid programs try to provide for more than a foundation program, leaving to the locality the decision as to the extras that they may wish to provide. In some states, however, the great bulk of the program is financed centrally.

In the case of federal grants to the states, current programs have been largely on a matching basis with a minimum of the equalization element. If some greater degree of equalization is called for in the future to take care of education, highways, and health, some greater emphasis must be placed upon the differential grant. If this is done, the best measure of capacity would seem to be personal income payments in the state. Current figures are available in the national income accounts, and no better measure seems to be available. The great stumbling block here is resistance of the wealthier states to the diversion of their tax receipts to those states in a less advantageous position. Although in the long run they have as much to gain as anyone in the growth of the standards in all of the United States, they may well tend to take a narrow view.

The continued vitality of our federal system of government depends upon the crontinuance of healthy states and local governments. Whether this health can be maintained in face of cur-

CHAPTER XIV

Summary

The main conclusions of this study can be stated briefly. Underlying all of them is the fact that government finance will continue to play a role of overwhelming importance in our economy. Individuals and business are vitally affected by government.

The reasons for this growth in the role of government have been the depression, the war, the continuation of the cold war since the end of World War II, and the growth in the complexity of modern society with its great urban concentrations. It is also true that there are many wants that must now be satisfied collectively through government rather than by the individual. Our great wealth; the rise in birth rates; the automobiles; the growth in the mobility of the population; needs for water, power, resource conservation; and the realization of the principle of equality of opportunity have also been factors affecting the role of government.

The second main conclusion is that these trends will not be reversed. The growing recognition of the needs of the country for a more productive work force, for the training of technicians, executives, and scientists makes the problem of education alone one of the most pressing issues of the day. Defense requirements will probably not diminish. The need for roads and the use of water will increase more rapidly than the population. The demand for parks and other recreational facilities will also grow as leisure time increases. And through housing and other programs the government will be expected to secure a minimum standard of living for its citizens.

The third main conclusion is that government finds it difficult to use its power wisely. The difficulties of gaining the sort of coördinated policies that are required within government is one of the major problems. Senators and congressmen tend to represent their individual constituencies rather than consider the nation as a whole. The executive office of the President realizes that to stay in power some groups cannot be offended and that in some cases little can be done to prevent excessive expenditures or tax concessions. Pressures brought to bear on the government by regions or by interest groups may overwhelm the best senator or congressman. The President wishes to have a strong party to back him up in his appeal to the people. He may find that building a strong party requires him to act in ways contrary to the best interests of all the people.

One of the greatest problems arises from the growth in the number and power of special-interest groups. This makes it difficult to discuss political issues intelligently in the United States. Too many people are thinking of the best way of using government to gain advantages for their own group. They seldom worry about the tendency to abuse the powers of government. Yet these abuses, if not checked, could destroy the productivity and freedom that has made this country the one place in the world where there is a high degree of mobility and a reasonably satisfactory standard of living for all. The danger of the politicalization of the economy at the cost of productivity remains one of the most serious threats to the preservation of those things that are good and in the best tradition of the United States.

Even if there were intelligent and unselfish discussion of public economic policies and even if the government were well coördinated and alert, government still would not find it easy to make wise decisions in economic matters. No economist can predict events that will be of major importance to the government in its planning for the next few months. And if it is difficult to predict economic developments, it is even more difficult to predict what the response of the public will be to any counter action taken by government to meet these developments. A tax cut may generate increased spending, and it may drift into idle balances. A tax increase may be desirable, but the size of the increase required to accomplish the necessary result is difficult to predict, depending upon the attitudes of the public and the extent of their balances, their access to credit, and the degree of tightness of the banking system. All this suggests the necessity of a flexible policy so that there can be rapid response to changing conditions. We must realize that governments should be allowed to change their policies with reasonable speed and to correct for known deficiencies and excesses. They should not be required to concentrate all their economic efforts on actions designed to prevent any economic disturbance. Much can be done to strengthen the economy by preventive action, but the need for flexibility will still remain.

The methods chosen by the government to achieve its economic ends will permanently influence the social, political, and economic system that we will enjoy in the years ahead. Conversely, the government's choice of means will be influenced by the nature of our society. The problem uppermost is that of the limited capacity of government to be able to satisfy all of the people all of the time. This is one of the prices of democracy and must be accepted if either our economic system or our political system is to be preserved. The danger is that the individual citizen expects too much from his government and is unwilling to realize the limitations of governmental powers. This means that the reaction to any condition other than perpetual boom will be adverse and have in it the seeds of a major reaction against the party in power. The use of political power as a means of improving one's income position has already gone far enough to make a reversal of the trend mandatory if the essence of our economic system and the political traditions of the United States are to be preserved.

One of the most important developments has been the rise of labor and agriculture to a position where they can bargain on equal terms with industry. The new balance of power among these three groups has created pressures with inflationary implications. Labor has been able to win sufficient power so that it can bargain with the government on equal terms with industry. Agriculture has been able to insulate its sector of the economy from paying the full price of variations in demand and from the effects of changes in the weather and foreign markets. Add to this the low tolerance of the public for any departure from continuous boom conditions, and the dangers of inflation are evident. One of the greatest problems is the development of a new belief in the dangers of any downward price adjustments, enforced by the powerful interests of labor, agriculture, and industry. If the only method of transferring resources is by upward adjustments in prices, then the tendency for perpetual inflation will be greater than ever before in the history of the country. If prices are to remain stable, some prices must go down while others rise.

Two other problems must be mentioned. The first is the need for a thorough revision of the federal and state tax laws. The tendency for differentials to develop in our tax laws, so that the burden of taxation varies with the source of income, can undermine the tax base, and limits the possibility of effective enforcement of our tax laws. A wise policy would be to reduce the top rates of the individual income tax and to force all individuals who have equal incomes to pay equal taxes. Unless this is done, there is danger that the problem of tax collection will become increasingly difficult at the cost of both political and economic stability.

The second issue is the growing problem of financing state and local government. Due to the great increase in the severity of federal tax burdens, the rise in the birth rate, and the tendency for industrial and residential communities to be separated, state and local governments have been finding it difficult to raise the revenue required to finance their local services. The youth of the nation has no less potential in the south than in the north, yet the ability of the southern states to finance a well-designed education program is inferior to that of the north. The interest of the wealthier states in this matter should be clear, as many of the future workers, managers, and scientific personnel must come from the poorer southern states. They have surplus population and will continue to send a large part of this surplus to the north. The one solution of this problem compatible with preservation of our federal system is for the federal government to increase the amount devoted to grants-in-aid to the states. This is the best method of raising the level of education and is clearly a responsibility of the federal government due to its interest in the status of all citizens, not just those who are fortunate to live in wealthy states.

The discussion above leaves us with a problem of devising more effective means of accomplishing the legitimate functions of government. There is no magic solution, and the difficulties to be faced are formidable. All of us want the free services provided by government—few of us like to pay the price required. Even when the abstract principle of pay-as-we-go is accepted, most of the public find irresistible the temptation to seek special favor from government, either through subsidy or tax relief. All of us realize that there are many functions of government which are inadequately served, yet we resist the taxation requested to pay for them. One solution is to follow the path of inflation. This would reflect a degree of political irresponsibility that would prove to be a serious threat to the stability of both the political structure and the economy. Inflation reflects a breakdown in capacity to govern and a failure to resolve through any orderly procedure the basic problem of the distribution of the total product of the economy.

Inflation is difficult to avoid, because the measures necessary to prevent it are resisted in periods of boom. Increased taxes, higher interest rates, lack of credit availability to meet profitable business opportunities will anger many and hurt some. It is not easy to determine just who is to be hit hardest by the necessary restraints. Both taxes and credit restrictions must apply somewhat unevenly and may adversely affect some sectors of the economy where the boom has been particularly strong. When one adds to these complications the fact that the agencies involved may be fearful of taking action that could cause them to accept the blame for breaking the boom without full ability to guarantee the restoration of the previously existing prosperity, it is a wonder that we do as well as we do.

It is clear that it is the President who must take ultimate responsibility for both the checking of inflation and the initiation of action to stop a depression or restore favorable conditions in the event of a minor slump. The Federal Reserve Board cannot generally prove to be as effective in offsetting a depression as it can in checking a boom. On the other hand, it is difficult to use taxation or expenditure reductions to check a boom in a period of great prosperity. The two methods of indirect control must complement each other; but in spite of the flexibility granted the Federal Reserve, it cannot have much faith in the willingness of Congress to act with dispatch in the event its actions force too great a reaction. Only as the President uses all his powers of persuasion can rapid action be taken. In this, his position has been improved by the addition of the Council of Economic Advisers to his office. But he must be willing to take action that may not be popular. This is the rub. His job is a strange mixture of the leader of both his party and the nation. In the process of resolving the conflicting interests of his office he may act too slowly or sometimes even in the wrong direction. If he is weak, or has strong advisers in his cabinet who have some special interest to

serve, he may even find that his desire to act with wisdom will
be offset by the conflicting testimony of his staff.

If inflation is not to be the solution to the conflicts of public
opinion over governmental finance, a much higher degree of
leadership must be forthcoming, particularly on the part of politicians. How this can be produced in view of the conflicts of
interest to which they are subject is difficult to see. Perhaps the
greatest hope would be the success of a single politician who
chose to stress equity and stability at the price of special favor
for some constitutent. The public can be appealed to on grounds
of equity and a reasonable distribution of the tax burden. Otherwise, there would be less use of the individual income tax and
more stress upon indirect taxation. Stress upon equality of opportunity can also be appealing. This has both a positive and a
negative side. The positive side requires the offering by the state
of reasonable educational facilities, health and basic public
services. The negative side requires that no groups be unduly
favored by government so that they gain a head start in the competitive struggle for profits. But neither possibility will be forthcoming if the public is led to believe that the costs of government
are too high and that most of their money is being wasted.

In this regard the business community has a major responsibility. The generally hostile attitude taken by business toward government has hurt and has led to a generally negative attitude about
governmental requirements. The fact remains that there is probably no more waste or inefficiency in government operations than
there is in the typical big business. In fact, a strong case can be
made suggesting that dollar for dollar, the public gets more from
its tax dollar than it does from its dollar spent for the highly
stylized products of industry. No one can prove such an assertion,
but it is just as valid as the much more frequently made assertion
that government expenditures are too large and that the future
health of the economy requires a drastic reduction at once. What
bothers business as well as the individual is the size of the tax

bill. Some business groups have even gone so far as to suggest that taxes should first be lowered as a means of forcing a reduction in expenditure levels. This suggestion is an open invitation to inflationary financing, for those who vote appropriations are not going to be impressed by the fact of tax cuts.

When one adds to the general criticism of government the cynical pursuit of special favors from government typical of the average business lobby and the steadfast refusal to favor the increase in government salaries to make the career of the governmental official more attractive, the full dimensions of the problem become evident. Now that labor, agriculture, and well-organized produced groups of all types are active, the wonder is that the level of governmental performance is as high as it is. The one saving grace is the bright light of publicity and the possibilities of investigation under which every governmental official now lives. More subtle pressures, such as job offers and the like, may be used; but it is still remarkable that there is as high a standard of morality as continues to exist in the government of the United States.

A Positive Program of Reform

The greatest need at the present time is for the growth of a more articulate philosophy of the role of government in the social, political, and economic structure of the United States. The public tends to hold to an outmoded belief in the virtue of limited government. Few individuals are interested in questions of government except where they are directly affected. Yet the price of failure to alert more people to the issue of the proper role of government will be an increase in the frequency with which special-interest groups find it possible to gain personal advantage by use of political power. There is also danger of growing discontent as more people find that their government is not acting in the general interest but is being manipulated by special groups.

The problem is to find means of stimulating such an interest and the means of giving to it the degree of publicity that it requires. The person best able to do this is the President, given the vast power of his office and his almost unlimited access to the press, radio, and television. But to be effective, the President must have an articulate philosophy and be able to defend it not only in prepared speeches but in a rough and tumble press conference. In recent years, there has been no President with such a philosophy or interest. What is called for, therefore, is the rise of a new sort of statesman who can achieve the office of the President. In view of the peculiar qualifications that permit someone to rise to high office, there is no certainty that such an event will occur within the foreseeable future. We can hope, but it is only a hope, that leadership will come in this particular form.

Short of the rise of a really effective leader in the office of the President, the job of drawing attention to these issues and formulating a reasonable set of objectives must be the job of lesser men and women. This book is one attempt to call attention to the problem. Other social scientists must be willing to make similar attempts and divest themselves of the cult of pure objectivity. The debate must also range over the area of more than a single discipline. In this day of specialization, individuals with more than a single interest are less and less frequently found in institutions of higher learning. The more discussion of these matters is pursued by academic writers, the more frequently will popular writers find means of carrying the essence of their findings to the public at large.

One encouraging development has been the rise in business of some outstanding leaders who have developed a real philosophy of government and its relation to the society and economy. One such group is the Committee for Economic Development which has worked closely with the best talent available in economics to formulate a position on many matters of national interest. Even here, however, there is a basic distrust of government and a tendency to suggest cuts in government programs that are both unrealistic and unlikely to be achieved. It is also true that because varied interests are represented in such a group, there are certain subjects that cannot be discussed or on which public pronouncements cannot be made. But in this effort there have been developed some outstanding business leaders who are well in advance of the public at large and who can prove to be a great asset in any public debate over the evolution of governmental policies in the future. It is on these individuals rather than large organizations that the hope of the future rests.

Still another source of satisfaction is the growth in the popularity of training programs for top business executives which include considerable emphasis upon the role of government and its influence upon the society and the economy. More and more businessmen are finding that they will profit from a greater degree of knowledge in the field of national income accounting, government tax policies, debt management, and credit controls.

We are still left with the issue of the direction in which we will move over the next decade or two. The final result will be determined by the political forces and the degree of leadership in the political field. So we must return to the hope that we will develop some statesmen who can alert the public to the dangers of abuse of government and lead it to demand a resistance to power grabs and other distortions. The job is made more difficult by virtue of the size of today's government, but it is not an impossible one.

This leads to a discussion of the quality of government officials and the shortage in most areas of persons best qualified to do the jobs required by government. When governments have risen to the level of importance they now command, there is no excuse for a policy of poor pay and inadequate opportunities for advancement. With the exception of a few states, there is too little offered to make a career in government attractive to the most able. Much interest has been expressed in the shortage of teachers—the problem would not exist if they were paid more. There is also danger in the adequate staffing of important offices. For example, more than the additional salary could be recovered if more internal revenue agents were added to the staff of the Treasury Department. Although there is some question of the ability of the Treasury to hire more at current pay scales, there is no question that if salaries were more attractive the additional personnel could be obtained. The salaries of legislators should also be increased to attract more able persons to this important task. Fairer apportionment would also help, as there can be little attraction in becoming an assemblyman or state senator when the over-represented rural areas tend to dominate the legislative procedure. An extreme example of this state of affairs is found in Georgia where the county-unit rule gives a minority of the population the majority voice in the legislature.

At the federal level, the additional cost of higher salaries would not loom large in terms of the total budget. At the state and local level, the increase would be relatively more noticeable, as it is at this level that government employment is more closely related to total costs. Salaries will have to be raised to bring to government the necessary additions to personnel now required or foreseeable in the near future. The issue therefore is not the fact of some increase, but whether it will be large enough, and whether the top salaries will be sufficient to attract the most able men and women and keep them. A recent study of the turnover among military personnel arrived at the conclusion that if an efficient military service was to be maintained it would be necessary to increase substantially the salaries of officers and men to keep them from seeking more attractive jobs in private industry. In view of the costs of training a qualified soldier or officer, this would seem to be the only way of assuring the maintenance of an efficient force. A similar point can be made with regard to the civil service, where many of the most able men and women leave for better-paying jobs just as they have achieved full knowledge of the intricacies of government operations. Although there are many other reasons for the relatively high turnover of government workers, the rate of turnover could be substantially lessened if pay and advancement opportunities were more attractive.

The most troublesome issue now facing the federal government is its obligation to maintain economic stability. To many, this means the preservation of a perpetual boom. To others, the obligation is for a much less ambitious program but one designed to prevent any major deviations from the ideal of full employment. The first group tends to favor government intervention as soon as unemployment exceeds two to three million, while the latter group would permit unemployment to reach five million before action would be required. If perpetual boom is the objective, there is little question that either elaborate direct controls must be used or inflation will be the rule. The experience in World War II and again in the Korean period suggests that direct controls are difficult to administer, are impossible to apply equitably, and are subject to manipulation by powerful interest groups. In a period of inflation, a similar process develops. Powerful interest groups can gain to the disadvantage of the less well-organized, and there is a premium placed upon organization strength rather than productive contribution. Yet the public enjoys a boom and would like to see it continue. Thus, at the outset, the basic issue becomes one of gaining acceptance for a policy of government intervention that does not equal the expectations now commonly in the public's mind. The almost uninterrupted improvement in economic conditions from 1940 to date suggests to the average person that if we have enjoyed a boom for years we may have it for another indefinite period. What has been is good, and there seems to be no reason to accept anything less than the best. That we do not know enough to prevent some deviation from perpetual boom is not generally realized by the public, and the divided viewpoints of economists can be cited to prove either side of the argument. That we may delay in taking the sort of action necessary to offset the decline is also a possibility. That external events may prove to be disturbing is not widely understood by the voters. The one hope is that in spite of our desire for pereptual boom the efforts of the government to preserve this condition will fall short.

The critical question boils down to the capacity of any economy to sustain a perpetual boom. Too many uncertainties exist to give any assurance of this happy state of affairs continuing any length of time. Although no government can accept blame for a downturn, governments now must accept responsibility for taking all possible steps to restore favorable economic conditions, once a depression has begun. The most critical issue is, therefore, the limit of tolerance that governments will be allowed in the pursuit of the ideal of full employment. If, as is widely believed, this limit is very low, then trouble is bound to develop, either as the result of failure to prevent some deviation from the ideal or as the result of inflation or direct controls. There is no government that can guarantee perfectly ideal conditions at all times. It is also true that even in a generally favorable market there may be some industries that are lagging behind. If attempts are made to subsidize these areas, then real trouble is bound to follow. If they are ignored, protests will arise in that particular sector.

We have already seen that under current conditions there is a dangerously high level of public expectation, a limited power of government to deliver up to the public's expectations, and a danger of overcompensation leading to perpetual inflation or the multiplication of direct controls. How the public can be led to accept a more reasonable level of employment as the norm, is the question that must be answered. One device that can help is improvement in the terms and conditions offered under unemployment insurance. If in addition a general disability insurance program is developed, then some of those most adversely affected could survive a reasonably long period of unemployment. Other provisions that could help include some generalization of the dismissal pay provisions of certain industries; improvement in the Old-Age and Survivors Insurance provision for the aged, who are most likely to be without work; and some guarantee that, in the event of the exhaustion of the state unemployment compensation pool, the federal government would be able and willing to make available funds for continuance of regular payments. All this adds up to a statement that if a wider tolerance for economic uncertainties is to be generated it will be necessary for the public to have assurance of adequate minimum levels below which no one will be permitted to fall. In other words, under current conditions there is real reason for welfare programs to be strengthened. Yet even this course has its dangers, as there is the implication that if everyone is guaranteed a basic minimum then those gainfully employed should be treated much better. The one hope is that the provision of unemployment insurance, disability insurance, and old age and survivors' insurance, are sufficiently separated from the market and job to permit these payments to be divorced from the attempt to gain a larger share of the total product by political pressure. So long as economic conditions remain favorable, this may well continue to be the case, but in the event of another depression of some duration, the growth in the number of aged, unemployed, and underemployed suggests that there may be another attempt to bring about recovery by excessive payments to the nonproductive members of the society. The strength of the Townsend Plan in the 1930's suggests the vigor which such programs can develop.

We must again assert that there is no one who will be able to save us from our own self-destruction if that is what we wish to do. No simple solution can be offered to guarantee that we will not ruin what has been one of the most productive and progressive economic systems of all times. In the end, it will be the quality of leadership that will offer the best opportunity to save us from foolish action. But it is just as possible to be misled by foolish leaders as to be saved by wise ones. Unfortunately, many persons wish to believe that they can have their cake and eat it too. If this is the course we are to follow, then there will be difficulties. If we are wise and exercise restraint, we can maintain the best of the current system without many of the unnecessary hardships associated with the early days of capitalism.

There is no question that in a dictatorship the rate of economic progress can be as high as the government believes it possible to force the people to accept. In a country that has never had much luxury, such as Russia, this can be very effective. But in the United States today, there is generally a drive to live beyond one's means and to use any device to improve one's position. Under these circumstances, there is little chance of our either accepting a minor role for government, now that it has assumed the role of protector of the public welfare, or denying many attempts to make raids upon the government as a means of bettering one's economic position. What can be hoped for is the realization that one raid leads to another and that no one will gain advantage in the end. If, on the other hand, attempts are made to achieve equality by means of granting to all the exceptions now available to the few, then there is little hope of maintaining either a stable government, a stable economy, or a stable society.

It is clear that there should be some means found to increase the flexibility of response granted to the government to meet changing conditions. How this can be done and at the same time preserve the necessary democratic power over taxation and expenditures, is the issue. New concepts of government operations are required that do not do violence to the concept of adequate response to known difficulties. The possibility of gaining acceptance for such a program will be determined in part by the skill with which the plan is written so as to minimize the possibilities of abuse. If there could be action in the fiscal area that did not require the reopening of all the questions of tax-burden distribution and expenditure levels, then there could be more delegation of authority. Until such power has been delegated to the executive, there will have to be primary reliance placed upon monetary

controls and hope that in the event of a major crisis Congress
would act with sufficient dispatch to prevent the disturbance from
gaining momentum.

Governments of the size of those existing today cannot be
made neutral. They have the capacity either to improve or grossly
distort the distribution of income and the rate of growth of the
economy. More attention to long-run objectives is essential.
Otherwise, there is danger of drifting into a condition incom-
patible with the preservation of the market as the primary
determinant both of the character of output and of the direction
in which new growth is desired. If the public wishes to live in a
state-controlled economy, it should choose this course with
its eyes open. But if the public is reasonably content with the
performance of the economy and does not wish to be subjected
to detailed controls, then it should see that some types of government intervention are inconsistent with its objective.

There is a legitimate complaint in many sectors about the inflation of the past years. In the process there have been severe
changes in the relative income status of many individuals who
are dependent upon retirement income, those who are employees
of endowed institutions, and in general, the civil service employee
who has seen his or her income rise less rapidly than that of comparable workers in private industry. All holders of fixed-dollar investments, including insurance, have suffered; and many have been
encouraged to invest in common stocks when this is a gamble
they should not take. The danger in all this is that there is a
tendency for pressures to develop to prevent any downward
adjustment of any prices. Under these circumstances there will
be no possibility of increases in productivity being reflected in
lower prices, and all increases in demand will be reflected in
price increases. This is the perfect formula for perpetual and
cumulative inflation.

There is little time left if the advantages of a free economy
are to be preserved, while at the same time each citizen gains

more equal opportunity. The productive genius of the United States can be the source of the millennium sought by all peoples at all times: the elimination of poverty without the loss of individual freedom. The answer must be sought not in the pure science of economics but in the revival of political economy. The issues that are most troublesome are now those of pressure groups and power blocs that have learned to use their strength to gain a temporary advantage from government. Such policies cannot be pursued for any period of time without deterioration both of public morale and of political morals. The consequences of such action are bound to be disastrous to both the stability of the government and the economy and will lead to a popular reaction that will force some change likely to lead to radical departures from both democratic principles and those of a free economy.

To achieve the reforms required is a problem of leadership. First the public must be alerted to the problem, and then the alternatives must be presented for debate and consideration. There is no certainty as to the final outcome, but there is need for discussion of the direction in which we are to move over the next few years, a choice made on the basis of the best evidence available.

INDEX

Acheson, Dean, 54
Agricultural Adjustment Agency, 86
Agricultural Marketing Act of 1929, 3
Agriculture, Department of, 28, 128
Agriculture, under Eisenhower's administration, 86
  price support program for farms, 12
  and World War II defense preparations, 24-25
American Federation of Labor, 3
Arnold, General Henry H., 26
Assessments, full market-value, 270
Assets, during Korean War, 78
Authorities, appraisal of, 268
  for general financing and administration, 267
  rapid growth of, 268
  as solution of state and local financial problems, 269

Banks, failures of, 14
  and the public debt, 16
Benson, Ezra Taft, 86
Berle, A. A., Jr., 116
Beveridge, Lord, 187
Blough, Roy, 40, 211
Bonds, financing of, 222-223
  issues of, 264
Boom, continuation of, 290-291
  of 1951, 81
Budget, and administrative obstacles, 189
  annually balanced, 196
  balanced, 186-187
  better management of, 191-192
  democratic control of, 125
  fads' and fashions' influence on, 198
  federal, between 1946 and 1950, 60
    deficits in, 17
  importance of, 93

interdependence among components
    of, 110
  process, proposals to improve, 119,
    190-191
  separation of expenditure and revenue
    sides of, 189-190
    from stabilization fund, 161
  size of, 192-193
  stabilizing influence of, 135, 177
  unlimited variation theory of, 187
  various aspects of, 119-120
Bureau of the Budget, 28, 67, 128, 129
  Fiscal Division of, 17
Bureau of Internal Revenue, 71-72
Business, marginal support for, 13
Butters, J. Keith, 210

Capital gains, 212
  preferential treatment of, 218-219
  taxation of, 218
Capital losses, 213
Capitalism, democratic, limitations on
    power of, 131-132
  welfare under, 115
Chandler, Lester V., 40, 41
Clark, J. M., 14, 59, 117
Collective bargaining, 158
Committee for Economic Development,
    15 n., 287
Commodity Credit Corporation, 47-48
"Concept of Countervailing Power," 94
Congress, action on tax bills by, 44-45
  and executive department, 25, 90
  limitation of powers of, 26
  resistance to tax reduction by, 246
Conservation, federal programs for, 18
Consumer demand, and tax relief, 233-
    234
Consumer price index, 146
Consumers, spending habits of, 78

Controls, administration of, 140
  breakdown of, 51
  danger of, 38-39
  direct, 14, 29-39 ff.
    difficulty of administering, 290
    general impact of, 38
    limitations of, 73, 138-139, 140
    in 1951, 77
    and savings, 41
    stabilizing effect of, 29-30
  and economic capacity, 78
  farm price, 30
  general, wise use of, 140
  indirect, instruments of, 33
  over investment, 115
  of materials, 77-78
  1950 economic, 70
  power blocs' abuse of, 138
  to prevent inflation and unemployment, 138
  price, 50-51
    resistance to, 35-36
    and wages, 139-140
  program of, 33
  public reaction to, 37-38
  rent, 30
  and special interest pressures, 34-35
  during World War I, 38
Corporations, common law for, 116
  double taxation of income of, 221
  governmental, 125
  high rate of savings by, 219
  as means of financing and administering local services, 267
  public responsibility of, 159
  retention of income by, 219, 252
  welfare responsibility of, 116-117
Council of Economic Advisers, 14, 59-60, 62, 80, 128, 129, 284
  and 1953-1954 recession, 87
Credit, control by banks of, 153
  importance of cost and controls of, 155
  necessity for maintaining adequate supply of, 154
Curtice, Harlow, 159
Cycles, 177
  financial, 20-21
  and public works, 181-182

Debt, limits of, 264
  national, rise in, 87, 88

Debt management, 147-152
  initiation by Treasury of, 147
  and public debt, 148
Defense, expenditures for, 19, 188
Defense Plant Corporation, 46
Defense Production Act of 1950, 69, 79
  control section of, 84
Deflation, 9
Democracy, limitations of, 121
  representative form of, 97
Democratic Party, disunity of, 82-83
  and Franklin Delano Roosevelt, 19-20
Depression, government intervention during, 175
  Great, 1, 6, 11-21 ff.
    impact of, 133
  mild, measures to prevent, 12
  of 1937, 3
  psychosis of, 39
  reserve funds for, 199-200
De Salle, Mike, 69, 70
Desegregation, federal grants and, 266
Dividend, credit on, 220
Douglas, Paul, 80

Economic analysis, and government expenditures, 169-170
  and government policy, 197-198
Economic policy, changes in, 137
  of 1939-1946, 40-42
  of 1951-1958, 81-92 ff.
  politicalization of, 33, 46-48
  public responsibility for, 195-196
Economic product, maximization of, 107-112
Economic progress, objective of, 99
  rate of, 31-32, 293
Economic Report of the President,
  January, 1957, 59 n., 63 n.
Economic stabilization, 177-186
  balanced budget as instrument of, 151-152
  central bankers in relation to policies of, 156
  determination of policy of, 143
  and direct controls, 140
  factors in, 160
  maintenance of, 290
  as policy guide, 133-166 ff.
Economic Stabilization Agency, 69, 70, 75-76, 79
Economist, The, 38-39

Economy, contemporary, inflationary
  bias of, 100
  current interpretation of, 101
  danger of politicalization of, 280
  dynamic nature of, 139
  effects of monetary and banking sys-
    tem on, 153
  free, maintenance of, 209-210, 294
  future predictions in, 136-137
  impact of government on, 131
  long-run stability of, 157
  periodic inflation of, 101-102
  and restraint by expenditure cuts, 144
  state-controlled, 294
  total, variations in, 158
Education, financing of, 261, 262
  problem of, 279
Eisenhower, Dwight David, 26
  campaign of, 82, 83, 84-85
Employment, 12
  commitment to maintain, 115
  full, 12
  government, cost of, 184
    and security questions, 88-90
  influence of government on, 7-8
  reasonable level of, 291
  stability of, 111-112
  variations in, 164
    See also Unemployment
Equity, in taxation, 214-227
Excess Profits Act of 1950, 69
Excises, elimination of, 162, 230
  in 1950-1951, 76
  reduction or removal of, 234

Fair Deal, 54, 58
Family, public expenditure demands of,
  171
Farmers, political power of, 94
  in postwar era, 37
Federal Housing Administration, 150
Federal Reserve System, 45
  banks of, open-market operations of,
    153
  Board of Governors of, 8, 30
    debt issues by, 148-149
    and inflation checks, 284
    policies of, 198
    restriction of open-market opera-
      tions by, 149-150
  debt management policies of, 41

increased prestige of, 153
  monetary policies of, 42
  1951 policies of, 81
  Open Market Committee of, 41
  restoration of power to, 80
  reversal of policies of, 62
  tightening of credit by, 159
  Treasury domination of, 59
Federalism, new form of, 124
Finance, deficit, 16
  of states and local governments, dif-
    ficulties in, 260
  reforms in, 256
Fiscal policy, 140-147
  basic theory of, 140-141
  between wars, 59
  difficulty in management of, 141-142
  relationship of monetary policy to,
    141
Ford, Henry, 242
Foreign aid, 5
  increased, 61
Foundations, charitable, 242
Friedman, Milton, 243
Full Employment Bill, 199
Full Employment in a Free Society, 187

Galbraith, J. K., 77, 99, 117
Goldenweiser, E. A., 40
Goode, Richard, 221
Government, ability to measure economic
    conditions, 98
  adjustment to new responsibilities of,
    132
  administrative aspects of, 125-130
  analysis of economic effects of finance
    of, 104-112
  balance between states and, 123-124
  and basic living standard, 122
  bonds and private investment, 149
  borrowing by, 147
  concentration of power of, 124, 185-
    186
  concepts of operations of, 293-294
  conflict between branches of, 96, 128
  costs of, 125-126, 285-286
  danger of abuse of power by, 165
  as determinant of employment, in-
    come, and prices, 110-111
  economic framework of, 104-132 ff.

Government, ability to measure economic conditions—*continued*
  economic influences of, 8-9
  economic nonintervention by, 2
  economic policy of, and the President, 129
  educational purposes of activities of, 108-109
  employment of land, labor, or capital by, 105
  executive branch of, and Congress, 90
    as defender of the public interest, 121
    delegation of powers to, 19, 25-27
    personnel of, 88-90
  expenditures by, 6-7, 105-106, 109, 143-144, 167, 169-177
  factors affecting role of, 278
  federal structure of, 122-125
  finance, pervasive influence of, 130
  financial policy of, 104-132 ff.
  functions of, 18, 283
  and future economy, 94-95, 134
  growth in the role of, 1-2, 95
  improved salaries of officials of, 289-290
  justification of programs of, 111
  justification of services of, 108
  limitation of powers of, 281-282
  and minimum subsistence for all, 114
  patronage system in, 91
  policy coördination of, 127, 128, 129-130, 280
  political framework of, 104-132 ff.
  public commitments made by, 98-99
  public control of policies of, 120-121
  public understanding of policy issues in, 97
  quality of officials in, 185, 288-289
  and responsibility for debt management policy, 148
  reversals of fiscal policy by, 142-143
  size of, 172
  and size of tax burden, 151
  stabilization by, 134-135
  state and local, financing problems of, 7, 282-283
    reorganization of jurisdictions of, 276
    service functions of, 262
    tax problems of, 259-276 ff.
  valuation of services of, 109

Government contracts (1939-1946), 45-48
Grants-in-aid, differential, 277
  federal, 275
    arguments against extension of, 266
    and state, 263, 265, 277
  general and permanent, 265
  as part of stabilization program, 265
  social issues involved in, 266
  standards for, 200
Great Britain, parliamentary system in, 119
  taxation in, 254
Gross National Product, 49-50
Growth, and corporate saving, 250
  and incentives, effects of taxation on, 247-253
  problem of, 249
  real, lower rate of, 251
Guffy Coal Act, 86

Hansen, A. H., 15, 133-134
Hiss, Alger, 65
Home Owners' Loan Corporation, 19
Hoover Commission Report, 65
Hopkins, Harry L., 27
House of Representatives, Ways and Means Committee of, 120
Housing, financing of, 12-13, 150

Ickes, Harold L., 184
Incentive, danger of destruction of, 173
  and growth, effects of taxation on, 247-253
  studies of, 248-249
  tax, for industries, 253
Income, distribution of, 168
  equalization of, 217, 240-241
  gains in lower brackets of, 56
  national, accounting of, 131, 134
    change in relative distribution of, 99-100
  personal, decline in, 162-163
  preferential treatment of certain sources of, 218
  real, increase in, 93-94, 176-177
  stabilization of, 133
  taxable and true, differences between, 236-237
  total taxable, 216
  variations in, 164
Income tax, averaging scheme for payment of, 213

community property provisions of, 215, 229

corporate, 43-44, 146, 208-209, 220-221

current features of law on, 228-230

and discriminatory burden on single persons, 231-232

equitable exemption policy for, 227

flexible features of, 225-226

forms of relief from, 234-235

individual, 43, 220
    exemptions and deductions under, 223-224, 231
    and fluctuations, 225

as means of income redistribution, 226

progressive, 224

and revenue requirements, 224

revision of, 57

shift in, 4

state, 7, 271-272
    and federal, 272
    trends affecting, 254-255

uneven coverage of, 162, 232

Industries, dependence on government orders of, 7

extractive, tax position of, 212-213

tax exemption for, 270

Industry, relationship to labor and agriculture, 282

and wage demands, 32

Inflation, 9

attempts to curb, 12, 62, 100, 138, 162-163

dangers of, 282

difficulties of avoiding, 283

final result of, 36

and general tax relief, 233

and individual income status, 294

and international implications, 102-103

labor-management responsibility for, 102

pressures toward (1951), 79

as preventative of unemployment, 137-138

in price of homes, 150

and recession (1953-1954), 87

as underlying current in United States, 73

Institutions, change in policy and administration of, 95-98

economic structure of, 164

political, preservation of, 176

repercussions of failure of, 116

Interest, low rates of, 14, 16
    variation in rate of, 154-155

Internal Revenue Service, funds for, 220

International Bank, 61

International Monetary Fund, 61

Investment, adverse effects of progressive tax on, 240-249

high rate of, and taxes, 209

public, 16

as a tax savings, 242

Isolationism, 23

Joint Committee on Internal Revenue, 91

Joint Economic Committee, 129 n.

Kaiser, Henry, 45-46

Kaldor, N., 152, 187

Keynes, J. M., 15, 134, 154
    analysis of short-term saving and investment propensities, 101
    system of autonomous and dependent variables, 109-110

Keyserling, Leon, 14, 59, 80

King, Adm. Ernest J., 26

Korean War, consumption function during, 110
    impact of, 65-80 ff.
    inflationary developments caused by, 137
    level of production during, 67
    1947-1951, 56-80 ff.
    price and wage rise during, 68
    Treasury and Federal Reserve policies during, 69

Kuznets, Simon, 135

Labor, demands for higher wages by, 32
    draft of, 30
    and New Deal, 24
    political power of, 94
    postwar struggle with management of, 37

Labor unions, 30

Leadership, and economic action, 292
    and problems of finance, 285
    by seniority, 196-197

Lerner, A. P., 243

Life insurance policies, irrevocable, 241-242

Lintner, John, 210

Livingston, Joe, 76

Losses, carry-over and carry-back of, 249

Lubell, Samuel, 58

MacArthur, Gen. Douglas, 67
MacIver, R. M., 121, 185
Mack, Ruth, 243
Markets, finance and security, 2, 3
    government, 168
    and shifts in production factors, 183
Marshall, Gen. George, 26, 54
Marshall Plan, 61
Mellon, Andrew, 242
Missiles, 6
Monetary policy, as instrument to prevent
        inflation, 155
    restrictive strength of, 155-156
    revival of, 153
Monetary theory, basic, 153-154
    improvement in, 152-157
    problem of, 156
Money, cheap, 14
    discounting of, 16
    easy, 15
    necessity of maintaining adequate
        supply of, 154
Mortgage, credit for, 150
    easy money for, 13
Murphy, Henry C., 40

National Bureau of Economic Research,
        134
National Industrial Recovery Act, 3, 19,
        86
New Deal, 15
    and business community, 17-18
    modifications of, under Eisenhower,
        85-86
    and stabilization program, 28-29
Nimitz, Adm. Chester W., 26
Nourse, E. G., 59, 117

Office of Price Administration, 28, 30
    basic prices under, 52
Office of Price Stabilization, 69, 79, 80
Old-Age and Survivors Insurance, 18,
        41, 87

Paul, Randolph E., 40
Pearl Harbor, 23-24
Percentage depletion allowance, 212
Political economy, versus economics, 295
    recurrent problems of, 91-92
Political parties, and responsibility for
        budget analysis, 191
    and responsibility for public expendi-
        tures, 193-195

Population, growth of, and public works,
        182
Port of New York Authority, 267-268
Potter, David M., 177
Power, aggregates of, 99
    countervailing thesis of, 99, 117
President, and responsibility for checking
        inflation, 284
    statesman, 287
Price Control Act, 50-51
Price indexes, and tax variation, 247
    institutional barriers preventing ad-
        justment of, 160-161
Price stabilization, 12, 159
    in conflict with full employment, 157-
        163
    barriers to adjustments in, 158
    downward adjustments of, 282
    general freeze of (1951), 70
    in a sellers' market, 157-158
Production, capitalistic system of, 121-
        122
Productivity, growth of, 158
Profits, protection of margins of, 80
    undistributed, and tax avoidance, 222-
        223
Public assistance, program of selective
        aid for, 183
    and transfer expenditures, 173
Public debt, 16
Public expenditures, 167-201 ff.
    budget process of, 188-189
    built-in flexibility of, 178-179
    conclusions concerning, 200
    manipulation of, 178
    political and administrative aspects of,
        188-200
    and revenue variation, 199
    and shifts in demand, 183
    See also Government
Public finance, 107-108, 251
Public health, expenditures for, 171
Public opinion polls, 97-98
Public services, costs of, 170
    expansion of, 172-173
    retarded rate of increase in, 174
Public works, countercyclical program
        of, 179-180
    dangers of, 182-183
    direct federal program of, 180
    federal grants to states for, 181
    political and administrative aspects of,
        184-185

reservoir of, 180-181
Public Works Administration, 266

Recession of 1953-1954, 73, 153
    of 1949, 62, 65
Reconstruction Finance Corporation, 13,
    19, 46-48, 86, 267
Reconversion, 48-55 ff.
    and wage-price policies, 50-51
Recovery, and World War II defense
    program, 24
Recreation, financing of, 261, 262
Regional planning, 124-125
Regulation "W," 76
Renegotiation Act, 43
Reorganization Act of 1939, 20
Republican Party, and Eisenhower Ad-
    ministration, 85-92 ff.
Revenue, capacity of state and local gov-
    ernments to raise, 255
    and equalization of individual tax
        burdens, 240
    policy of variation in, 144-145
    and stabilization policy, 243-245
Revenue Act of 1950, 69
    of 1954, 211-212
Revenue system, appraisal of, 253-257
    and broadening income tax base, 225
    built-in flexibility of, 256
    of California, 264
    of New Jersey, 261
    of New York, 261
    of Pennsylvania, 263
Roosevelt, F. D., 15, 19, 20, 23, 26-27,
    54, 58
Rural Electrification Administration, 86

Savings, and high taxes, 209
Schools, consolidated, 276
Seltzer, Lawrence H., 219
Sherwood, Robert, 27
Shoup, Carl, 243
Sloan, Alfred P., 242
Social security, development of, 135
Social Security Act, 18
Stabilization, see Economic stabilization;
    Price stabilization
Stabilization policy, 243-247
    multiplier and acceleration principles
        of, 163-164
    and revenue measures, 243-245
    between wars, 58
Stagnation thesis, 134

Standard of living, increases in, 176-177
States, broad-based taxes for, 271
    and countercyclical credit programs,
        200
    diminished powers of, 19-20
    financing difficulties of, 7
    growth in federal grants to, 262
    reorganization of boundaries of, 276
    service functions of, 262
    tax problems of, 259-276 ff.
    ultimate control of political power by,
        123
Stevenson, Adlai, 82, 83, 84
Subsidies, 13
Supreme Court, 19

Taft, Robert A., 83
Tariff, 206-207
Tax burden, distribution of, 204-205,
    216
Tax Foundation, 238
Tax policy, 202-222 ff., 228-258 ff.
    1939-1946, 43-45
Tax Reduction Act of 1948, 63
Taxation, administration of, 126
    basic postulates of, 205
    as basis of benefit or user charges,
        235-236
    built-in flexibility of, 245
    and business expense allowance, 219-
        220
    changes in interpretation of laws on,
        151
    congressional action on, 44-45
    corporate, credit on, 222
        and revenue changes, 244
    current issues and possibilities of
        reform of, 214-227
    dangerous results of, 250-251
    devices for minimizing burden of,
        237
    and distribution by income class, 236-
        243
    and effects on incentives and growth,
        247-253
    and effect on savings and investment,
        208-209
    equity of, 214-227
    on estates, 241-242
    exemption of bottom groups from,
        239
    flexibility and stability conflict in, 245

Taxation, administration of—*continued*
  on gifts, 241-242
  in Great Britain, 254
  Harvard studies of effects of, 210
  high rate of, 33, 210
  ideal system of, 211-214
  incidence of, 203-204
  incidence theory of, 215
  as instrument of economic stability,
    247, 255-256
  as instrument of social control, 205-
    206
  limits of, 207-210
  long-range policy of, 212
  of lower-income group, redistribution
    of burden of, 233
  modification of, 222-223
  necessity for flexible policy of, 281
  positive program of reform in, 286-
    295
  preferential rates of, 217-218
  prevention of differential impact of,
    239-240
  probable increase in, 257
  progressive system of, 72, 216, 237-
    238, 241
  proportionate system of, 216
  and regressiveness of tax burden, 238
  and repercussions on prices, 106
  revision of state and federal laws on,
    282
  states versus federal government on,
    123
  theory of, 203-207
  undesirability of total exemption
    from, 240
  in the United States, 202-203
Taxes, broad-based, 271
  cuts in, 61, 190, 207-208
  cycle-sensitive, growth of, 7
  distribution of, increases in, 145
  excess profits, 43-44
  gross-receipts, 274
  high, continued need for, 57
  maximization of stimulus for cuts in,
    145
  property, administration of, 269-270
    local, 260
  rate of, effect of expansion on, 264
  receipts of, countercyclical variations
    in, 163
  remission of, 146-147
    to new industries, 260

  retail-sales, 272-273
  state and local regressive, 239
  sales, federal, 146
    rejection of, 44
  value-added, 274
  variation of, 146
  withholding, on industrial profits, 222
    See also specific taxes, such as
      Income tax.
Tennessee Valley Authority, 18, 86
Transfer payments, 105-106
Transition period, *see* World War II
Treasury, Department of the, 28
  and bond supports, 5
  control of gold and silver policy by,
    148
  debt issues by, 148-149
  debt-management policies of, 41
  fiscal policy of, 61
  fiscal program of (1951), 70-71
  and income controls, 30
  and influence on monetary policy,
    16-17
  1951 accord with Federal Reserve
    System of, 73
  and relationship with Congress, 90-91
Truman Committee, 34
"Truman Doctrine," 61
Truman, Harry S, 54, 64, 82, 83, 84-85
Turner, Julius, 177

Unemployment, federal grants-in-aid for,
    265
  government intervention and, 290
  insurance against, 291
  state insurance against, 18
U.S.S.R., and U.S. mobilization, 75
United Nations, in Korea, 65
United States economy, 1958, 93-103 ff.
United States government, *see* Government

Valentine, Alan, 69
Viner, Jacob, 85-86

Wage Stabilization Board, 74
Wages, barriers to adjustments in, 158
  contracts in, 207
  higher, attitudes toward, 32
  rise in, 74
Wagner Act, 3
War debts, 23
War Labor Board, 28, 30

War Production Board, 34
Welfare, analysis of determinants of, 112
  basic ideas of, 113-114
  commitments to achieve objectives of, 115-116
  criteria for maximization of, 170-171
  decisions by élite for public on, 117-118
  economic, and government expenditure, 169-177
  equity in, 114
  increase in government expenditures for, 175
  payments and subsidies for, 99
  political, maximization of, 118-122
  promotion of general, 114-115
  public responsibility and, 117
  revision of value judgments of, 112-115
  social, maximization of, 112-118
  strengthening of programs of, 292
White, Melvin I., 142, 243
Works Progress Administration, 266

World War I, 29
  controls during, 38
  depression following, 49
World War II, controls during, 31
  economic situation of United States at outbreak of, 22-23
  emergency programs of, 139
  financing of, 40-55 ff.
  and growth of government influence, 2
  impact of, 22-39 ff., 48
  to Korean War (1947-1951), 56-80 ff.
  post-transition period, 51-52
  and revenue requirements, 224-225
  spending during, 142
  transition period (1945-1946), 48-55 ff.
    budget during, 51
    conclusions concerning, 54-55
  financial problems during, 55
    reassertion of Congress during, 53
    savings during, 52
  U.S. defense preparations for, 23
Wright, David McCord, 210